Market Timing For Dummies®

WITHDRAWN

Cheat Sheet

Rules of the Road for Market Timing

You're not going to make money every time you trade, but you can increase your odds of staying sane and solvent by following a few rules of the road.

✔ **Practice patience.** You can get burned if you jump into every trade that looks great at first glance.

✔ **Trade with the trend.** You're unlikely to outsmart the market — at least not for any length of time — but you can benefit by keeping your trades in line with the trend.

✔ **Time with your charts, not your emotions.** There is only one absolute truth in the markets: price. If price is in your favor, stay with the position. If it's going against you, get out by following your trading rules.

✔ **Protect your money by diversifying your investments.** As I see it, diversification means that sometimes you own no stocks at all; sometimes your portfolio sits in a money market account waiting for better times. Diversifying your investment portfolio cuts your potential risk of a catastrophic loss.

✔ **Limit headaches by limiting losses.** Knowing how big a loss you're willing to take is a key part of any timer's trading plan. A fairly common loss limit in the stock market is 5 to 10 percent, depending on your risk tolerance and how often you want to trade.

✔ **Trade reasonably.** If you have only a little money, there's no point in taking big risks. And even if you have a lot of money, there's no point in being foolish.

✔ **Set low expectations.** No trader is right all the time. Most don't even get their picks right half the time. Having low expectations enables you to keep a lid on the emotions of trading that come from the highs, the lows, and the dull periods that you encounter and to continue to trade well.

✔ **Enjoy it or quit.** Aside from making money, I enjoy trading and market timing, because it lets me put my wits up against incredible odds and the collective investment opinion of the entire trading world. If I ever stop enjoying the preparation, analysis, and management of a trade, I'll quit. If you don't enjoy it, find something else to do.

Making Market Sentiment Work For You

✔ Keep tabs of market sentiment surveys. Several of them are available to help you pick out market tops and bottoms.

✔ Use the data from the options markets to analyze extremes in the markets. The put/call ratio can be a very useful indicator.

✔ Listen to the water cooler talk. If everyone is talking about something being the hot topic, it's often a sign that the trend in that investment may be about to change.

✔ Volume and volatility are excellent sentiment indicators. Too much of both or either of them could be a sign that the market's trend is about to reverse.

✔ Never trade on a hot tip. Always do your own work.

D0796637

For Dummies: Bestselling Book Series for Beginners

Market Timing For Dummies®

Cheat Sheet

Essential Economic Reports to Monitor as a Market Timer

- The monthly employment report
- The Consumer Price Index
- The Producer Price Index
- ISM and regional purchasing manager's reports
- The Beige Book from the Federal Reserve
- Housing Starts
- Index of Leading Economic Indicators
- Gross Domestic Product
- Oil Supply Data

Why Exchange-Traded Funds Are Your Best Bets for Timing the Markets

- You can use them to time just about any asset class, stocks, bonds, metals, currencies, or commodities — and you can go long or sell short with a point and a click of your mouse.
- Unlike mutual funds, when you use ETFs you don't have to wait until the end of the day to enter or exit any position.
- You can trade options based on many ETFs, which can give your timing another dimension.
- Technical and fundamental analysis techniques are easy to adapt to ETFs.

What to Look For in an Online Charting Service

- **Accessibility:** The service needs to be available to you virtually anywhere, either online or by the use of a convenient online interface.
- **Charting tools:** The charts provided by your charting service must be easy-to-read and user-friendly. You shouldn't have to punch five or ten keys or toggle your mouse for 10 minutes while trying to make your chart look right.
- **Live charts:** If you're going to trade, you need access to *live charts* that actually change with every tick (up or down movement) of the market.
- **Multiple indicators:** Make sure that the service to which you subscribe lets you plot price charts and multiple indicators at the same time.
- **Real-time quotes:** Market timing without real-time quotes is a sure path down the road to ruin.
- **Support:** Make sure that the service offers a toll-free telephone number to call for support and that it provides online support.
- **Time-frame analysis:** Make sure that your charting service enables you to produce intraday charts. You want to be able to look at different time frames simultaneously.

For Dummies: Bestselling Book Series for Beginners

Market Timing FOR DUMMIES®

by Joe Duarte, MD

WILEY

Wiley Publishing, Inc.

Market Timing For Dummies®

Published by
Wiley Publishing, Inc.
111 River St.
Hoboken, NJ 07030-5774
www.wiley.com

Copyright © 2009 by Wiley Publishing, Inc., Indianapolis, Indiana

Published by Wiley Publishing, Inc., Indianapolis, Indiana

Published simultaneously in Canada

For general information on our other products and services, please contact our Customer Care Department within the U.S. at 800-762-2974, outside the U.S. at 317-572-3993, or fax 317-572-4002.

For technical support, please visit www.wiley.com/techsupport.

Wiley also publishes its books in a variety of electronic formats. Some content that appears in print may not be available in electronic books.

Library of Congress Control Number: 2008939707

ISBN: 978-0-470-38975-1

Manufactured in the United States of America

10 9 8 7 6 5 4 3 2 1

WILEY

About the Author

Dr. Joe Duarte (www.joe-duarte.com) is best known for his candid, no-nonsense, and prescient expert commentary on the financial and commodity markets, such as his on-the-money call on CNBC, June 4, 2008, when he correctly noted that oil had made a top and that a fall below $110 would take prices to $100 or less. By September 2008, oil had broken below $100. He is a widely read analyst and writer and an active trader. His daily Market IQ column is read by thousands of investors, market timers, and professional traders around the world.

Dr. Duarte is the author *Futures & Options For Dummies, Trading Futures For Dummies, Successful Biotech Investing,* and *Successful Energy Sector Investing.*

His combined expertise in health care, energy, and the effects of politics and global intelligence on the financial markets offers a unique blend of insight and information to thousands of active investors and political and intelligence aficionados around the world on a daily basis.

Dr. Duarte's Market Moves column is syndicated to a global audience through FinancialWire, a leading independent syndicate of financial information. He is also a featured columnist on the popular investor Web site Stockhouse.com.

Dr. Duarte is a frequent guest on CNBC and is an original CNBC Market Maven. He is a regular guest on the *Financial Sense Newshour with Jim Puplava* radio show, where he comments on the energy markets and geopolitics.

Dr. Duarte has been writing about the financial markets since 1990. His articles and commentary have been featured on Marketwatch.com and in *Barron's, Smart Money, Medical Economics,* and *Technical Analysis of Stocks and Commodities* magazines. He has been quoted in the Associated Press, CNN.com, *The Wall Street Journal, Smart Money Magazine,* and *Investor's Business Daily.*

In 2003, Dr. Duarte received second place in the professional section of the Medical Economics Investment Challenge with a 12-month return of 42 percent.

Dr. Duarte published the critically acclaimed market-timing newsletter "The Wall Street Detective" from 1990–1998, when it became an exclusively electronic publication. It later was converted to Joe-Duarte.com. His daily market commentary "Joe Knows" appeared on Financialweb.com from 1998–2000. Dr. Duarte served as senior columnist for Investorlinks.com from 1998-2001. He is a registered investment advisor and president of River Willow Capital Management.

He lives in Dallas, Texas, plays a Gibson ES-135, and loves his vintage Völkl tennis racket.

Dedication

To family, friends, and market timers around the universe.

Acknowledgments

Writing a book is a unique, lonely, and personal experience, and very few but the author, the editor(s), and those who share the space-time continuum with them can understand this. During this one, I had my share of ups and downs as well as rewards. So I can't complain. Still, I couldn't have done it without the usual gang that helps me on a daily basis. So here's a big thanks to:

My family, my office staffs from my other life, the Wiley editorial staff, especially Stacy and Traci who helped shepherd me to the final goal, nearly on time for once.

Grace "the wonder agent" and purveyor of recurrent gigs. Thank you for sticking with me.

Frank "the master of all things Web-related," without whom there would be no Joe-Duarte.com. Too bad you couldn't come along on this little expedition.

To Stone Barrington, Michelle Maxwell, and Sean King, Gabriel Allon, Oliver Stone (the literary character, not the movie director), and other inhabitants of pages and audio books that help me stay sane as I work and travel.

As always coffee, tea, vitamins, sports drinks, nutrition bars, and the game of tennis also help.

Special thanks to those who read my books, subscribe to my Web site and have kept this thing going for 18 years. Who'd've thunk it?

And also to two longtime friends, John and Greg, whose interactions with me always prove to be worthwhile and interesting, to say the least.

My patients who so graciously come back the next day even if I've had to run out of the office in a hurry to be on CNBC.

If I've forgotten to mention anyone, it wasn't intentional. I'm not as young as I used to be.

Publisher's Acknowledgments

We're proud of this book; please send us your comments through our Dummies online registration form located at www.dummies.com/register/.

Some of the people who helped bring this book to market include the following:

Acquisitions, Editorial, and Media Development

Project Editor: Traci Cumbay

Acquisitions Editor: Stacy Kennedy

Copy Editor: Traci Cumbay

Editorial Program Coordinator: Erin Calligan Mooney

Technical Editor: Tim Ord

Senior Editorial Manager: Jennifer Ehrlich

Editorial Supervisor & Reprint Editor: Carmen Krikorian

Editorial Assistants: Joe Niesen, David Lutton, Jennette ElNaggar

Cover Photos: Blend Images

Cartoons: Rich Tennant (www.the5thwave.com)

Composition Services

Project Coordinator: Katie Key

Layout and Graphics: Nikki Gately, Sarah Philippart, Christine Williams

Proofreader: Christine Sabooni

Indexer: Word Co Indexing Services

Publishing and Editorial for Consumer Dummies

    Diane Graves Steele, Vice President and Publisher, Consumer Dummies

    Kristin Ferguson-Wagstaffe, Product Development Director, Consumer Dummies

    Ensley Eikenburg, Associate Publisher, Travel

    Kelly Regan, Editorial Director, Travel

Publishing for Technology Dummies

    Andy Cummings, Vice President and Publisher, Dummies Technology/General User

Composition Services

    Gerry Fahey, Vice President of Production Services

    Debbie Stailey, Director of Composition Services

Contents at a Glance

Table of Contents

Introduction

. . . .

*W*hen I started trading, I had no idea that I was a market timer. The whole concept that you could actually maximize your gains and avoid major losses by managing your portfolio was foreign to me, given the fact that Wall Street's buy-and-hold mantra is the first thing that anyone ever hears about. But after nearly 20 years in the business, every time there's a bear market or a market crash, I'm glad that I took it upon myself to learn the craft.

Martin Zweig, a legendary money manager from the 1980s, changed the way I looked at investing when he promoted his book *Winning on Wall Street* (Grand Central Publishing) in the early days of financial television. The phrases "don't fight the Fed" and "don't fight market momentum" were so intriguing that I bought the book and became a market timer.

With this book, I hope to humbly contribute to opening more readers' eyes to a new reality — that of being able to avoid catastrophic losses and to maximize stock market gains by actively managing their portfolios.

About This Book

Market timing is the most essential aspect of all trading and investing endeavors. If you think about it, timing is the key to success in many things you do. Try to hit a tennis ball without timing your stroke. Or try to run a yellow light before that camera goes off behind you without timing.

So why is it that if you're talking about getting married or buying a house, people say that "timing is everything," but when you talk about market timing, people roll their eyes and tell you that it's impossible? In fact, market timing isn't just possible; it's central to successful trading because whenever you mistime an entry or an exit to any trading or investing position, you run the risk of reducing your profits or losing money outright.

Indeed, because market timing is so misunderstood and maligned, it's still an area of trading that few people practice — openly, anyway. Its shady reputation gives the successful timer an advantage over the financial planner, the retail broker, their unsuspecting clients, and their buy-and-hold strategy. As others hold on to falling stocks through bear markets and see their assets dwindle, you'll be able to make money or preserve more of your bull market gains by applying the market timing techniques in this book.

Am I guaranteeing you gains? Of course not; you don't get guarantees on anything in life. You wouldn't stay on a sinking ship in the middle of a hurricane, yet millions of investors decide to ride out massive bear markets and stock market corrections, pinning their hopes and their retirements on that old adage "the long-term trend is up."

Being different could make you money if you consider market timing a viable alternative to the old Wall Street "buy and hold" swindle. If you have any doubts about considering market timing, remember that Wall Street has also given us things like portfolio insurance, the savings and loan crisis, the Internet bubble, and most recently the subprime mortgage crisis. Each of these little gifts from the guys who tell you that holding stocks for the long term is the only way to fly has also led to major bear markets where investors have lost billions by holding on to their investments too long.

Sure, the market came back. But in many if not all cases, the best that most buy-and-hold investors got was all their money back. Those who sold early in the start of the down trend had more money to invest when the market turned up. Better, those who sold the market short actually made money when the market fell. And because of new products, such as exchange-traded mutual funds (ETFs), short selling is as easy as buying shares of stock through your online broker with one click of the mouse.

This book is about staying with the overall market trend. It's about knowing when to get in and out of your trading or investment positions with enough time to preserve more of your hard-earned money. Accomplish that, and when things turn around, you can start in a better place than someone who rode the bear market all the way down to the bottom and is only likely to get her money back — if she's lucky enough and has enough time.

Conventions Used in This Book

To assist your navigation of this book, I've established the following conventions:

✔ I use *italic* for emphasis and to highlight new words or terms that I define.

✔ I use `monofont` for Web addresses.

✔ Sidebars, which are shaded boxes of text, consist of information that's interesting but not necessarily critical to your understanding of the topic.

If the book seems to be a little heavy on jargon, it's because there is no other way of saying what I'm trying to say. Believe me, this book was heavily edited, and carefully combed through in order to make it as accessible as possible to you.

Foolish Assumptions

In order to write this book, I had to make assumptions about who you might be. Market timing isn't rocket science, but it's not for preschoolers, either, and I have done my level best to walk the line between basic and technical information that gives readers what they need to go forth and confidently time the markets. As I did that, I assumed that you

✔ Know something about trading and have some experience. (I'm actually hoping that you have more than a little experience; this topic is difficult for beginning investors and may be a fairly risky practice for those with little savvy.)

✔ Don't mind working hard and spending time analyzing the markets on a regular — even daily — basis in order to be successful.

✔ Will set time aside on a regular basis to develop your trading skills, and will run your trading as a business, keeping accurate records of your trades, both winning and losing, and reviewing them on regular basis.

✔ Are well financed enough to be able to take some risks with your money without impairing your long-term finances or your family's well being.

✔ Are interested in trading with the prevailing trend of the stock market but not quite interested in day trading.

✔ Are tired of missing opportunities and waiting too long to take profits and so would like to improve your ability to enter and exit markets.

✔ Would like to expand your trading beyond the stock market but are more interested in trading commodities and futures through exchange-traded funds than in trading futures or options directly.

✔ Want to be able to make money when the market enters a down trend but don't really want to go through the hassle of opening a margin account or a futures account.

✔ Have or would like to develop the market analysis skills that enable you to be patient in order to recognize outstanding opportunities and don't mind some break-even, lose-a-little, or gain-a-little trades along the way.

✔ Recognize that this is a global marketplace in which futures, stocks, bonds, and currencies influence each other and that you need to be well versed in the vagaries of international markets in order to maximize your profit potential.

✔ Have access to top-of-the-line computing equipment, an online trading account, and a high-speed Internet connection, as well as the ability to check your trades when you're not in front of your trading station.

How This Book Is Organized

To make this book easy to navigate, I've organized it into five parts. The following sections give you a quick rundown of what you find in each.

Part 1: Stepping Into the World of Market Timing

In this part, I ease you into the wide world of market timing, introducing you to its basic tenets and showing you the tools you use to time the markets. You find out about the principles that market timers use, and the charts they use to get the timing job done. Read this part to stock up on the raw materials of market timing.

Part II: Market Timing's Methods and Strategies

Here you get into the meat of timing. I tell you how to prepare for and decipher the economic reports that matter. Believe it or not, timing in January can be different from timing in July, and in this part I introduce you to some of the seasonal and cyclical patterns you find in the markets.

Your primary directive as a timer is finding the prevailing trend in the markets and making trades according to that trend. But the market reacts not just to facts and realities but to how traders, financial experts, and consumers *feel* about those trends, and I tell you about how to assess the sentiment as well as the trend.

Part III: Applying Timing to the Markets

What happens when the all the timing principles I cover in Parts I and II come together in a trade? I kick off this part of the book by taking you through every step of my actions and thinking as I executed a real trade. Your mileage may vary, but glimpsing the way the parts come together gives you great insight into the planning and evaluation that are timing's hallmark.

The later chapters run through the various markets you might want to dip your toes into, from the stock market you probably already know and trade to the specifics of currency, commodity, and many more markets.

Part IV: Timing the Sectors

Opportunities run through the stock market all the time; your job is to find them, and in this part I take you on a tour of some of the major divisions within the market. You find out about timing technology stocks, for example, as well as the energy, financial, and health care sectors. This part is one of my favorite sections of the book, as I get into the very specific characteristics of each of these very profitable sections of the stock market.

Part V: The Part of Tens

In every *For Dummies* book, you find chapters that give you quick tips for the topic at hand, and right here is where you find them. In this part, I give you a rundown of many more than ten resources that I turn to most often as well as ten ways to keep your timing practice on track without losing your shirt or your sanity.

Icons Used in This Book

I use icons to emphasize and reinforce information throughout the book. Here's a list of the icons you find and what you can expect from the text they highlight.

When I present a concept that is important for you to keep in mind as you read, I include this icon beside it. This icon directs you to bits that enable you put together key concepts.

Feel free to skip over information highlighted with this icon. I use it to point you toward information that goes deeper than you need. You might find these advanced tidbits interesting, but you can come away with a complete understanding of market timing without them.

A tip is something that you can use right away in your trading practice. Tips save you time or money and give you the benefit of my many years of trading experience.

This bomb icon reminds me of funny old cartoons and the Pink Panther movies, but its message is hugely important. I use this icon to identify practices or notions that could cause damage to you or your trading accounts.

Where to Go from Here

In short: Anywhere you want. *For Dummies* books are written so that you can jump in at any point that interests you. Want to find out how presidential elections affect your investments? Head straight to Chapter 6. Interested in browsing the various market sectors? Part IV has what you want. If you're brand-new to market timing or just an overachiever, turn to Chapter 1 and don't stop reading until you get to the index.

I've been a market timer for 20-plus years and have found the concepts that I've put forth in this book quite useful. I hope that you do, too.

Part I

Stepping into the World of Market Timing

The 5th Wave   By Rich Tennant

"Volatility bands? Trend reversals? I say we stick the money in the ground like always, and then feed this guy to the sharks."

In this part . . .

New to market timing? This part of the book takes you through the basics you need to get started. In it, I show you how to think like a market timer and how to use the tools that lead to successful timing. You get a good view of the work required to anticipate timing situations and an insider's view about what to expect in this often misunderstood world of trading.

Chapter 1

Becoming a Market Timer

. . . .

In This Chapter

▶ Understanding market timing

▶ Getting a handle on timing's jargon

▶ Glimpsing the importance of technique

▶ Finding the whys of market timing

▶ Getting ready and diving in

▶ Keeping your expectations reasonable

▶ Enjoying the process — and the results

. . . .

An old market cliché says "there's always a bull market." In other words, if you look hard enough you can find a market that is trending, up or down, and that you use to make money.

Because there's always a bull market, market timing may be the trading method of the 21st century, given the potential for volatility in the world and the markets, and the change that's likely to follow as humanity progresses toward its next stage of development.

Although the topic may seem daunting, you have plenty of reasons to consider adding it to your investing arsenal, given what may lie ahead. For one thing, the world is moving from a North American and Eurocentric focus to one that includes Asia and the emerging economies of South America, specifically, China, India, and Brazil. Resource-rich nations such as Russia and Venezuela are also participating in the mainstream markets.

That change alone — the spreading of power and influence to more places around the globe — is enough to create opportunity for market timers, who now operate in a world where money travels at the speed of light and the 24-hour news cycle has created a world where information is available at any time to anyone who has access to a computer and an Internet connection.

The bottom line is that buy-and-hold investing, the more traditional method for everyday folks to increase their wealth, is losing its appeal as the ability to move faster in and out of trading positions, and to trade markets that are rising or falling profitably, is increasingly important to long-term investors. The net effect is that investors who can adapt to this new world are the ones who will have the best chance of success.

But don't let all that stuff about change get you down. With this book, you can find out how to profit from the market's perception of and reaction to events by timing the markets. In this chapter, I introduce you to the world of market timing and show you how you can be in control of your investment results.

Defining Market Timing

Market timing is the act of entering and exiting trades (buying and selling at the most opportune time) in any market, whether, stocks, bonds, futures, or options. When timing the markets your goals are to

- **Decrease your exposure to risk.** As a market timer you want to stay with the dominant trend, whether up or down; you want to swim with the tide by buying stocks in a rising market, and selling or selling short in a falling market.

- **Maximize your profit potential.** If you can make money when the market goes up and when the market goes down, you have twice the opportunity to make money, and you decrease your chances of losing money when the trend goes against you.

- **Increase the consistency of your results.** Non-timers confuse consistency with frequency of trading. Market timing isn't day trading. It's about recognizing opportunities early, moving into positions using well-planned strategies, and monitoring the process on a daily or more frequent basis. It's about doing your homework, being prepared, and setting exit strategies before entering any position. And it's about recognizing when you've made a mistake early so that you can exit a position with as much capital as possible so that you can trade again.

- **Avoid heartburn and feelings of misery.** Anyone who's ever sat through a three-year bear market, such as the 2000–2003 implosion of the dot-com boom, knows that holding on to your favorite stocks during such a period is a sure recipe for heartburn and high blood pressure. If you had followed sound market timing techniques during that time, your losses would almost certainly have been less than if you held your positions during that period.

✔ **Make responsible investment decisions.** Some investors watch every single tick of a trade and sweat the details constantly, compounding their mistakes and increasing their suffering as their trade turns against them and the losses mount. Finally, when they can't stand it any more, they sell in a panic and remain miserable for months after their experience when they have no one to blame but themselves.

Timing is about seeing the intermediate-term trend, which lasts for weeks or months, and staying with a position as long as it meets the criteria that you've set forth in your trading plan. It's also about getting out of your position when your goals are met or when your exit strategy is triggered.

✔ **Diversify your opportunities.** What makes timing one of the most useful trading methods is that you can use the techniques to time stocks, bonds, mutual funds, futures, options, and exchange-traded funds, which means that there is one or more timing vehicles for every possible personality, level of expertise, or risk profile in the investment universe.

Timing is as much a state of mind as a combination of trading methods, and it requires knowledge of fundamentals and technical analysis, the latter being as much as 80 percent of what will help you pull the trigger consistently and become successful.

Terms of Engagement for Timing

I use a lot of terms in this book that sound jargony (and *man,* do *For Dummies* editors hate that). These terms are at the heart of market timing, though, so you might as well get used to them. You encounter more terms (defined wherever they first appear) throughout the book, but this small list of critical lingo gets you started:

✔ **Going long:** Buying assets, be they stocks, bonds, or futures, in hopes that they will rise in price.

✔ **Selling short:** Borrowing stocks (usually from a broker's stocks) in hope that the stocks will fall in price, at which time the short seller buys the stock back and returns the stock to the lender. The short seller pockets the profits gained from the stock having fallen in price. In turn, the lender receives dividends accrued by the stock during the time the stock is being sold short.

Short selling is very risky: Any time the stock rises, the short seller loses money. And stocks can fall only to zero, but they can theoretically rise forever.

✔ **Bull markets:** Markets that are rising.

✔ **Bear markets:** The opposites of bull markets; the tendency of prices during these periods is for markets to fall.

✔ **Leverage:** The practice used by traders in which less than the full amounts of money let them participate in the full price action of the underlying contract. Leverage is similar to credit. And like credit, it can be very detrimental when it goes against you.

✔ **Margin:** In the stock market, margin is like a down payment on buying stocks. In futures, it's more like a good-faith deposit. In all cases, margin is a form of leverage that lets traders buy larger positions without putting up the entire price.

✔ **Futures contracts:** Contracts between buyers and sellers that specify how much of an underlying asset will be delivered to the buyer at a certain time in the future.

✔ **Options:** Contracts that give those who possess them the option to buy or sell an asset at a certain time in the future. I don't go into great detail about futures and options in this book, but I do mention them when the time is right. You can get *Trading Futures For Dummies* (by yours truly) and George A. Fontanills's book *Trading Options For Dummies* for the full details.

✔ **Market sectors:** A specific area of the market, such as technology or health care. Market timing of individual sectors of the market is essential in both bull and bear markets and can be very profitable. See Part IV for more details on sector investing.

✔ **Trends:** Time periods in the markets where prices head primarily in one direction for a period of time. The **dominant trend** refers to the one direction in which the market heads over a very long time, even though it includes periods where it heads in the opposite direction. See Chapter 4 for more about trends and how to time them.

✔ **Sell stops:** Price limits that you specify to your broker when you buy a stock. You use sell stops to decrease losses by selling your shares when they hit the price that you specified as the stop. Sell stops are an important part of market timing, and I discuss them throughout the book.

✔ **Buy stops:** Price limits used to limit losses when you're selling stocks short. Sell stops are limits placed below the price of the stock you own. Buy stops instruct your broker to buy back the stock you sold short at a price above the price of the stock. You should adjust your buy and sell stops as the trade develops.

Timing Technique: The Secret of Success

The secret of all experts, although few will tell you this outright, is their technique. Their better-than-average results aren't the result of magic or of experience alone. Even talent isn't enough. Success is based on their long hours of practice, review of that practice, and constant attention to detail that leads to the slow and steady adjustment of technique until it becomes nearly flawless. And when your technique is flawless your chances of success rise significantly. Notice how I said *chances* of success. There are no guarantees in this business, especially when you're up against other people who have perfected their own trading techniques. But in timing, as well as in life, all you can do is the best that you can. Everything else is up to the vagaries of chaos and the universe.

I had a guitar teacher once who was kind enough to teach me about technique when I was in my early 40s. (Old dogs *can* learn new tricks.) I had been playing guitar since I was 14 and had even played semi-professionally in college and high school, making a nice tidy sum, not to mention compiling an interesting chunk of experiences over a couple of summers.

My teacher, Jim, saw me struggling with a scale during a lesson, and he asked me how I practiced. I showed him how I would place my hand on the guitar and started to play. He looked at me and started to shake his head as he told me an interesting story.

He had spent some time in Spain during his early 20s, attending seminars and classes with some of the best Flamenco guitarists of the time. One day in Spain, Jim was walking down the street heading for a class when he heard a guitar playing from a second-floor window. But this was no ordinary guitar. It was the guitar of Paco de Lucia, a Flamenco master and internationally recognized guitarist and performer.

Jim stopped to listen. But he didn't hear Flamenco notes pouring off of the guitar at the speed of light. Instead he heard the single tones of a guitar string being struck in time with a slowly ticking metronome.

Paco de Lucia was playing a C-major scale — the simplest of scales — over and over again at a very slow speed, following the metronome. As he listened carefully, he told me, it was as if he had been hit by lightning. Every note was perfect, every time the finger struck the string. Over and over again, slowly moving, perfect single notes, up and down the fingerboard. My teacher stood under the window for some time and heard no variation in the playing.

What de Lucia was doing and what all masters do to perfect their technique is to slowly repeat the movements required to hit the perfect note every time. By doing this slowly, thousands of times per day, the muscles in the hands learn to recognize the amount of pressure required to hit that perfect note, and the brain remembers it. The ears recognize what a perfect note sounds like and can tell when something is not right. And the master's ability, over time, continues to improve.

Jim began to incorporate the practice modality into his own routine, and over several weeks he began to notice improvement. I incorporated the exercise into my own routine and also started to notice improvement. More important, I began to enjoy my playing more, as my fingers were able to play notes and chords that were impossible a few weeks earlier. To this day, I start my own practice sessions by playing slow C-major scales. And even though I don't play as often as I used to, my playing now is better than it was several years ago when I used to play more often.

Why? Because I have better technique than I used to. This is the secret method of the masters. Slow and steady repetition of the perfect movements, over and over again over years, will lead to improvement. It works for musicians, athletes, dancers, and so on. More to the point, it works for market timers.

Here's what you can do to improve your technique and to start your quest for the perfect trade:

- **Look at market charts every single day.** You can't ever look at enough charts. Even when you've looked at millions of them, as I probably have, you can always discover something new, a new nuance with an oscillator, or a new wrinkle on something that you thought you knew.

- **Watch CNBC and other business channels and listen to what the experts are saying.** Then compare what they're saying to the reality of the moment. This will do two things: First, you'll eventually figure out which of those folks who are on TV all the time really know what they're talking about. Sometimes they say something that's worth checking out, and if you don't know whether they're trustworthy or not you may miss something important. And second, listening to them will give you ideas as to what to look for and how to go about doing your own work.

- **Read as many books as you can on trading and investing.** Some are good; others are terrible. Either way, reading them is time well spent because it helps you develop your own trading sense.

- **Find good sources of information and spend the money to become a subscriber.** Think of a subscription to *The Wall Street Journal* and *Investor's Business Daily* as part of the cost of doing business. Spend some money on a good charting Web site. There is no substitute for real-time charts when you're a timer. Chapter 22 lists some of my favorite information sources.

✔ **Never stop learning and adjusting.** This is the key to developing and improving your technique. If you stop looking for ways to improve your skills, you eventually see your results decline.

Running Down Reasons to Market Time

The only reason to become a market timer is to save yourself heartache and anguish while saving your portfolio significant losses. You can do this by using the methods that I provide in this book and studying the markets on a daily basis with the goal of anticipating significant changes in the overall trend of the markets and then acting upon them decisively before they advance to the point where you've missed a significant opportunity to make money.

Before you become a market timer, you need to understand trading, which is what market timing is all about. It may help you to think of trading as investing for different time frames.

For example, if you're a traditional buy-and-hold investor, you have been conditioned to think of your portfolio as something to hold on to forever. You may be an asset allocator, an investor who always has some of his portfolio invested in several areas of the market, with some of your holdings in bonds, others in stocks, and others in cash.

You may hold individual stocks, mutual funds, exchange-traded funds, or mixtures of all three. Yet, as a "long term" investor, you aren't very likely to change either the allocation or the components of the portfolio. If you're lucky, that may work out in the long haul. But in a world where conflict and competition for resources is the underlying fundamental, your mix of assets and your lack of flexibility are likely to cost you money in the short and perhaps in the long haul as well.

As a trader, you don't want to be lucky. Instead, you want to do everything you can so that your money grows, and to ensure that it's there when you need it. In other words, the difference between trading and investing is twofold: First, traders are more likely to make periodic changes to their portfolios and second, different times call for different trading methods and asset allocation.

For example, you may run into times when your portfolio should have zero stocks and bonds, or periods when gold, oil, or foreign currencies should be the major holdings. More important, at certain times you should be selling some of the markets short, or betting that prices will fall.

As a traditional stock investor who only reviews quarterly statements and forgets about them until the next batch arrives, you're very likely to miss, or fail to anticipate, key turning points in the markets. By the time a financial market story makes the cover of *USA Today* or the Drudge Report, the trend is well on its way, and you may have missed a significant opportunity to profit or to protect your money, resulting in significant losses.

Successful market timing depends on the following:

- **Commitment:** Make a conscious decision to become a market timer and to give up buy-and-hold investing. Just because you become a timer doesn't mean you'll become a day trader. It just means that you make a conscious effort to optimize your entry and exit points from your positions and that you take responsibility for watching your money and making the necessary changes to its composition whenever the market environment calls for it.

- **Discipline:** Your trading plan is useless if you aren't disciplined enough to follow it. Trading often isn't likely to net you any better results than the trader who trades once or twice a year. Successful timing isn't about quantity; it's truly about quality.

- **Patience:** Give timing an opportunity to work for you. Some markets are impossible to time and are better skipped altogether, with your money earning interest as you wait for the next opportunity. I always tell inexperienced investors that 2 percent in your pocket is better than 10 percent of your money in someone else's pockets.

- **Follow the rules:** Execute the trade every time your system gives you a buy signal. Sure, you're going to be wrong some of the time. Sometimes you're going to be wrong for a while, and you'll start to worry about your trading ability. But anyone who follows baseball or any sport knows that slumps are part of the game. When what you normally do isn't working, it means that you may have to fine-tune or retool your system. But if you only take some of your buy signals and avoid others, you run the risk of missing big profits or never knowing how good your system really is.

 The game is the same on the sell side. You may get away with ignoring your sell signals some of the time, but one day you'll be sorry that you ignored them. It's better to miss that last 5 percent on the up side than to lose a big chunk of what's already in your pocket.

- **Manage your money:** This is the hardest of all concepts to pass on to a budding timer, and it has three parts.

  - First, know yourself. If you don't handle risks well, don't risk all of your stake on any one trade, and don't put your entire nest egg into your timing strategy.

- Second, be diligent about limiting your risks. You do this by using sell stops and by being diligent in adjusting them as the market changes.

- Third, keep adding money to your trading stake. The more money you have available, the more opportunities that you have to trade larger positions as well as to get back any losses by earning interest. Never stop adding to your trading stake.

✔ **Diversify:** Consider timing different markets at the same time, and consider *going long* (betting that something will rise) while *going short* (betting that something will be falling in price) at the same time in another market. Doing so is a good way to hedge against risk.

Your success depends more than anything else on how you prepare yourself financially, intellectually, technologically, and personally through the development of a detailed and easy-to-implement trading plan.

The Nuts and Bolts of Market Timing

I'm a top-down analyst, which means that before I do any trading I get my bearings as to where the market's major trend is and what are the general conditions that could affect the odds of my making money.

I have a ritual that over the years has served me well and that I describe to you in detail in the section "Setting your timing ritual." I'm not telling you that this is what you need to do for your own trading, although I recommend that you develop some kind of routine that gets you in the groove, and that you follow this routine when you've got money in the markets. A timing routine is an important part of your success and the faster you start developing one, the better off you'll be.

Financing your possibilities

Before you get started with timing you need several things, the most important of which is money. And the inevitable question is, how much? Timing the stock market is not the same as trading futures, where your trading stake is highly leveraged and you need to be very well bankrolled. That doesn't mean that you should start timing with $100 and expect to become as wealthy as Warren Buffet in a few months.

You can have a modest start and still be successful if you apply yourself and keep adding money to your account. For example, I started my timing career with just a little over $1,000 dollars when I was 25 years old and through timing and saving, my stake has grown significantly over the years.

Large accounts don't guarantee large profits but can lead to large losses if you're not careful. Successful timing is more dependent on trading technique and your ability to establish positions early in a trend and remain in them for as long as possible to let time work for you.

Here are some key steps toward building your trading stake:

- ✔ **Live within your means:** The less you spend, the more you have to save and invest. Living on your credit cards and paying interest is a constant drain on your resources and on your trading stake.

- ✔ **Minimize your debt and be creative:** Use cash as much as possible or pay your card balances every month if you can. I use one credit card for over 90 percent of all my expenses and pay it off every month. It's also a reward card which means that at the end of the year I have something nice coming, like maybe a few free nights at a hotel or a free pair of plane tickets to somewhere worth going to.

- ✔ **Set aside a minimum amount every month for timing:** Put as much away as you can and make your tax deferred account, IRA, 401(k), or 403(b) the first priority. If you're self-employed you have the opportunity to put larger amounts away for retirement in your SEP-IRA. As a rule I try to maximize the amount that I put in my SEP-IRA every year. I've even borrowed money to do it a few times, and it's paid off nicely as the account has grown.

- ✔ **Adapt the size and change the types of positions as your account grows:** When I started timing, I limited my activity to mutual funds. But over the years as my account grew I moved on to individual stocks and more recently expanded to exchange-traded mutual funds (ETFs). I traded futures for a period of time but could never work my lifestyle to the point where I could give those markets the constant attention that they deserve.

- ✔ **Avoid leverage at all costs:** Margin traders, those who use borrowed money to trade, tend to take bigger risks than they should and often pay the price for it when the market turns against them. As a general rule, use only the amount of money that you have in your account to trade. A nice general rule is that you should always leave some money in the account. For example, I find that when I have over 60 to 70 percent of my stake in the market at any one time, I have a hard time managing the number of open positions.

The one exception to the no leverage rule is when you're using an ETF that has leverage as part of its design. For example, some stock index funds, such as the Ultra Series, are designed to move at a 200 percent clip to the underlying asset. I use those kinds of funds frequently in order to maximize the return on the trade for short periods of time. That's not something I recommend for you at the start of your timing career, but it is worthwhile as you gain experience. Check out my book *Trading Futures For Dummies* (Wiley) for a good overview of leveraged ETFs and how to use them for timing. Parts 3 and 4 of this book also give you more detail on using ETFs for timing individual sectors of the market.

Analyzing the markets

Most of timing has to do with preparation, research, and analysis, which can be summed up in one word: planning. The rest of it is execution of the plan and then management of the trade.

In order to analyze the markets you have to have a good grasp of some of the general principles of macro analysis and chart analysis. See Chapters 4 and 5 for more on charts and analysis. Here are some general principles:

- **Get comfortable with technical analysis.** Technical analysis has gained wide acceptance over the past few years with the advent of trading software and the improvement in trading results that can be yours if you learn to spot key characteristics in chart patterns.

  See Chapter 4 for a complete overview of the basics of this important aspect of market timing. The bottom line is that you can't time the markets without using charts, as indeed a picture is worth 1,000 words.

- **Sort out which reports and fundamental indicators are important and which to ignore.** You find numerous reports of economic data whose release is usually a market-moving event. I describe them in detail in Chapter 5. I recommend that you become familiar with each of these reports and that you clearly understand the kind of effect that they may have on the market.

- **Familiarize yourself the way sectors of the stock market tend to move when the stock market is at each particular stage of its cycle — bullish, bearish, or in a transition stage.** I suggest that you do the same with any commodity market that you're going to enter, as seasonal variations can govern these. I cover seasonality in Chapter 6.

- **Identify the dominant trend of each market or sector that you time.** There is no substitute for swimming with the tide in any form of investing. But trading with the trend is imperative in your timing endeavors, as is the ability to spot any time that the dominant trend is in danger of reversing.

✔ **Get a feel for market sentiment.** Market sentiment is a pretty esoteric thing, yet it's quite useful, and I cover it in detail in Chapter 8. Market sentiment has to do with having your fingers on the pulse of the market. Money moves from one extreme to the other — from greed to fear. When you sense that you are at one extreme or the other, you can be almost certain that the trend is about to change.

Greed is what you see at market tops, and fear is what often marks a market's bottom. That's when you start looking at your positions very carefully, and you start checking your charts looking for the signs of impending danger or a future opportunity to make money.

✔ **Be diverse in your ability to time the markets.** Don't limit yourself to any one market, and don't be afraid to sell the market short if the dominant trend is down. By the same token, you need to be proficient in one aspect of trading or individual market before moving on to the next.

Setting your timing ritual

After you have enough money to trade and a good grasp of technical and fundamental analysis, it's time to put all of that knowledge to work.

Like most professionals, in sports or any line of work that requires discipline, I've developed a ritual. No, it doesn't involve any scratching or spitting, but it does involve doing the same thing in just about the same order every day. Otherwise, I'd miss something, and in this business, if you miss something, there's a good chance that you'll pay for it later.

I start every day in a similar fashion, waking up at 4:30 a.m. and canvassing the landscape. As my computer boots up, I check CNBC World, and Bloomberg on the T.V. in my office. I then hit the Internet and start scanning a handful of important Web sites that have great amounts of information.

In about twenty minutes I check the headlines at *The Wall Street Journal* (www.wsj.com), *Investor's Business Daily* (www.investors.com) if I haven't checked it the night before, and Marketwatch.com (www.marketwatch.com) along with The Drudge Report (www.drudgereport.com). On occasion I also visit Stratfor.com (www.stratfor.com) if there is a geopolitical story that's affecting the markets, and during the election season I visit the Rasmussen Reports (www.rasmussenreports.com) to see what the latest political trends and opinion polls show.

Once or twice a week I also look at the *New York Times* (www.nytimes.com), the Washington Post (www.washingtonpost.com), and *The Washington Times* (www.washingtontimes.com). I work the *Los Angeles Times* (www.latimes.com) into the mix on occasion.

I do all this site-checking for two reasons. One is that I write a daily analysis column, Market IQ, for my Web site, Joe-Duarte.com. The other reason, which is equally important, is that aside from the recommendations that I make on the Web site, I also usually have thousands, if not hundreds of thousands, of my own dollars in the markets at any one time, so it's my business to know what's going on.

If things look attractive, I begin to look at different areas of all the markets. I canvass stocks, bonds, and commodities in general. I look at what happened in overnight markets. And I look to see what the stock index futures are predicting for the open on Wall Street.

I look at the trading calendar and see what the economic reports of the day will be, and whether any significant companies are due to report earnings, as well as what happened in after-hours trading the day before when important companies reported their earnings.

I then check all of my open positions and decide whether any of them require significant action, such as modifying sell stops, or whether I should consider closing out any positions.

After I've done that bookkeeping I look at the stocks that made my list the night before when I checked *Investor's Business Daily's* "Stocks in the News" section for charts that looked attractive. If conditions are right and I find anything worth risking, I put in orders to buy, to sell, or to sell short.

Then, I sit back and watch what happens, knowing that I've got a trading plan that works, and that I've done all that I can to give myself the best chance of making money.

Setting Realistic Expectations

If you think that just because you make the commitment to timing you're going to be rich tomorrow, you're going down the wrong road. If you're *very good* at timing, you'll make big profits anywhere from 30 to 50 percent of the time. In fact, what you'll see most of the time is what the pros call *scratch trades,* or trades that lose a little or make a little. And that's why most people give up on the market. What you'll see over time, though, is that once in a while, you'll get everything right and end up with a very nice trade or group of trades that more than make up for your break-even, lose a little, or gain a little trade.

You can't predict the future

No matter how much hype newsletter and *black box trading system* (secret trading systems pushed by tricky salesmen) types put out, no one can predict the future. So don't waste your time trying to do it, and don't beat yourself up when you make a bad trade.

Your best bet is to watch the market on a daily basis and to have good tools available that help you spot significant changes as early as possible, and then you have to be able to make the right trading decisions by always executing your trade based on what the indicators are telling you. If you're wrong, you should accept that as yet another scratch trade, and move on to the next trade after carefully analyzing what didn't go right with your last trade.

You can't win every time

If you and I made money every time we traded, you wouldn't have to read books like this, and I wouldn't have to write them; we'd both be in Tahiti soaking up rays and living large. In fact, very few people ever reach that kind of trading result. And even those who do often end up losing much of what they gain, as they fail to realize that a good portion of the gains had to do with good fortune.

I'm not saying that market timing is about getting lucky. What I'm saying is that you get only a handful of opportunities in your trading life to make huge gains. But if you don't take every opportunity that presents itself, you'll never be in a position for those few shots at making huge gains.

Do yourself a favor: Get well grounded, get a thick skin, and realize that market timing will be hard work but that you can be successful if you apply yourself and make it a long-term project.

Measure your success reasonably

As a market timer you will have periods of very rough going. You may even get some big losses because you forgot to put in your sell stops, or because the market opened way above or below where you had set your stops.

You can beat yourself up pretty handily if you don't get a proper view of how your fortunes ebb and flow as early as possible in your career as a timer. Think about this before you start the self-flagellation that can undo your trading. Look for the reason that you lost money and figure out whether it's because of something you did or because of something someone else did. That distinction is hugely important and could make the difference between staying in the game or giving it up altogether.

Here are some good points for keeping your trading practice in perspective:

- **Measure your results reasonably:** Making money in the markets every day is difficult. But if you measure your success every week, month, and then every 12 months, you're more likely to get a better picture of how well you're doing.

- **Don't try to beat the market:** The media and Wall Street are fascinated with *beating the markets* — having your portfolio gain more than the major indexes, such as the Dow Jones Industrial Average, at any given time. But doing so on a regular basis is difficult. Instead, concentrate on making good trades consistently. If the market goes up 15 percent and you made only 10 percent, you're doing quite well. Rather than obsessing over beating the market, work on trading with the trend and being consistent.

  If the market is going up and you're making money, that's success. If the market is going down and you're not losing money that's success. If the market is going down and you're making money as a short seller, that's outstanding success.

- **Dollars versus percentages:** Measure your gains or loses with the right perspective. Percentages work better for small accounts. A $2,000 change in a $20,000 account is a big deal. But, if you have a big account, measuring your success or failure in terms of dollars and cents is better. For example, if you have a $500,000 portfolio, and you make $2,000 in a few days, you've done well, even if your gain is only 0.4 percent. You made $2,000 in a short period of time. Don't beat yourself up because you could have made more or because you made only a few percentage points.

Enjoying the Process and the Fruits of Your Labor

This chapter gives you an excellent overview of market timing. More than anything, market timing is a process, and one that, at least for me, has developed into a lifetime commitment. Timing is part of what I do every day, and it's something that my friends and family have come to expect of me.

And I enjoy the hell out of it. Even if I'm not making money, timing offers me a challenge on a daily basis. Sometimes I win, and I celebrate. Sometimes I lose and I try to figure out where I made my mistakes, so that I don't get caught with my pants down the next time something similar happens.

But no matter what, I look forward to analyzing the markets, writing my daily columns, and trading my own account. If you get into this vocation and find that you don't enjoy it, it's either because you're not doing it right, or because you're not meant to do it.

Don't give up if you're not successful right away. Take your time and set realistic goals. Practice your timing trades on paper before you put real money to work. And don't let what others say influence you without checking their advice out for yourself first.

When you have a good day, celebrate a little. Have that glass of wine, or treat yourself to an extra delicious desert. Life is short and worth enjoying. If you've had a bad day, let it go. You can review your mistakes the next day. The important thing is to learn to leave the trading at the office, or at your trading station at home.

Remember, if Flamenco master Paco de Lucia can play one note at a time very slowly, you too can look at one chart at a time and savor every single tick on that chart, glean every single ounce of knowledge from it, and put it to good use.

Chapter 2

Peering Inside the Mind of a Market Timer

· ·

In This Chapter

▶ Looking behind the curtain at Wall Street

▶ Understanding the effect of the Fed

▶ Digging in to the psychology of timing

▶ Creating and evaluating a trading plan

· ·

Wall Street doesn't want you to make money. Wall Street wants to take your money.

That's why the Wall Street marketing machine harps on about the randomness of the market, long-term investing, and other drivel. But ask mutual fund managers what they do with their own private accounts, and most of the good ones tell you that they trade aggressively, and that means they time the market.

In this chapter I wipe away the myths and the half-truths that are part of the market's lore but that do nothing but help you to lose money.

Finding Out How Wall Street Really Works

In order to understand how Wall Street works, it pays to understand what it is — a giant sales machine. And what it sells is potential for gains and losses. Wall Street accomplishes its primary goal, making money for itself, by taking on risk, packaging it into products, and then selling them to institutions, such as pension funds, mutual funds, insurance companies, foreign governments, and the public. Furthermore, it collects fees along every step of the way, serves as an intermediary at stock and futures exchanges, and offers money management, advisory, and analytical services to anyone who can pay for them.

So, why do hedge funds collect management fees on top of taking 20 percent of any profits that they generate? Why do some financial advisors sell you only the mutual funds that generate the highest fees for them, regardless of the funds' performance? Why do mutual funds collect fees whether they make money or not? And how is it possible that some mutual funds charge you money to get in, while they hold your money, and as you exit?

Basically, because they can. Because Wall Street is the best distribution system for money in the history of the world. No entity in history has been more efficient at transferring wealth from one place to another — and enriching itself handsomely along the way.

 Wall Street is also in the business of trading vehicles, instruments, and situations that allow it to collect money for itself. If you happen to make money along the way, it's mostly incidental and considered part of the cost of doing business.

The best way they do all of what they do is by creating products that are difficult to understand, such as derivatives based on arcane indexes and weird securities that they can market to the unwary. A perfect example is the subprime mortgage crisis, where worthless paper was bundled into mortgage-backed securities with good mortgages and given top ratings in order to sell them and get them off their books.

These practices are part of a Wall Street business model integral to the boom and bust cycle that defines the global economy. And the bottom line is that market timing is essentially the antidote to the bubble-generating hype and marketing machine designed to rid you of your hard-earned money.

Introducing the Federal Reserve

Think of Wall Street and its creation, the financial markets, as a point of convergence where the output of the Federal Reserve — interest rates and money supply — all available economic and financial data, and the collective sentiment of all investors come together. From a trading standpoint, all the economic data generated on a daily basis is little more than the catalyst for the market's short-term gyrations. What really moves the markets is how investors interpret the data and how they decide to allocate their money in response to the information. As a market timer your most important focus is how the market responds to or anticipates events, such as the release of key economic or earnings reports.

The *Federal Reserve* is the United State's central bank; it was created in 1913 to prevent the boom and bust cycles of the early industrial age. The net effect of the Federal Reserve's actions on the markets is twofold.

On one end, *bull markets,* markets where prices rise for extended periods of time, tend to last longer than they might without the Fed's stimulation by the net effect of lower interest rates and readily available credit.

Big hedge funds and even some mutual funds that use *margin* (the practice of establishing positions with only a portion of the stated value of the position) as part of their trading strategies tend to run their business on borrowed money. That strategy usually holds up fairly well until interest rates begin to rise and money is no longer easy to get. That leads to *margin calls,* where the lenders want their money back and the borrower either has to pay from its reserves or sell assets in order to meet the margin call. When enough margin calls hit simultaneously, markets can fall precipitously as big margin-fueled trades are unwound, often by the big players being forced to sell their most liquid assets, blue chip stocks — those of high-quality companies, such as the ones in the Dow Jones Industrial Average.

On the other side, *bear markets,* markets where prices generally tend to fall for extended periods of time, tend to last too long, as highly leveraged players sell their assets in waves in order to meet their loan repayment obligations.

Making matters worse, these big institutions tend to wait until prices bottom out, at least temporarily, before they start unloading their next wave of sell-ing. This is the major reason for the volatility and the haphazard nature of trading usually seen in bear markets, as these often desperate players are trying to get out of their leveraged positions or their liquid positions at the best possible time. The Federal Reserve often starts and exacerbates bear market periods by raising interest rates and continuing to do so over extended periods of time. Higher interest rates tend to make less volatile, interest-earning investments such as money market mutual funds more attractive than stocks; traders can make money with less risk in those instruments, as compared to stocks.

The Fed is by no means perfect but, especially since the 1980s, has done a reasonable job of meeting its two mandates: keeping the economy growing, and maintaining full employment. The central bank, in the past 30 years or so, has been directly and indirectly involved in the inflationary spiral in the 1970s, the early Reagan years' bull market in stocks, the 1987 crash in the stock market, as well as the creation and implosion of the dot-com boom. The Fed has also engineered several recessions as well as several significant economic recoveries during that period and has mostly done a fairly credible job of meeting its mandate, although its record is far from perfect.

The most recent example of the Federal Reserve's intervention in the markets was the subprime mortgage crisis, a situation that took several years to develop but came to a head in 2007. After the September 11, 2001, attacks on the World Trade Center, the Federal Reserve feared a deflationary spiral and so lowered interest rates very aggressively and kept the benchmark Fed Funds rate at 1 percent until 2004. During that period of low interest rates, two things happened:

✔ Money flowed out of the United States and made its way to the emerging economies of Asia, mostly China and India.

✔ Low interest rates, a weak U.S. stock market, and easy credit led to a boom in housing and commercial construction in the United States that also spread to other areas of the globe, including Europe.

Eventually, the artificially low interest rates, speculative excesses, and inflation began to creep into the U.S. economy. The inflation was also influenced by increased demand for commodities in the emerging economies of the world, which had benefited from the capital flight away from the United States after September 11, 2001. In 2004, the Federal Reserve began to raise interest rates. But rates were so low that it took quite a long time before the market began to feel the squeeze of higher rates.

Wall Street, always looking for a way to make money, was no slouch this time around and hooked investors with the mortgage-backed securities market. Mortgage-backed securities are just mortgages that are grouped into bonds so that they can be sold to investors. The practice of grouping many mortgages into one bond also increases the attractiveness of the bond to investors, because if one mortgage in a group of, say, 100 mortgages packaged into one bond doesn't pay, the other 99 help to defer the risk.

The securities sold well. Investors took comfort in the fact that most people in the United States pay their mortgages before they pay any other bills — homes traditionally are their owners' number-one investment.

The problem with this strategy, at least this time, is that the housing boom went on so long that the quality of the mortgage loans began to fall, as banks and mortgage brokers dropped their lending standards just to make sales. All that finagling added up to people with low-paying jobs and no real prospects of improvement in the future buying million-dollar homes and often paying as little as $1,000 per month in mortgage payments.

Many of the low-quality loans were adjustable-rate mortgages made to totally unqualified buyers. Adjustable-rate mortgages have a low introductory rate in order to attract buyers but eventually reset to higher interest rates. After a while, Wall Street started grouping high-quality mortgages, where the homeowner could make payments, with low-quality mortgages, where the homeowner would not be able to make payments after the low introductory interest rate rose.

Clever and downright crooked mortgage vendors continued to push adjustable-rate mortgages on unqualified buyers. And Wall Street kept lumping the good mortgages with the bad mortgages into single bonds. When the low interest rates on the adjustable mortgages reset to higher rates and the homeowners stopped paying their monthly payments, the bad mortgages lost value, and in many cases were defaulted on, leading to a high home foreclosure rate. Because these bad mortgages were lumped with the good mortgages into bonds, when the bad loans became worthless, they took down the value of the good loans, and the whole thing collapsed.

The bottom line is that the Federal Reserve, by keeping interest rates too low for too long, gave Wall Street an opportunity to make too much of a good thing in the mortgage securities market. What was once an excellent risk-management practice — the bundling of mortgages into bonds in order to decrease risk of default to banks and mortgage lenders — backfired when the lending standards were lowered too far, and too many high-risk mortgages were sold to high-risk homeowners and to investors.

The whole thing unraveled when the Fed began to raise interest rates and the adjustable-rate mortgages sold to high-risk clients reset to higher interest rates, making it impossible for those homeowners to make their payments.

The Fed and its relationship to the markets is your best set of friends as a market timer. Understanding and watching this relationship and combining it with technical analysis equips you to make better timing decisions. Make sure that you

✔ **Keep track of what the Federal Reserve says.**

Federal Reserve governors and the Federal Reserve Chairman are always making speeches; they often give interviews to the press and testify in front of Congressional committees. They rarely give away the house during any of these appearances, yet they give fairly good clues about their individual thinking. Deciphering this information can be tricky because some Fed players are outside the majority, and you can get false clues. Still, monitoring what the Fed says and how the market responds to it is important.

✔ **Keep an eye on the Fed Fund Futures at the Chicago Board of Trade (www.cbot.com).**

Fed Funds are overnight deposits that one bank lends to another bank in order for both banks to square their books. The Fed Funds rate is the benchmark for all rates in the United States.

Fed Funds futures allow banks to lock in rates for future overnight loans. This process, by which the market tries to predict what the Federal Reserve is going to do, is not an exact science, but it shows you the market's expectations for the future of rates. If the rates on these futures contracts are falling, then the market is expecting the Fed to lower rates. If they are rising, then the market expects the opposite. What's really important is what actually happens. If the market expects the Fed to do one thing, and the Fed does another, there could be a change in the trend of the markets.

As a market timer, you always want to trade *with* the Fed, not *against* it. When interest rates are falling, a rally in the stock market is likely at some point in the future. This relationship is variable, as making the markets rally can take significant amounts of interest-rate lowering. But the odds of a rally tend to rise when the Fed primes the pump enough — via lowering interest rates and other maneuvers to help increase liquidity and ease credit. In other words, when the Fed lowers rates, look to buy stocks and when the Fed raises rates, look to sell stocks.

Uncovering the Psychology of Timing

The major reason to become a market timer is to save your portfolio significant losses by studying the markets on a daily basis and anticipating significant changes in the overall trend of the markets, and then acting upon them decisively before they advance to the point of creating those losses. But before you can do all that — before you become a market timer — you need to understand trading.

The markets operate at two extremes — greed and fear. You see the former at market tops where speculation runs rampant. Stocks are making multi-point moves to the up side on a daily basis and the market seems to have no direction to go but higher. That's when the Wall Street hype machine is at its finest, with analysts raising price targets and selling initial public offerings (IPOs) on a daily basis. If you took part in the Internet bubble in December of 2000 and the housing bubble late in 2006, you understand what greed feels like.

Evaluate your open positions carefully when you recognize the signs of greed gone wild.

Fear arises when the market has nowhere to go but down. The news is bleak; the economy is in recession; job losses are mounting; politicians are running around creating programs and holding hearings; and the 24-hour news channels, the local news, newspapers, and the Drudge Report are blaring sensational headlines and comparing the current set of issues to those that preceded significant economic disasters in the past.

As a market timer, the times when you recognize that the markets are in the midst of a bubble are the times when you should be the most careful and put the timer's triad — vigilance, preparation, and execution — into full swing.

Vigilance: Being a steady, not a fast Eddie

Being vigilant means that you're watching the trading action carefully, that you're aware of your surroundings with regard to the market, and that you can translate what you observe into a plan of action. You should develop, implement, and fine-tune a market analysis routine and go through it on a daily basis. I run mine every night after the market closes and I get ready to update my Web site, www.joe-duarte.com. Here's a summary of my routine:

✔ In a notebook, I log the prices of all the major indexes, all the major sector indexes, as well as the prices my portfolio of active stocks, and exchange-traded mutual funds (ETFs). I update this notebook by hand every day, and I make notes about key developments in each of them as applicable.

✔ I scan my favorite news and information sources: *The Wall Street Journal* (www.wsj.com), *Investor's Business Daily* (www.investors.com), and yes, The Drudge Report (www.drudgereport.com), along with other sources for clues as to what's lurking out there.

✔ I make careful notes and record changes in all my open positions, as well as those of my subscribers. I look at all my notes and observations and then adjust any sell stops and do other bookkeeping chores, so that I'm ready to go.

I run through the routine again when I wake up in the morning. In other words, I am meticulous about my trading and make my decisions based not on whims or emotion but on preparation.

Preparation: Acknowledging the Boy Scout in all of us

Staying vigilant enables you to step confidently into the preparation phase, during which you formulate your trading plan. A trading plan is the blueprint for how you make your trades. It takes out the guesswork of when, how, and why you enter and exit trading positions. It also lets you review your trading activity, often pinpointing where you made your mistakes or earned your success. In *Trading Futures For Dummies* (Wiley), I describe the full details of a trading plan that is perfectly adaptable to any market.

Follow these basic steps when you create your own trading plan:

✔ **Use only risk capital.** Make sure that you are financially able to sustain the risk of market timing. In other words, have your family and yourself well insured, have your saving plan in order, make sure that your bills are covered, and use only risk capital for timing.

✔ **Study the markets before you trade.** Understand the characteristics of your chosen market, and get comfortable with it before you move on to another area. If you decide to trade stocks and stock ETFs, get to know each sector of the market well. Do some *paper trades,* where you write down what your trade would be but don't actually make the trade, before plunging in with your capital. Paper trades let you test out strategies and get your feet wet in timing with no risk.

✔ **Pin down your time frame.** Decide ahead of time whether you want to risk your money for hours, days, weeks, or longer. Your time frame makes a big difference when you're deciding how far you'll let a position run.

✔ **Stay flexible.** No strategy works every time, so get comfortable with more than one way to trade. For example, sometimes picking up stocks at low prices is a good idea, and sometimes buying them when they're showing significant signs of strength — momentum trading — works better.

✔ **Determine your exit strategy before you put your money in.** Know how much you'll buy, or short. Know how much more you'll add to the position and when, and how you'll get out of a trade before you make your trade.

✔ **Review your results.** This is where you evaluate the steps, decisions, and processes that you went through while making a trade. Whether you did well or poorly in a trade, reviewing it is likely to help you to do better in the future. If you don't make mistakes, then you're probably not trading enough.

✔ **Apply what you've discovered.** If you don't study the results of good and bad trades and use what you find, you never become as successful as you could be. Take notes, review them, and use what you discover.

Execution: Pulling the trigger on the trade

Execution is the part of trading that gets the headlines but that can be disastrous if you don't stay vigilant and prepare adequately. I give you more details about what happens when you pull the trigger on the trade in Chapter 9.

The execution phase of a trade is divided as follows:

✔ **Being diligent in your preparation and committed to finding the opportunity to make the trade.** If you're well prepared, you will recognize the chart setup that you're looking for.

✔ **Pulling the trigger.** When you recognize the opportunity, you have to pull the trigger. This is where all that vigilance and planning pays off. Buy the stock or the ETF. If you're right, then the trade will move in the direction that you expected, up or down, and you move on to the next phase. If you're wrong, preparation should also save you trouble, because you have an exit strategy in place.

✔ **Managing the trade.** Execution doesn't end when you enter your position. You need to monitor the trade and, as things progress, put the rest of your plan into effect by adding more shares based on the criteria you develop in your plan, as well as how the trade develops. Don't be afraid to adjust to changing market conditions. Finally, when your criteria are met, either you've met a profit target or you've been stopped out of the trade, and you go back to your results and study them, to see why things went right or wrong.

Picking Your Battles and Battlefields

Perhaps the hardest aspect of market timing is deciding what to trade and how to go about it. Experience will show you which markets you enjoy trading and which ones you don't.

If you don't understand something, don't trade it. That general rule has served me well during my 20-plus years as a trader.

If you're a long-term stock investor looking for a market to time, stick with stocks or instruments such as stock index futures, or stock options. If you're a bond investor, start by studying the bond market and its timing aspects. In other words, you're likely to be a better trader if you choose a market that you're already familiar with, as long as you're willing to make the necessary changes in order to be a timer, not a buy-and-hold investor.

Consider the following when you choose markets to time:

- **Spend some time studying multiple markets.** See which ones intrigue you, and do some research and some paper trading. Get all the information you can about what moves that market, such as which reports tend to have more influence on the way the market moves.

- **Trade what you know first.** If you're a software engineer, why would you want to start your timing career trying to trade energy stocks or precious-metals ETFs? Use what you know to your advantage, and get specific in your trading.

  I like to think of timing in terms of efficiency; using what I already know and can bring to the table is an advantage. I'm a physician, so I'm always paying attention to the medical sector. And you might be surprised to learn that I haven't traded too many health stocks in a very long time. Why? Medicare began to cut reimbursements to physicians and hospitals in the 1990s, and the drug companies began to cut back their research and marketing budgets, reducing the chance of delivering blockbuster drugs.

- **Consider your personality.** If you're a conservative investor who's happy with mutual fund–style returns and don't have a lot of time, you're not really cut out to be a timer. Stick with what you know, and good luck. However, if you spend all your time trying to figure out what moves the currency markets, start right there with paper trading as you learn the ins and outs of that volatile market.

  If you pick up new things fast and like to be aggressive, then you can look at some of the sectors of the stock or commodity markets, such as metals, the energy sector, and other areas that you can time via ETFs. See Part IV for more details on the more aggressive style of timing required for sector trading.

Stocks and ETFs that cover broader ground, such as broad indexes like the S&P 500 may be the best middle ground for the rest of us, especially because timing is all about spotting trend changes and trading with the trend as early as possible. Individual stocks are still the most widely used instruments in market timing, and now ETFs have opened up a whole new world to timers, because they can trade stock indexes, bonds, oil, natural gas, gasoline, and individual sectors in the stock market through an online brokerage account.

Market timing is a state of mind that requires studying, preparation, and following up on your strategies to figure out why they worked or didn't work in any particular situation.

Chapter 3

Preparing Yourself and Your Finances for Timing

In This Chapter

▶ Working timing into your financial plan

▶ Making sure you're on solid financial ground

▶ Taking personal matters into consideration

▶ Assessing your financial starting point

▶ Setting up your timing equipment

Market timing without preparation is likely to get those who try it into trouble, given the complexity of the task and the required attention to detail. Get your timing practice off to the best start by taking the time to learn the ropes and put together the infrastructure required to be successful at it. Timers need several kinds of tools. But software, hardware, and information are only a small, albeit important, part of what you need.

In this chapter, you find out what it takes to prepare yourself for a potentially rewarding trading strategy.

Defining the Role of Timing in Your Financial Plan

When I was 26, I became obsessed with the stock market and read everything I could about it. From day one I timed the markets with my entire retirement portfolio, which began with a humble $1,500 in a mutual fund account. At any time I may have as much as 80–100 percent of my money invested, while at other times, I may not have a dime invested.

There is no tried-and-true formula to help you decide how much of your money you should dedicate to timing. But here are some important questions to ask yourself as you decide how much of your portfolio to use for timing:

✔ **What do I want to gain from timing?** When I started, I wanted to turn a little money into a lot of money in a hurry. But it didn't take long to figure out that timing is more of a grind than a path to quick riches.

Timing is more like a baseball game. You go to bat, look for a good pitch or two, take your best swing, and hope that the ball falls in for a hit. You'll hit timing home runs, but it's better to play for base hits, doubles, and sometimes just to get on base on a walk or an error. Think about that boat, or that nice vacation. But don't fool yourself into believing that you'll get there every year by timing — unless you're truly gifted and very fortunate. If you were, you'd probably be writing this book or spending time on your private island, not reading this book.

✔ **How much money do I have?** I had $1,500 when I started. I had to become a timer or my entire stake might have been wiped out with one bear market or even a couple of bad trades.

If you have a big portfolio, say one that is over a million dollars, you may want to use only a small portion, say 30 to 50 percent, for timing, and allocate that according to your risk tolerance, market conditions, and whether you need money in the near term or further out. As a general rule, it seems prudent that anyone with a portfolio of less than $50,000 should consider timing.

✔ **Is the money in a tax-deferred account?** Conventional wisdom says that retirement accounts should be placed in mutual funds and managed by professionals. But tax-deferred accounts are perfect for timing, for they generate no taxes, no matter how many trades you make. The flip side is that in a non-retirement account, you have to pay capital gains taxes every time you sell a position for a profit. Most people won't sell anything if they have to pay taxes on it, which makes timing difficult.

✔ **How much time should I devote to timing?** The answer is *enough,* and it may vary from person to person or period to period. If you have a job that requires your full attention on a daily basis and no opportunity to check the markets carefully at least once or twice per day, timing is likely to be a dangerous enterprise for you.

Although you don't have to spend all your time in front of a trading screen to find timing success, you should make time in your schedule for at least one daily check of your portfolio. On days when I'm not in front of my screen and have positions open, I usually check before I leave the house, during any break that I have from whatever I'm doing during the day, during lunch, and again at least 30 minutes before the market closes, in case I have to make changes.

✔ **What price am I willing to pay in order to become successful?** I decided that I would be willing to pay whatever the price was to time the markets successfully and to turn timing into a second career. I chose to put up with losing trades, frustration, and constant worries about my account, because it was a challenge that I couldn't run away from. You may or may not ever run into such dramatic circumstances in your timing endeavors. But you should ask yourself the question before you start, and you should repeat the question on a frequent basis.

In other words, it makes sense to know yourself well before you start on the path to market timing.

Working with a professional

If you like the idea of being out of the market during bad times, which is the basic tenet of timing, but you don't have the time or perhaps the fortitude to manage your trades yourself, you might decide to use an advisor or a broker. But unless you have a sizeable account — usually larger than several million dollars — few true timers will even consider taking your money under management.

If you find someone who will take a modest account, you probably won't get the kind of service that you think you deserve, as your account will likely be lumped in with all the other accounts that the broker or timer uses for timing.

Depending on your agreement, your broker may have to call you and ask your permission to trade on your behalf. If instead you give your broker discretion to make trades on your behalf, you may not like the risks she takes with your money. You may face some conflict down the line if your broker is unscrupulous or not very talented.

In my experience, finding a broker, investment advisor, or financial planner who is willing to time the markets and can actually do it successfully is very difficult. Another option is to put your money in a mutual fund that times the markets. There are very few of those, and even

fewer that do it well. Here are two that have had good records:

✔ **CGM Capital Appreciation** is very aggressive. It doesn't say that it times the markets in its prospectus, but it actually admits to "frequent trading" and higher "transaction costs" due to the increased trading volume. That's code for market timing.

✔ **PMFM** offers two different timing strategies, the Managed Strategy and the Core Managed Strategy. The Managed Strategy is pure market timing and is based on a technical asset allocation model of the stock market. This approach to the markets can lead to market exposure of 0 percent up to 100 percent, depending on the model's reading, and the market's interpretation of the model. The Core Strategy always has a minimum exposure of 50 percent to the stock market but can have up to a 100 percent exposure. PMFM manages individual accounts and offers mutual funds.

My point here is not to recommend CGM or PMFM, although if you're looking to time the markets passively, these institutions aren't a bad way to go. My point is that you can time the markets, and that there are professionals out there that can do a credible job for you.

Financing Your Timing

You need money to make money, and certainly you need a source of money to get started in trading, as well as to buy or upgrade equipment, and to obtain reliable trading and timing information.

If you have to borrow money to be a timer, such as using your home equity or credit card advances for your trading stake, you shouldn't market time. The money you use for timing needs to be money that you can afford to lose, money that is left over after you've covered your savings, expenses, and other necessities. Your goal is to keep your losses as minimal and as infrequent as possible, but the reality is that the markets are risky.

You may have to develop a savings plan over several years to finance your new endeavor. That means that you may need to make changes in your spending habits, such as missing a vacation, driving a more modest car, or eating at fewer fancy restaurants. No matter how you do it, the best way to time the markets is with your own money. When it's your money that you're trading, you're more likely to be extremely careful about what you do with it.

Before you start timing, make sure you have the following matters under control and accounted for:

- **Living expenses, especially food, mortgage, rent, and car payments:** If you can't live the way you want on what you make, looking to market timing to save you from your current situation is not prudent. You have to have enough money for the basic necessities before you do anything else.

- **Life insurance coverage:** You can find basic life-insurance calculators online to help you determine how much coverage you need.

- **Health insurance:** The amount of health coverage you need is based on your family and your individual needs. Figure a worst-case scenario to be on the safe side.

- **Retirement plan:** Don't time the markets unless you have adequate amounts of retirement funds available. I do trade my retirement fund, but I have done it for many years and am a professional trader. You have to be quite good at this before you start to do the same.

Do not put 100 percent of your retirement money into any single asset class. Diversify, and time the markets based on your experience and knowledge of trends and indicators.

- **Savings plan for other needs, including vacations, day-to-day surprises, and especially your children's college educations:** Plenty of financial advisors and Web sites may be useful in giving you guidelines. Eric Tyson's book *Investing For Dummies,* 5th Edition (Wiley) does a good job of helping you through this very important point.

 ✔ **Emergency fund:** You can never have enough money stashed away for emergencies, but three months of monthly expenses is a fairly good start.

Use your tax returns, credit card statements, and include all your monthly bills to determine where you stand financially.

After you take care of the matters in the bullet list, take as much debt as you can off the books. If you've got anything left over, you can start your timing endeavor. If you're not there yet, you can prepare for that happy day by putting together your trading plan and doing some paper trading to test your mettle.

When you add up your expenses, include a special section for surprises like car repairs and dental bills. Those unexpected bills have a knack for popping up, and they can add up in a hurry.

Considering Personal Matters

Pretty much anything is possible in life, and you should be diligent in your preparation for timing, as well as living. Consider the following aspects of life before you start:

 ✔ **Age:** If you think that you won't live long enough to make your money back if you have a disastrous trade, market timing isn't for you. Give yourself some room to recover, as well as to understand why you failed.

 ✔ **Health:** Make sure that you're in good physical and mental shape before you start. The stress of timing may truly be hazardous to your health if you have high blood pressure, heart disease, diabetes, or any other such condition that is not well treated.

 ✔ **Dependents:** If you have a family and are the only breadwinner, more conservative investing methods might be best for you.

 ✔ **Job security:** A steady job is your best source of trading income. Make sure that you're secure in your occupation before you start timing.

 ✔ **Your family situation:** Make your spouse or significant other aware of your intentions and gauge his or her attitude. A cold stare from the person you're sharing a home with is a good reason to paper trade as you gain experience or to start out with small lots.

 ✔ **Know your own limits:** If failure makes you mental, this isn't for you, at least not until you get the hang of it and can come to grips with the fact that you won't make brilliant trades every single time you step up to the plate.

Determining Your Net Worth

Calculating your net worth helps you to reach your final decision about whether you can actually afford to become a market timer.

Your *net worth* refers to the assets and cash you have after you subtract all your liabilities. And it's the number that can tell you whether trading futures is a good idea.

Calculating your net worth is simple. You can do it by using easy-to-find software programs, such as Quicken, getting on the Internet and finding a calculator, or filling out a form from your bank or broker. You find a thorough explanation of how to calculate net worth in Eric Tyson's *Personal Finance For Dummies,* 5th Edition (Wiley).

Pay special attention to the amounts you have in the following:

- ✓ **Cash:** The amount of money you can get your hands on quickly. This is the stuff that you have in money-market funds, bank accounts, your pocket, or in the cookie jar.

- ✓ **Real estate:** Your home, rental properties, second home, and even partial stakes in vacant lots, and so on.

- ✓ **Stocks, bonds, and retirement accounts:** You need to count this money because it's there, not because you're likely to use it, unless you're planning to time with your retirement fund. It's foolish to cash these in and use the funds for timing, as the penalties are too high.

- ✓ **Business assets:** Include these assets but remember that — except for something like accounts receivables (cash owed to your business) — they're likely to be difficult to cash in. Better to underestimate than overblow this category.

- ✓ **Credit card balances, second mortgages, and adjustable-rate mortgages:** This dangerous category requires your utmost attendance. Be as complete here as you can, and consider the worst-case scenarios, such as your low-rate adjustable-mortgage payment resetting and rising significantly.

If your net worth is less than $200,000, you shouldn't be trading at all, much less trading futures.

Differentiating between timing and investing is important. If your net worth is $200,000 or less, using managed timing strategies such as those used by mutual funds is perfectly acceptable.

Never risk more than 10 percent of your net worth as a trading stake. If you have a net worth of at least $500,000 and you're a well equipped, stable, and experienced trader, you can take more risk and use 20 percent of your net worth to trade, provided your expenses and long-term investments are covered. However, risking more than 25 percent of your net worth in any one trading venue is a crapshoot and will likely get you into trouble.

Getting Tooled Up for Timing

You need two significant tools in order to be a successful market timer: a trading account and the right trading setup. The former is easy enough to set up, with a phone call or even through a Web site. The latter requires a bit more thought and expense.

Setting up your trading account

A timer's trading account has two parts, the money market fund and whatever you decide to buy and sell with the money you place in the account. I prefer online trading accounts because they enable me to enter just about any asset class with a few clicks on my mouse. I get instant order fills 99 percent of the time, and I get instant notification and proof of my order, which market maker the trade went through, how many shares I bought, and at what price.

The money market account is the hub of your account because it's the first account that you open with your broker. It's not just easy to use, it's required. Aside from earning interest, its only other purpose is to be a place where your money waits for your next trade. Money will move in and out of this account as you trade, instead of your having to wire money to and from another account, such as your bank.

You can set up a money market account through any of several brokers. Three reliable and long-standing options are

- ✔ Fidelity (www.fidelity.com)
- ✔ Charles Schwab (www.charlesschwab.com)
- ✔ Ameritrade (www.ameritrade.com)

Your commission per trade, if you trade stocks or exchange-traded funds, usually is less than $10 per trade. That's $10 or less to get in, and another $10 or less to get out. That's not always the case, and I suggest you check each individual broker's fee schedule. Some brokers charge more if your account doesn't have a minimum amount. On the other hand, the more you trade, the more likely you are to get some sort of discount.

Money market funds charge a management fee but also pay interest. The management fee is taken out on a daily basis, before your interest is calculated.

Building your timing toolkit

Detailed analysis and discipline make you a successful timer. But it doesn't hurt to have the best tools at your disposal. Consider the following:

- ✔ **First and foremost, you're going to need a fast computer with as much memory as you can get.** Most trading rigs now require at least 2.5MB of RAM (random access memory) to run large programs at high speed, and over 100MB of hard drive to store data. You'll be running real-time quotes, reading charts, and looking at information from multiple sources simultaneously.

  Ideally, a setup that lets you run two or more monitors is best. If you don't have enough money to buy more than one monitor initially, it's still worthwhile to get a computer that will let you run two monitors so you can expand your setup down the road.

- ✔ **Get comfortable.** Your furniture should include a good desk and chair. A television set with cable and access to multiple news sources is also essential. I keep CNBC on all the time when I'm trading, with the sound off a fair amount of the time. This lets me look up once in a while to see whether something important is happening.

- ✔ **Have backup systems.** Aside from a good telephone setup, have at least one mode of reliable high-speed Internet connection available and a regular modem. I use both DSL and cable in my setup, as well as a backup laptop with all my data in it and a handheld PDA that can give me access to the markets and my trading account if all else fails.

Trading and analysis software

You can find a lot of good programs out there, including E-Signal and Worden.com, as well as a bunch of Web-based trading sites that have good access to charts and indicators.

I give you more detail in Chapter 22, but here are a few of the ones that offer both free and paid charts and indicators: Stockcharts.com, Askresearch.com, Yahoo Finance, BigCharts.com, Prophet.net, and Marketwatch.com. Most of these programs and Web sites have all the basics, including real-time charts and the ability to run a good selection of analytical tools.

At the very least, your software should

- ✔ **Be easy to access.** If it's not on the Web, it's not worth it. And if it's always down when you're ready to trade, get another provider.

✔ **Have all the major indicators available.** Make sure that you take the free trial of the service before pay for it and that you try everything — moving averages, oscillators, trend-line drawing tools, and tutorials. If it's not easy to use, move along.

✔ **Be well supported.** Test all the support methods: chat, toll-free telephone, e-mail, and anything else that the service provider gives you. If they don't take care of your problems fast, you know what to do.

Information sources

This is not as big a deal as it used to be, since the Internet will let you find whatever you want about an individual stock or news item, often for free. But for a subscription fee you can get *The Wall Street Journal* (www.wsj.com) or *Investor's Business Daily* (www.investors.com). And to me it's worth subscribing to these two Web sites, as I get a lot of good background information and company data there. *Investor's Business Daily*'s Web site is all about timing the stock market and is worth the price I pay every year.

Chapter 4

Charting Your Course: The Market Timer's Edge

....

In This Chapter

▶ Looking for the mother of all trends

▶ Watching for four critical signs

▶ Grasping timing's crux: How to read the charts

▶ Getting to know important oscillators

....

Without charts and technical analysis, timing the markets would be nearly impossible. Market timing is about anticipating and preparing, not forecasting, and you find the best tools for the trade in the annals of technical analysis, where a picture is indeed worth a thousand words.

In this chapter, I show you how to develop your technical analysis arsenal and how to hone your skills to levels that enable you to recognize three key events and give you the market timer's edge. I develop each particular set of indicators individually and then summarize their simultaneous use at the end of the chapter, as you put your technical analysis method together. I also give you a concise library of technical formations that gets you off on the right foot as you dive into market timing.

Defining the Primary Trend

The primary trend is the number-one thing you're looking for within your charts and the most important of all trends in market timing. The *primary trend* is the direction of the market that offers the least resistance toward making money. When you follow the primary trend in a bull market, you look for opportunities to buy strong stocks, and in bear markets you look for stocks that are showing weakness.

Knowing the primary trend and trading along with it increases your chances of achieving success as a market timer. You use the following tools to define the primary trend:

- ✔ **Trend lines** are as simple a device as you can find. Knowing how to draw and use them gives you an excellent start on any trade.

  To correctly draw a rising trend line, start at the lowest low in the chart and connect to the lowest low preceding the highest high without taking the line through prices between the two points. (See Figure 4-1.) To draw a down trend line, draw the line from the highest high to the highest high preceding the lowest low without passing through the prices between the two points. The arrows in Figure 4-1 illustrate this technique.

- ✔ **Moving averages** smooth out the market's trend over any given period of time and serve as important support and resistance levels. *Support levels* are areas where prices stop falling and buyers step in. A break in prices below support levels is a sign of weakness and an indication that more weakness may be ahead. By the same token a break above *resistance areas* — areas above which prices have not risen for some time — is a sign of a strong market.

- ✔ **Oscillators** are graphic depictions of points derived from mathematical formulas that are plotted below price charts. These formulas are not as important as the fact that they produce useful data that can help your timing.

  The main function of these indicators is to let you know whether the market is overbought or oversold, and whether the momentum of the primary trend is still adequate or there is a potential change in the primary trend ahead. The upcoming section "Trend and Momentum Oscillators" tells you about two commonly used oscillators, the Relative Strength Index (RSI) and the Moving Average Convergence Divergence (MACD) histogram indicators.

- ✔ **Bollinger bands** are also known as volatility bands or envelopes. These bands offer you visible evidence when markets have traveled too far in any one direction, as well as good visual cues about important exit and entry points into positions.

  Bollinger bands are calculated by plotting points one or more standard deviations above and below a moving average. (For more on moving averages see the section "Understanding Moving Averages" later in this chapter.) The classic Bollinger band is calculated by plotting points two standard deviations above and below the 20-day moving average. But you can use any moving average to calculate Bollinger bands.

  You use these bands primarily to predict when a big move is coming in the markets. I tell you more a bit farther ahead in this chapter. See the section "Getting a Grip on Bollinger Bands."

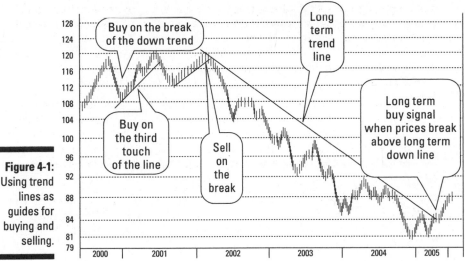

Figure 4-1:
Using trend
lines as
guides for
buying and
selling.

Key support is an area above which prices have held for some time. Key resistance is an area above which prices have not been able to rise for some time. A market breaking above key resistance or above key support signals a new trend. As a rule, you want to be out of the market or selling it short as soon as it's clear that the market has broken below key support. You want to buy into a market that has broken above key resistance.

After you identify the primary trend, you have to decide what your trading time frame will be. For most market timers, that will be the *intermediate-term time frame,* which is defined as a period of time that lasts for weeks to months. These time frames are sort of vague, but if you need a number to hang your hat on you can use roughly three weeks to six months as a reference, although there is no fast-and-hard rule.

Other important time frames include the *short term,* which for timers is usually a few days or weeks, and the *long term,* which is longer than six months. There is a time to invest in the short term, and a place for long-term investing. But both of those approaches are difficult to reproduce, unless you're an avid and able day trader or a very patient investor — I'm neither, which is why I became a market timer. Real market timing is usually about the intermediate term.

During the intermediate-term trends, you can make the most money in the smallest amount of time while still controlling your risk. If you're lucky, or patient, you can hold a stock for five years and double your money. But if you hold the same stock and catch it while it's hot for six weeks, you may make significant amounts. It's not unreasonable to expect to make 20 to 40 percent or more in any one stock or sector over a few weeks, provided that conditions are favorable for such gains. Not every trade will yield such results, but applying sound principles of timing may enable you to achieve those kinds of results in a significantly shorter period of time while cutting out the risk associated with the inevitable changes in the trend that are likely to happen in a five-year holding period.

Introducing the Four Amigos: Signals That the Trend Is Changing

Being right about the primary trend is paramount, because you want to get in on that trend early. The big money is made by those who correctly identify a change in the trend the earliest, jump on board, and hang on for the ride. And that's where the four amigos — trend reversals, breakouts, breakdowns, and momentum failures — come in handy.

Taking stock of the trend reversal

A *trend reversal* occurs when a price trend that is heading in one direction turns in the opposite direction. It's a fairly common market phenomenon and one of the most misunderstood by the non-professional or rookie timer. Most people are rarely sure whether a market break is significant, thus they hang around until it's too late and end up selling after losses have mounted. On the other side, too many people wait too long to enter a market that has bottomed and can get whipsawed (taken in and out of positions) — a situation that leads to heartburn and can take a big toll on the market timer's confidence. Figure 4-2 shows you an excellent set of examples of trend reversals.

The key to successful management of a trend reversal is to develop solid criteria upon which to act. When an up trend line is broken, as in Figure 4-2, take it seriously. As a general rule, the longer the trend line, the more significant the break above or below it. For example, if a market were to break above a down trend line that's been in place for five years, that break generally is more important than a break of a trend line that's been in place for two weeks, although your final decision about what action to take should take your trading time frame into account.

Apply the same approach to a bear market that's been in place for several years. When that down trend line is broken, it's a good idea to make that shopping list of stocks that you want to buy, as the break above such a long trend line is very likely a signal that the bear market is over.

Figure 4-2:
Trend line
analysis of
the Nasdaq
100 index
(NDX). Note
the trend
reversals.

Chart courtesy of BigCharts.com.

Refer to Figure 4-2, and you see that the rising trend line was in place from August until November — long enough to qualify as an intermediate-term trend line. Most timing decisions involve the intermediate-term time frame; a break below such a trend line is significant, as the Figure 4-2 clearly shows — the NDX index lost some 500 points over the next four months before recovering.

A trend reversal to the up side works in similar fashion, but in the opposite direction. Figure 4-2 shows such an event. On March 17, 2008, NDX bottomed out, and by April, a new rally was under way. By May, NDX had climbed over 300 points. Without drawing trend lines you could have missed the first signal that the trend had reversed.

Riding the highs of breakouts

A *breakout* — when prices break decisively above resistance — is about as exciting a development as there is in timing. It's a sign of rising strength in a security, and much of the time signals that prices are going higher. Market timers looking to make money in a rising market look for breakouts. Generally, breakouts are best when

  ✔ **They follow a fairly long period of prices that move sideways — a basing formation, which ideally lasts at least several weeks.** Bases describe markets that are moving sideways, and their purpose is to grind out all the indecision from a stock. When a base ends, the path of least resistance is either up or down, depending on whether the sellers or the buyers get the upper hand. When sellers win, prices fall from a base. When buyers win, prices move higher from a base.

✔ **They are accompanied by rising trading volume, compared to the average daily volume in the base.** If a base resolves to the upside, rising volume means that a lot of new money is coming in and that the chances of higher prices are much higher. When a stock moves sideways for a few weeks to months and breaks down accompanied by rising trading volume, it's a very negative development.

Figure 4-3 shows a base building in Intel, followed by a breakout. Notice the following:

✔ **The stock bottomed out in February** and began to move sideways (forming a base) until March, when it made its first attempt to rally. The attempt failed, but the stock eventually gathered itself, slowly rallied, and built enough momentum to deliver a breakout in May.

✔ **The breakout came with rising volume,** as did the final bottom (signaled by the *doji pattern* — where prices on the second day of trading in the rectangle in Figure 4-3 shows that prices reversed by the close of trading as buyers came in. Note how the stock started rallying on the following trading day; see the section "Candlestick charts" later in this chapter for more on the doji pattern).

This double bout of volume signifies that sellers panicked when the selling took place. This trading pattern is called a *selling climax,* and it means that the sellers were exhausted at this point, a notion proven by the fact that on the very next day the stock gapped higher, as there was no overhead resistance to the rise in prices triggered by unopposed buyers.

✔ **The stock then built a small consolidation shelf.** A *consolidation shelf* is an area of very tight prices that move sideways with volume decreasing as stock moves sideways. Check out Figure 4-3 to see a consolidation shelf defined by the support and resistance lines.

Support is where prices find a base, and it's where buyers come in. Resistance is an area above which prices are rejected — where the sellers are waiting.

Getting through the lows of breakdowns

If a breakout is about success, then a *breakdown* — the fall of prices below a support level — is about failure. When a stock or an index fails, you see a complete breakdown in confidence on the part of the buyers followed by a rise in strength on the part of the sellers.

Figure 4-4 illustrates a market that ran out of gas. The S&P 500 had bottomed in March 2008 after suffering a multi-month decline resulting from the subprime mortgage crisis. The index recovered as the Federal Reserve lowered interest rates. Still, the rally clearly ran out of gas as the index reached its 200-day moving average.

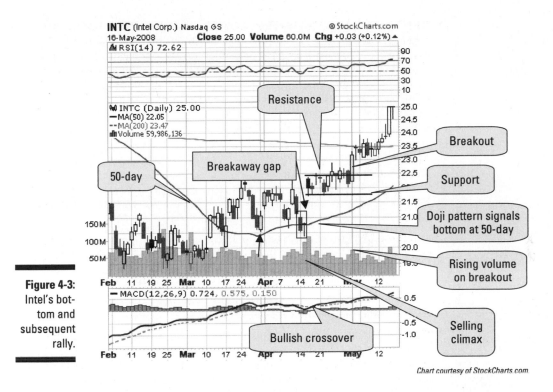

INTC (Intel Corp.) Nasdaq GS
16-May-2008 **Close** 25.00 **Volume** 60.0M **Chg** +0.03 (+0.12%) ▲
RSI(14) 72.62

Resistance

Breakout

INTC (Daily) 25.00
—MA(50) 22.05
—MA(200) 23.47
Volume 59,986,136

Breakaway gap

Support

50-day

Doji pattern signals
bottom at 50-day

Rising volume
on breakout

Selling
climax

MACD(12,26,9) 0.724, 0.575, 0.150

Bullish crossover

Chart courtesy of StockCharts.com

Figure 4-3:
Intel's bot-
tom and
subsequent
rally.

Breakdowns are harder to spot than breakouts, as they usually follow a period where the market has done well and most participants are feeling pretty confident about the future. Here are some important things to remember about recognizing breakdowns:

✔ **Tops are usually preceded by a period of consolidation.** A market that goes straight up and then breaks is fairly rare, although it can and does happen.

✔ **Look for more than one top.** It usually takes one or two tops (or hills) on a chart before a major break develops. The second and third tops form on lighter volume than the first top — a sign that the buyers are less confident about the stock or the index.

Figure 4-5 gives you a good look at this phenomenon, as the month of May had two consecutive tops before the pre–Memorial Day failure. Arrows mark the two tops that preceded this breakdown.

✔ **Look at volume as the market rises and falls.** A rally needs volume to keep going. Volume failures are often preludes to declines in rising markets. The dark bar showing the volume from May 12 to May 19 illustrates that volume fell during this period, as the market rose just before it failed to move above its 200-day moving average.

✔ **Don't overlook other signs.** You can't ever have too much evidence when you're timing the market. If a key top or bottom is forming, you may see a doji pattern (Figure 4-5) at a key turning point. In this case, there is a doji pattern at the top in the S&P 500, as the market crossed the 200-day moving average on an intraday basis on May 19, before it failed. See the section "Candlestick charts" later in this chapter for more about dojis.

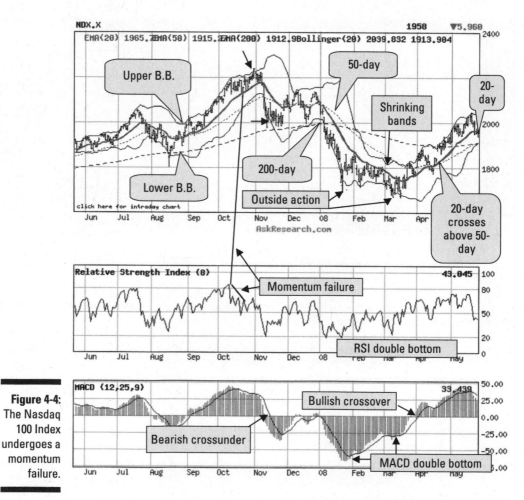

Figure 4-4:
The Nasdaq
100 Index
undergoes a
momentum
failure.

Charts courtesy of AskResearch.com.

Figure 4-5:
The S&P
500 paints
a portrait
of failure
ahead of
Memorial
Day in 2008.

Chart courtesy of StockCharts.com.

Also notice the following about the chart:

- The market broke below a key rising trend line very quickly after the market failed to rise above its 200-day moving average.

- Volume rose on the second day of selling — a very rapid loss of confidence.

- Compare the rise in volume in May to the steady volume when the index pulled back in April, as well as the way the rising trend line provided support. In May, the trend line gave up without any significant struggle, another sign of weakness.

Introducing Commonly Used Charts

There are four basic types of charts: line charts, bar charts, candlestick charts, and point-and-figure charts. Bar and candlestick charts are commonly used in stocks and futures trading, because they provide the most information with the least amount of analytical effort. A good chart will at least give you a good idea about the trend of the market, as well as let you plot out resistance and support levels.

Candlestick charts

The *candlestick chart* originated in Japan and has become very popular for market timers. Key features include color coding, as well as the ability of the chart to show key trading patterns that can predict changes in the trend. These charts are generally more useful for short-term trading, especially day trading, because they are color-coded, which enables traders to make quick decisions because they can glean information quickly. Speed is crucial in market timing, especially if you're day trading or trying to capitalize on a short-term set of developments.

In most charting programs, and on Web-based charting sites, candles that depict rising prices are colored green, and those showing falling prices are colored red. Refer to Figure 4-6 to see the basic characteristics of a candlestick.

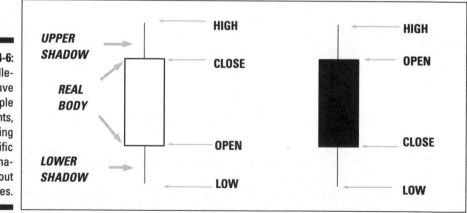

Figure 4-6: Candlesticks have multiple components, each giving you specific information about prices.

The *real body* is the box between the opening and closing prices depicted by the candlestick. The body can be white (green in full-color software) or black (also red). White or green bodies are bullish, meaning that the price depicted is rising. Black or red bodies are bearish, meaning that the price depicted by the candlestick is falling.

The *lower* and *upper shadows* are the thin lines that extend above and below the real body. The shadows, or candlewicks, extend to the high and low prices for the time frame.

Candlestick charts help you to

- ✔ **Spot trends faster.** A sea of rising green candles is an unmistakable sign of an up trend, just as a big glut of red is the opposite.

- ✔ **Spot trend reversals faster.** Specific patterns alert you to potential problems or significant positive developments in the future.

- ✔ **See shifts in momentum more clearly.** Oversold and overbought securities — those where sellers or buyers are exhausted — can show specific chart patterns. One such example is clear in Figure 4-3. The rectangle highlights a doji pattern. A doji is a candlestick with no real body, and can be a sign that a trend is near exhaustion. In Figure 4-3, you see a *dragonfly doji,* a thin line with a "T" bar across the top, and it means that prices reversed.

    Dojis don't mean much on their own. But if you can spot the entire setup, you can find yourself in a good position. In Figure 4-3, the doji came after two very large falling bars, which are signs of heavy selling. The appearance of the doji tells you that the stock was oversold, around the 21 price area. The next day, the stock gapped higher. A month later, Intel was up around 25, nearly 20 percent higher.

 For a more thorough overview of candlestick charting, including specific illustrations of patterns and how to interpret them, I recommend Barbara Rockefeller's book *Technical Analysis For Dummies* (Wiley).

Bar charts and associated tools

Bar charts are made up of slim bars that show prices from the open of trading until the close, but they are not color coded and don't form the kind of patterns that you see with candlesticks. Bar charts are most apt for longer-term trend analysis. For example, it can be difficult to make sense of a yearlong trend in a stock or an index with candlesticks, because of the potential clutter on the charts; the sleeker bar charts are easier on the eyes for those occasions. By the same token, short-term trend reversals can be hard to spot on bar charts, especially if they're subtle.

An excellent use of bar charts is *trend line analysis*. Figure 4-2 shows three trend lines on the Nasdaq 100 Index over a 12-month period. The one on the left shows an excellent intermediate-term up trend, ranging from August 2007 to November 2007. The market then clearly broke down until it regained its footing in the February to March 2008 period. The down trend line was finally broken in the late April, early May period. By late May, the intermediate term seemed to have turned lower once again, as the market had broken key support levels.

Bar charts and trend lines are a very simple combination of analytical tools that keep you on the right side of the dominant trend. But they aren't all that you need, as I show you in the next section, "Understanding Moving Averages" Here are a few basics to remember about trend lines:

✔ **Draw them without passing through the price action.** Note how my trend lines in Figure 4-2 connect the bottom of key prices in the up trend line, and the top of key prices on the way down. Draw your trend lines otherwise, and you get faulty information.

✔ **Use trend lines with other indicators.** Trend lines are excellent adjuncts to timing but aren't always your primary clue. Figure 4-4 shows you a group of indicators that together with trend lines make technical analysis even more useful. They are moving averages, the RSI and MACD histogram indicators and Bollinger bands. Together, this battery of indicators gives you about as complete a technical picture as you could want. I give you details on each of them in the upcoming sections.

Understanding Moving Averages

Moving averages are the lines that you see in Figure 4-4, and they are nothing more than an ongoing and defined set of points. For example, the 50-day moving average is made up of a string of the past 50 days of trading, plotted in a row. If you were to calculate your own 50-day line, you'd take the past 50 days of trading, average them out, and plot the number on your graph. For the next day, you'd plot the most recent 50 days, and so on.

As time passes, you start to build a line that averages out the market's movements over the past 50 days. Here are some important facts about moving averages:

✔ **Moving averages are great ways to smooth out the trend.** For example, rising moving averages confirm that you're in a rising trend. The down side to this use of these lines is that they're lagging, not leading indicators. This is in contrast to indicators such as RSI and MACD, which tend to be leading indicators. Oscillators usually signal a potential change in the trend prior to a moving average. Thus, you have to put the direction of the moving average into the proper context.

✔ **They serve as support and resistance levels.** You can use them to make decisions about when to buy, sell, or add to positions. For example, in an intermediate-term up trend, a stock may rise above its 50-day moving average, and then pull back and consolidate at the average. If it becomes clear that the stock will hold at this level, it's a great place to add to the position. You see this scenario in Figure 4-3, as Intel found support at its 50-day moving average three times before finally breaking out. The arrow (April) in Figure 4-3 illustrates a point where a moving average provides price support to Intel.

✔ **20 days:** The 20-day moving average traditionally is thought of as a short-term indicator in market timing. It is the default setting for Bollinger bands (see the section "Getting a Grip on Bollinger Bands," later in this chapter) in most analytical programs and charting Web sites.

✔ **50 days:** The 50-day moving average is considered a measure of the intermediate-term trend of the market. This one is very important for market timing and is often used as a place where you can either enter the market or add to positions.

✔ **100 days:** More pros are starting to use the 100-day average. The 100-day average gives you an edge, because most people tend to follow the 20- and 50-day lines. The 100-day average gives you a chance to participate in the market's action sandwiched between the very long term trend measured by the 200-day average and the shorter term periods measured by the 20- and 50-day lines.

✔ **200 days:** The 200-day moving average is considered the dividing line between long-term bull and bear markets. Use this average to make very long term decisions about the trend of the market. It's not the best place to exit the market, but it can be a useful entry point, especially in stocks that are reversing down trends.

Trend and Momentum Oscillators

Oscillators are graphs of mathematical formulas that help market timers and other fans of technical analysis make better decisions about trading. There are a great deal of them. On one Web site that I visit, subscribers have access to over 50 different oscillators. And although that sounds overwhelming, most of them do the same thing: tell you when the market is overbought or oversold, or when the odds of a trend change, a major bottom, or a major top are worth taking a risk on.

Oscillators are in fact excellent confirmatory instruments for trend lines, moving averages, and general chart watching. Everyone has their favorites, but mine are among the most popular, the MACD (Moving Average Convergence Divergence) and the RSI (Relative Strength) indicator.

The "Big Mac" of technical analysis: The MACD oscillator

The *Moving Average Convergence/Divergence (MACD) oscillator* is the result of a formula that's based on three moving averages derived from the price of the underlying stock or index. When applied to prices, the MACD formula smoothes out fluctuations of the price. You find two ways of looking at MACD, the original MACD oscillator, and the MACD histogram, which gives you similar information but produces blocks that let you confirm what the MACD oscillator is telling you.

Refer to Figure 4-3 to see what I mean: The Intel stock formed a base, and it eventually broke out and delivered a nice rally. Notice the bottom of the chart, where it says "Bullish Crossover." This marks an area where one MACD line is rising over another, a signal that momentum is moving toward the up side. Also note that it follows other bullish developments, such as the doji pattern, the breakaway gap, and the support provided by the 50-day moving average, just before the stock took off.

You most often use the MACD histogram to figure out when a bottom is likely to hold. Refer to Figure 4-4, where the two arrows in the March-April period point out what I call a *double bottom* — where a stock, an oscillator, or a market bottoms, rises for a while, and then makes a second bottom — in the MACD histogram. You can see that NDX made its initial bottom in January, but that it continued to slide into the March-April time frame. When NDX finally bottomed, making a lower low in March, the MACD histogram didn't make a new low.

In other words, a stock or index makes a lower low and MACD (RSI) make a higher low that produces a positive divergence. That's a big clue and an important point to remember. When the MACD or any other trend indicator, such as RSI, doesn't confirm a lower low in the market, or in the stock that you're analyzing, it usually means that the market is oversold. More importantly, it means that the chances of a rally are rising.

MACD, and other oscillators like it — among them RSI, Money Flow, Accumulation-Distribution, and many others — are designed to pick up subtle indications of momentum in the market. A market that bottoms for an extended period of time is accomplishing one thing above all, the exhaustion of the sellers. With fewer sellers around, selling pressure abates, and buying pressure starts to build. That's when you see the market start moving lower, but not the oscillator. And that's when you start thinking about a significant bottom forming.

MACD histogram also has other excellent uses. For example, when the indicator crosses above the zero line, it indicates that the rising trend is picking up steam. Figure 4-3 again shows you both a bullish crossover and a bearish crossunder by the MACD histogram, and how the market responded as you'd expect to the event. The cross under led to lower prices, just as the crossover led to higher prices.

Finally, note the following: The bullish crossover of the MACD histogram came just a few days before the 20-day moving average crossed over the 50-day moving average, a bullish crossover of the moving averages, and more evidence that the trend was toward higher prices.

Finding relative strength with RSI

My other favorite oscillator is the *Relative Strength Indicator (RSI)*. This indicator is all about momentum; it helps you see when the market is losing steam and headed for a momentum failure — where prices, after rising for some time, roll over and fall.

Refer again to Figure 4-4, where you see a momentum failure, and RSI's correct call of that event. In August 2007, the Nasdaq 100 Index (NDX) fell but found support at its 200-day moving average before rallying into November. The fall of the index to the 200-day moving average was preceded very nicely by the momentum failure signal from RSI, which is when the index rises to a new high, and the RSI fails to make a new high. This is called a *technical divergence* and is a signal that a trend change is ahead.

In this case, the continuation of NDX to rally, without the RSI index keeping up, was a signal that trouble was coming. And that's exactly what happened as the market topped out a couple of weeks after the RSI topped out. That means that, contrary to popular belief, you could have gotten out of the market before it fell, or at least protected your gains by tightening your sell stops (see Chapter 9 for more on sell stops), or lightening up some on some of your laggard holdings at the time.

Notice two things about RSI in this context:

- ✔ **RSI stopped rising before the market topped out** — an early warning.
- ✔ **RSI started to fall as the market kept rising** — as good a sign that trouble is ahead as any.

Getting a Grip on Bollinger Bands

Otherwise known as volatility bands, *Bollinger bands* are crucial to technical analysis and offer three major uses as

- ✔ Predictors of a big move ahead
- ✔ Support and resistance indicators
- ✔ Indicators of the major trend

Looking into the future

Bollinger bands aren't crystal balls, but they're pretty good warning systems about when the market is about to make a big move because they're measures of volatility. As the market swings wider, so do the bands. And as price behavior calms down, the bands tend to shrink.

It's in shrinking mode that Bollinger bands are most useful, as Figure 4-4 illustrates. There are two places on the chart where the bands are shrinking, signaling decreasing volatility in prices, and the potential for a big move ahead. The first is on the left of the chart, where the "Upper" and "Lower B.B." signs are. The second is on the right and is marked by arrows and the "shrinking bands" box. The *squeeze,* as I like to call this event, on the left preceded a rally, while the one on the right preceded an acceleration of the rally that had started a few days earlier.

Thinking outside the bands

Another great use of the bands is to see what prices are doing in relationship to them:

- ✔ **Use them as indicators of support and resistance.** Bollinger bands provide support and resistance to the market. As Figure 4-4 shows, prices "walked" along the upper bands on two occasions, from August to October 2007, and from March to May 2008. In these cases, the bands acted as price magnets, giving timers an indicator of a continuing trend.

- ✔ **Use them as a sign of a trend reversal.** Note the arrows in October (top), and November (bottom). In both these cases, prices moved outside the band. In October, prices rose above the upper band. This is usually a sign that the market has come too far too fast and that some kind of pause is ahead. The pause could be just that, a time when the market moves sideways. Or it could be a sign that a top of some sort is forming. In October, the trip outside the bands led to a top. In November, the arrow points to a move by prices outside the band, which led to a consolidation period that eventually resolved into another decline.

  Yet, in February, the box and arrow marked "outside action" proved to be a sign that a bottom was starting to form. By March, there were several more outside-the-band days, which proved to be quite of the rally that followed.

- ✔ **Watch them to signal that a big move is ahead.** When the bands shrink (see Figure 4-4), it signals that volatility is decreasing. Low volatility precedes a change in the trend. The "shrinking band" sign points to such a period and the ensuing big move — a rally — that followed.

As with any other indicator, Bollinger bands work best when you combine and confirm them with other indicators.

Making Technical Analysis Work: An Overview

Here are the key steps to understanding technical analysis as it pertains to market timing:

- **Define your time frame.** As a market timer, you want to look for markets that trend for weeks to months. Anything more volatile leads to heartaches, headaches, and losses.

- **Get familiar with the mainstream charting techniques.** You want to become very good at reading candlestick and bar charts. These are the tools of the timer. They are the two types of charts that give you the most information in the smallest amount of time and that you can find almost anywhere on the Web.

- **Get a handle on the basic indicators.** Become proficient with moving averages and trend lines. These may seem basic to anyone looking for thrills and spills. But any experienced timer will tell you they live by these simple tools.

- **Add a few oscillators for backup.** You can use any of numerous oscillators, but it's hard to beat MACD and RSI for consistency at calling the trend and the market's momentum — the two key variables for the timer. Learn how to use these two tools first, and branch out later.

- **Bone up on Bollinger bands.** Add these great indicators to your arsenal, as both primary indicators and also as confirmatory tools for your moving averages and oscillators.

- **Combine tools on one chart.** A combined chart can seem busy at first, but as you do this kind of analysis more and more, you'll be able to look at any chart with your indicators on them and make your decisions in seconds.

You can't have too much information with the battery of indicators that I describe in this chapter, but you can overdo it on data. If your charts are so cluttered that you can't make sense of what's happening, then they're not doing you any good. As you develop your own favorites, you'll find the balance point. I've been doing this for 20 years and have found these indicators to give me what I want in order to maximize my chances of success.

Looking for the setup

Market timers are like predators. They spend a lot of time poring over charts like a tiger cruising the jungle waiting to pounce. As when the tiger sinks his teeth into a good meal, they know when the wait for a good setup has been worth it.

A *setup* is the pause in prices before a big move. It can be anything from a base before a stock breaks out to a trend reversal to shrinking Bollinger bands. Price movement leaves a trail of activity, and the chart captures it. When enough time has passed, the trained eye sees a picture emerging. And when the picture is just about right, meaning that you can spot the early stages of a move in a new direction, then your setup is complete and you can start looking at support, resistance, oscillators, moving average, and the other important aspects of technical analysis I cover in this chapter.

Before you start looking for setups in individual stocks, consider the following:

- ✔ **Trade with the trend.** Are you looking to buy stocks in a rising market? Or are you going against the grain? The best-looking breakout could easily fail if the market is in a downtrend. And the best of short sales could blow up in your face if you happen to find it in the midst of a roaring bull market.

- ✔ **Is the market overbought or oversold?** If stocks have been rising for 10 to 12 days in a row, you have reason to be patient and wait for prices to cool off just a bit before moving in. I know it's tempting to keep buying as prices rise. I've done it, and I've regretted it — more than I care to talk about. Common sense dictates that you wouldn't go into a dark alley with scary sounds at the end of it on a night with a full moon. So why would you buy into a market that's almost certain to slow its rate of gain or even fall after a big advance?

- ✔ **Are you looking at strong or weak stocks in a strong or weak sector?** If you're in a bull market, you want to buy the strongest stocks in the strongest groups. If you're in a bear market, you want to short the weak stocks in the weakest sectors. That's all there is to it. Don't go against the grain when trying to time the market.

After you answer the big-picture questions, you can start to look at your setup and to make buy and sell decisions.

Buying on strength and on dips

Buying on strength is the easiest way to go in a bull market, as the momentum is on your side. You look for a stock that's been basing, or moving sideways. To buy on strengths and dips, examine the chart for the following key characteristics:

- ✔ **A stock that's been forming a base:** Bases shake out the sellers, making it easier for buyers to move the price up when critical mass is reached, such as when Intel gapped up in mid-April.

- ✔ **A generally positive look to the chart:** Refer again to Figure 4-3, and you see that the right side of the chart is clearly higher than the left side of the chart. That's a sign that momentum is on your side and that it's well established.

- ✔ **Rising volume on days in which the price of the stock is rising:** This is a sign of confidence on the part of buyers and is clearly pointed out in Figure 4-3.

- ✔ **Falling volume on down days:** This is a sign that buyers are feeling okay about their decision to own the stock and that they like the way the stock is acting. Comfortable buyers don't sell a stock too soon, thus the up trend has a better chance of staying intact.

- ✔ **A stock that has held at key support levels** and seems to find buyers at that support level: Intel meets the criteria in Figure 4-3. Steady or rising prices at support levels are a sign that buyers are still interested in acquiring this stock.

- ✔ **A good show of momentum:** In Figure 4-3, the breakaway gap in the middle of the chart is a great clue that momentum is on the side of the buyers. When a stock gaps up or down, it indicates that buyers (gap to the up side) or sellers (down side gap) have responded to some event in a very significant fashion. A breakaway gap is one that is accompanied by high volume and that is usually followed by higher prices. Gaps are also important as gauges of the commitment of buyers or sellers, as they act as support and resistance levels. Especially when gaps are tested on lighter volume than the day the gap was created. Light volume test of gaps shows the market doesn't have necessary energy to push through the gap. In this case, the top of the breakaway gap acted as an important support level.

When a stock meets these criteria you can place your buy order above key resistance levels, or as it holds up above key support levels. Intel offered several such chances during the period highlighted in Figure 4-3.

The figure has a textbook example of a chart breakout — a good place to buy, because the stock has momentum and has had plenty of time to show you that the rally is fake or weak.

The stock also gave you three good chances to buy as it tested its 50-day moving average three times before "gapping up" in mid-April. When a stock holds at support levels, it means that buyers are coming in at that price and it's a good example of "buying on the dip."

Using trend lines as buy and sell points

Trend lines can be very useful in timing, especially if you're using long-term charts. Refer to Figure 4-1 to see how these instruments can come in handy in letting you time the markets.

A good rule of thumb is to put your sell stop maybe 2 to 3 percent below the trend line, instead of putting it too close to the line. By giving yourself some room, you're buying some room for error, as stocks often bounce around, above and below trend lines, moving averages, and other support levels for a short period of time before resuming their up trends.

Running down other important technical formations

You'll run into three other chart formations on a regular basis — congestion patterns, complex tops and bottoms, and the exhaustion gap. These are good setups to look for when you're on the hunt for trading ideas. (The earlier section "Looking for the Setup" tells you more.)

Congestion patterns

A *congestion pattern* can be anything from a base to something more complex, such as a triangle. The key to congestion patterns is that they are a prelude to something — either a rally or a breakdown.

Figure 4-7 shows a congestion pattern known as an ascending triangle. This is an important formation because prices, as they form the triangle, are making higher highs and higher lows, a sign that the buyers are winning the battle against the sellers. In this case, the initial reaction after the triangle looks as if it's a failure, but as a bit more time passes, the stock finally breaks out.

ascending triangle eventually evolved into an intermediate-term rally and how — eventually — you could have sold out your position by placing your sell point below the trend line.

Complex tops and bottoms

Complex tops and bottoms are another form of congestion pattern, those that happen at the end of a price extreme or some kind of move. You find them when a trend in one direction has stalled. As a market timer, you should be attracted to complex tops and bottoms; they may indicate the start of an opportunity at some point in the future.

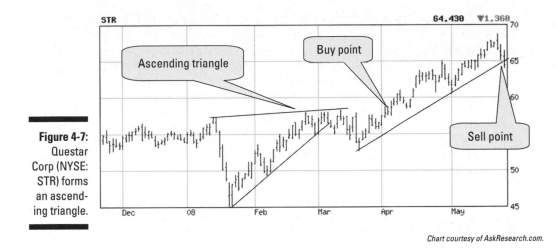

Figure 4-7: Questar Corp (NYSE: STR) forms an ascending triangle.

Chart courtesy of AskResearch.com.

You see the buy point in Figure 4-7, as well as a trend line. Notice how the Figure 4-8 of Cameron International illustrates a double top and a triple bottom. Notice how prices fell after the former and eventually rallied after the latter, as buyers were exhausted as the double top formed, and sellers were overwhelmed by buyers after the triple bottom. Trend lines in this figure reinforce their importance in timing, as once again they help you to best see when to enter and exit positions.

Figure 4-8: Cameron International (NYSE: CAM) forms a double top and a triple bottom and delivers an exhaustion gap.

Chart courtesy of AskResearch.com.

Exhaustion gap

Figure 4-8 also shows you a great example of an *exhaustion gap,* a chart formation that usually leads to breakdown. The truth is that you don't know when a gap is going to be a break-away gap, or when things will get ugly, as they did for Cameron International. To be sure, volume plays a role, as it tends to be big on a break away, and it tends to shrink during the development of an exhaustion gap.

Still, more important in these cases is what actually happens. In this case, prices fell into the gap instead of finding support above the gap, as they did in Figure 4-3, which illustrates a break-away gap.

Always supplement your chart analysis with as much other information as possible, such as trend lines, moving averages, and oscillators to confirm your impression.

Part II
Market Timing's Methods and Strategies

The 5th Wave   By Rich Tennant

"The one thing I've learned about investing is, timing is every... SMOOF!"

In this part . . .

*H*ere I take you through the strategies used by experienced market timers including how to make sense of economic reports and other reports that affect the markets. I show you how the markets sometimes cycle with the seasons and how to spot major market trends. You also find out about using what people think — via sentiment surveys — to spot key turning points.

Chapter 5

Timing with the Reports That Move the Markets

*T*iming is about trend recognition, and trends are influenced by events. Aside from intangible events, such as wars, accidents, and general geopolitical turmoil, a clear, predictable, and precise flow of information sets the tone for the overall trend of the markets, especially the stock, bond, and currency markets. Economic reports aren't the market's sole influence: The reports keep score on the state of the economy, and markets respond to the reports in their own way, based on the perception of all the participants that have access to a trading platform.

In fact, although some folks say that markets are random, the truth is that markets are efficient, as they factor in all the data available into current prices. They aren't always correct, and they aren't infallible, but they are efficient. Whatever is happening at the present is priced in and factored into what the future might hold.

The uncertainty about what's going on now and what might come in the future gives markets their inherent volatility and makes a good understanding of the global economy and its interplay with economic reports and the financial markets a key component of your market timing strategy.

This chapter gives you the tools you need to navigate difficult periods in the market that are made more dramatic and spectacular by the release of key economic data.

Understanding the U.S. and the Global Economies

The global economy is now a reality, with emerging markets driving the demand for commodities and heading toward the point where cheap labor is no longer a guarantee. After September 11, 2001, money flowed out of the United States into China, India, and other emerging markets, planting the seeds of economic growth and inflation in those areas as low-cost manufacturing combined with a real estate and building boom led to staggering growth in those economies.

Economic reality morphed; the major influences on economic trends moved from Europe, Japan, and the United States to China, India, Brazil, and a significant portion of the Middle East — especially Saudi Arabia, where petrodollars rule the roost, and Dubai, which has become the area's financial center.

Within that new framework, the U.S. economy remains the largest economy in the world and is dependent upon a series of delicately intertwined relationships to function. Keep these factors in mind to make the most out of timing the markets in relationship to economic reports:

✔ Consumers drive the U.S. economy and, to a significant degree, also drive the global economy, although the number of consumers worldwide is growing slowly but steadily.

✔ Consumers — around the world, but especially in the United States — need jobs to be able to buy things and keep their respective economies going.

✔ The constant flux in employment rates, credit availability, and supply and demand for goods and services drives economic activity up or down.

Generally, steady job growth, easy credit, and a balance between supply and demand are what the Board of Governors of the Federal Reserve (the Fed) likes to see in the economy. When one or more of these factors is out of kilter, the Fed has to act by raising or lowering interest rates to

✔ Tighten or loosen the consumer's ability to obtain credit

✔ Rein in a too-high level of joblessness

✔ Increase or decrease the supply side to bring it in line with demand

Homing in on an example

Figure 5-1 shows the reliable and important relationship between the growth rate of the economy (Gross Domestic Product, GDP), the unemployment rate, retail sales, and consumer spending. As the economy becomes sluggish — indicated by the highs and lows registered in GDP — the unemployment rate begins to rise. Eventually, retail sales slow, as consumer spending rolls over.

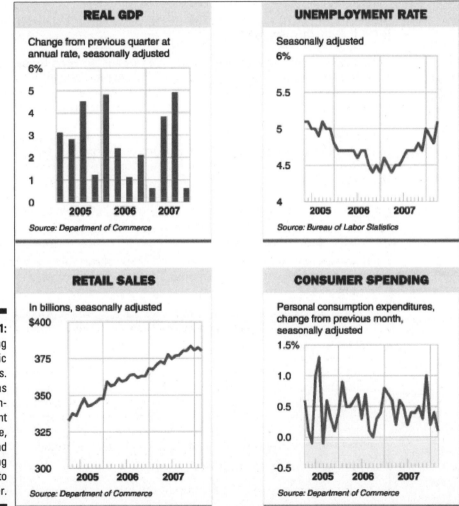

Figure 5-1: Comparing economic indicators. Note that as the unemployment rate rose, sales and spending began to falter.

Figure 5-2 shows the unique relationship between rising demand for oil and commodities in the global economy. Meanwhile, the downturn in the U.S. housing sector, resulting from the subprime mortgage crisis, eventually led to a collapse in U.S. consumer confidence.

The economic data highlighted in Figures 5-1 and 5-2 painted a difficult picture for the Federal Reserve, which had to pick a fight — beat back inflation, as shown by rising consumer and producer prices, or address an economy on the brink of recession, as highlighted by the collapse in consumer confidence.

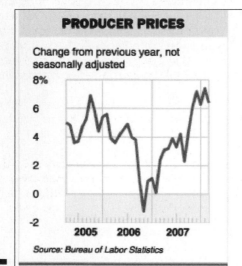

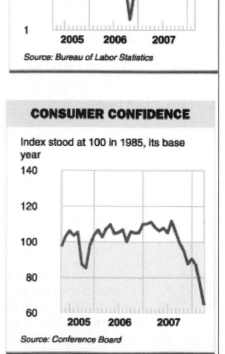

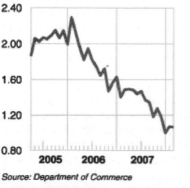

Figure 5-2:
Rising demand for commodities in emerging economies led to higher producer prices, which eventually led to higher consumer prices and the collapse in consumer confidence.

The Federal Reserve had to fashion a unique response to the change in economic activity that developed in 2007 and 2008, as the U.S. subprime mortgage crisis led to simultaneous inflation and a major decrease in economic activity. Economic factors moved like a set of dominoes tumbling: The mortgage crisis led to job losses and a subsequent decline in the number of people who could spend money. At the same time, the global economy — partially powered by emerging economies — slowed, but not to the same degree as the U.S. economy, at least not by the time I wrote this book.

The Federal Reserve chose to aim its bullets at the U.S. economy and to worry about inflation later. The central bank began to lower interest rates aggressively and to implement several other significant methods aimed at keeping the economy from a significant contraction. Among the unusual steps taken by the Fed were to engineer a buyout of Wall Street investment bank Bear Stearns by J.P. Morgan, as well as to provide discount-rate lending to investment banks, a privilege previously reserved for consumer banks.

The *discount rate* is the interest rate charged by the Fed to banks. It is considered a rate of last resort and is used by banks that have no other place to borrow.

On September 7, 2008, fearing a total global market collapse, the U.S. Treasury stepped in and placed Freddie Mac and Fannie Mae under receivership, essentially taking a controlling interest in both institutions, in hopes that this would provide a floor under the subprime mortgage crisis.

Keeping tabs on the data mill

Several government agencies and private companies monitor the economy and produce monthly or quarterly reports. These reports provide traders with a major portion of the road map they need for determining which way the general-direction prices in their respective markets are headed.

Trading, and specifically timing, is highly influenced by these government and private-agency reports and how the markets respond to them. Businesses are just pawns of the Fed and the markets, and their reaction to these changes in trend usually takes some time be noticed.

The overall focus of the markets is one thing: what the Federal Reserve is going to do in response to the report(s) of the day — lower or raise interest rates or produce new methods for dealing with whatever is ongoing. That combination of factors — the market's reaction to data and whatever the Fed does, or is expected to do at some point in the future — changes or maintains market trends. The essence of timing is trading along with the prevalent trend.

As a market timer you need to understand how each of these important reports can make your particular markets move and how to prepare yourself for the possibilities of making money based on the relationship between all of the individual components of the market and economic equation. I tell you more in the upcoming sections.

Getting a Handle on the Reports

Economic reports are important tools in all markets, but they're a big influence on market timers, because they can affect the general trend of the markets. Each market has its own set of reports to which traders pay special attention. Some key reports are among the prime catalysts for fluctuations in the prices of all markets and especially the bond, stock, and currency markets, which form the center of the trading universe and are linked to one another. Traders wait patiently for their release and act with lightning speed as the data hit the wires.

Some reports are more important during certain market cycles than they are in others, and you have no way of predicting which of them will be the report of the month, the quarter, or the year, but you can usually count on the following being important and highly scrutinized:

- ✔ Gross domestic product
- ✔ Consumer price index
- ✔ Producer price index
- ✔ Monthly employment reports
- ✔ The Fed's Beige Book, which summarizes the economic activity as surveyed by the Fed's regional banks

The Institute for Supply Management (ISM) report, formerly the national purchasing manager's report, is produced by the Institute for Supply Management and also is important. So is the Chicago purchasing manager's report, which usually is released one or two days prior to the ISM report. Many traders believe that the Chicago report is a good prelude to the national ISM report, and the day of its release can often lead to big market moves, both up and down.

Consumer confidence numbers from the University of Michigan and the Conference Board usually are market movers. Bond, stock, and currency traders pay special attention to them, because they can be very influential on the decisions made by the Federal Reserve with regard to interest rates.

Weekly employment claims data that come in far above or below expectations can move the market. Retail sales numbers also can move the markets, especially when they come from major retailers, such as Wal-Mart, or when several retailers report good or bad numbers on the same day. So can the budget deficit or surplus numbers. Consumer credit data can sometimes move the market as well, but that is fairly rare.

Cable news outlets, major financial Web sites, and business radio networks broadcast every major report as it is released, and the wire services send out alerts regarding the reports to all major financial publishers not already covering the releases. The government agencies and companies that are responsible for the reports also post them on their respective Web sites immediately at the announced time.

Economic reports find their way into political speeches in the House of Representatives and on the Senate floor. The president and his advisors, other politicians, bureaucrats, and spin-doctors quote data from these reports widely and often, using them to suit their current purposes.

As a timer you can best use economic reports as

- ✔ **Sources of new information:** When you combine the data in the reports with the market's reaction to that data, you end up with your best guide as to whether you open new positions, keep your current ones, or make changes in your portfolio.

- ✔ **Risk-management tools:** You can make costly mistakes if you ignore the market's reaction to the data. Each report has the potential to move the market — in your favor or against.

- ✔ **Further influences on the markets:** The headlines are only part of the story, mere clues about the meat of the report. Data hidden deep within a report can often become more important than the initial knee-jerk reaction to the headlines and cause the market to change direction.

- ✔ **Trendsetters:** Current reports may not always be what matters. The trend of the data from reports during the past few months, quarters, or years — in addition to expectations for the future — also can be powerful information that moves the markets up or down.

Trading solely on economic reports can be very risky and requires experience and thorough planning on your part. Make the reports part of your strategy, not the center of your strategy. It's still all about how the market responds to the reports and how the reports affect the overall trend of the market.

Exploring Specific Economic Reports

Some reports are more important than others, but at some point, they all have the potential to influence the market. In this section, I give you the tools to interpret the reports and to use them in your timing.

Using the employment report

By far, the most important report over the past several years has been the employment report. It is the first piece of major economic data released in the cycle — on the first Friday of every month — and is formally known as the Employment Situation Report. Bond, stock index, and currency futures traders are often on the edge of their seats as they wait for the release of the number at 8:30 a.m. eastern time.

The release of the employment data usually is followed by very active, often frenzied trading that can last from a few minutes to an entire day. Much of the action that follows this important number depends on what the data shows and what the markets were expecting. The report has become so important that it can set the overall trading trend for the financial markets for several days or even weeks after the release — especially if other reports confirm the status of the economy the employment report shows.

When consecutive employment reports show that a trend is in motion, the markets tend to follow that trend and act accordingly with regard to price action. When the trends in the employment report change, the markets also tend to change. Figure 5-3 shows that the stock market, as measured by the S&P 500, can take a good deal of bad news and keep moving higher. But, by 2007, too many negatives were in the mix, and when the unemployment rate began to consistently trend higher, the index began to falter.

The employment report is most important when the economy is shifting gears, similar to the way it did after the events of September 11, 2001, during the 2004 presidential election, and as the effects of the subprime mortgage crisis began to spread through the economy.

For timing purposes, the major components of the employment report are

  ✔ **The number of new jobs created:** This figure tends to predict the trend of the economy. Large numbers of people working and rising numbers of new jobs usually are positive for the economy. A declining number of new jobs usually indicates that the economy is slowing.

Generally, weakness in the employment report is a prelude to lower interest rates from the Federal Reserve, while a very rapid rate of growth in employment can be a signal that growth in the economy is overheating. The Federal Reserve sees too-rapid growth in employment as a potential prelude to rising wage pressures, inflation, and the need for higher interest rates.

✔ **The unemployment rate:** The month-to-month rate of unemployment is not always as important as the trend in the rate. The Federal Reserve gets concerned when the rate climbs or falls for several months and is accompanied by other signs of the economy rising or falling. For example, in September 2008, the unemployment rate rose above 6 percent, the highest level in many years, and it had risen above 5 percent in the previous month.

Two back-to-back months of rising unemployment is a signal that the economy is increasingly weak and that the Federal Reserve may have to consider lowering interest rates.

If the employment report delivers a number that would generally be seen as bullish (good job creation, stable unemployment rate) and the market sells off, look to your open positions and see whether they hold above their support levels, such as your 20- and 50-day moving averages.

Figure 5-3:
The S&P 500 from 2006–2008. As the unemployment rate began to climb in late 2007, the S&P 500 began to falter.

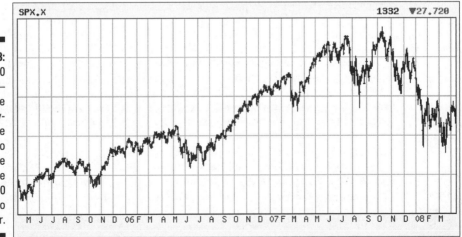

Chart courtesy of AskResearch.com.

Taking in the Consumer Price Index (CPI)

The CPI is the most important inflation report for the financial markets. Rising consumer prices usually lead to falling bond prices, rising interest rates, and increased market volatility, as fear of rising interest rates from the Federal Reserve take hold. This report is important because consumer buying drives the U.S. economy. Price changes at the consumer level change consumer behavior, and thus eventually affect the economy, as well as corporate earnings.

Here is some important information about the consumer price index and inflation:

- ✔ Consumer price inflation is most dependent on the ability of retailers to pass on rising prices. Increasing competition from discounters makes it much more difficult for traditional retailers to pass on their rising costs.

- ✔ Supply is often more important than demand, especially with trendy items like clothing or electronic equipment. A lot depends on what's hot at the moment. For example, if a retailer orders bellbottom pants in hopes that bellbottoms will be the back-to-school trend and the kids don't buy them, the discounting begins. Supply rises and prices fall.

- ✔ Inflation doesn't result from higher prices. Inflationary trends develop when too much money chases too few goods.

- ✔ Inflationary expectations and consumer prices go hand in hand with one another because inflationary expectations are built into the cost of borrowing money.

- ✔ Rising consumer prices develop late in the inflationary cycle and can be a sign of rapidly rising inflation in the financial system.

The real return on any investment is the percentage of the profit that you gain after subtracting inflation. If you make 10 percent but inflation is running at a 5 percent clip, your real gain is 5 percent.

Watch for reaction to CPI numbers in more than one market as interest rate, currency, and stock traders react and you can see moves in the bond, stock, and currency markets. If the report shows a significant amount of inflation, it could also move gold prices higher.

Perusing the Producer Price Index (PPI)

The PPI is not a critically important piece of data and usually doesn't cause market moves as big as those wrought by the CPI and the employment report.

The PPI measures prices at the producer level; it measures the cost of raw materials to companies that produce goods. The market looks for two things in this report:

- **The speed with which prices are moving up or down:** If PPI registers a sudden rise in prices, the market wants to know where it's coming from. For example, the February 2008 PPI report stated

  The Producer Price Index for Finished Goods rose 0.3 percent in February, seasonally adjusted. . . . This increase followed a 1.0 percent advance in January and a 0.3 percent decline in December. At the earlier stages of processing, prices received by manufacturers of intermediate goods moved up 0.8 percent in February subsequent to a 1.4 percent advance in January, and the crude goods index rose 3.7 percent after climbing 2.5 percent in the prior month.

  This report clearly suggested that inflation was well entrenched in the system, and that it had been so for several months. Refer to Figure 5-3 to note the overall poor performance of the stock market during the month of March when the report was released.

- **Whether inflation is being passed on to consumers:** The same report noted that the indexes for finished goods were mixed, with energy finished goods rising, but food finished goods falling, while other finished goods were on the rise. The overall tone, though, was that producers were starting to pass on costs to consumers, another sign that inflation was working its way into the economy at a steady pace.

Making sense of the ISM and purchasing managers' reports

The Institute for Supply Management's (ISM) Report on Business is quite important and is usually a market mover. The report is an excellent measure of how well the manufacturing sector in the United States is functioning. The data is compiled from surveys of purchasing managers across the United States and is summarized by the ISM. Find it at www.ism.ws.

The national report, known as the Report on Business, is different from the regional purchasing manager's reports, although the market pays attention to a few of the regional reports, such as the Chicago-area report, because they can serve as good predictors of the national data. However, the regional reports aren't used as a basis for the national report.

The ISM report has 11 categories. The most important market moving number, though, is the PMI index. Here's how to look at the ISM report:

✔ A number above 50 on the PMI means that the economy is growing. You want to know whether the main index and the subsectors are above or below 50.

✔ Watch the rate of movement of the index and the subindexes, up or down. The faster the ongoing trend is moving, the more likely that it will have an effect on the markets.

The March 2008 report noted a Purchasing Manager's Index of 48.6 percent, a sign of mild economic slowing, noting:

> *This completes the weakest quarterly performance for the U.S. economy since Q2 of 2003. Manufacturers' order backlogs continue to erode as the New Orders Index failed to grow for the fourth consecutive month. Additionally, manufacturers continue to experience heavy cost pressures, as the prices they pay are still rising even with slower overall demand. Some manufacturers are still benefiting from strong export demand and continue to see growth in export orders.*

The bond market remained stable. The dollar weakened. And stocks remained range bound, after suffering heavy losses in the preceding months. (Refer to Figure 5-3.)

Considering consumer confidence

Consumers play a central role in the U.S. economy, and so consumer confidence data is a good metric to keep your eye on. It comes from two credible sources that publish separate reports, the Conference Board, a private research group, and the University of Michigan.

The Conference Board Survey

The Conference Board, Inc., interviews 5,000 consumers per month in order to produce its monthly survey.

The three most widely watched components of The Conference Board survey are:

✔ The monthly index

✔ Current conditions

✔ Consumers' outlook for the next six months

In March 2008, The Conference Board's survey fell 12 points, a collapse that led to some market volatility. The report noted the following:

The decline in the Present Situation Index implies that the pace of growth in recent months has weakened even further. Looking ahead, consumers' outlook for business conditions, the job market and their income prospects is quite pessimistic and suggests further weakening may be on the horizon. The Expectations Index, in fact, is now at a 35-year low (Dec. 1973, 45.2) and at levels not seen since the Oil Embargo and Watergate.

When I read statements such as the one in The Conference Board's March 2008 survey, I wonder whether the markets have reached a bottom, given the pervasiveness of the negative sentiment. The key, though, is not to act abruptly. It's better to make money than to be right. Wait until enough people have the same idea that you have, and the market actually starts to rise — especially when the market moves above an important level such as the 50-day moving average, where other investors will also be confident enough to move back in and cause prices to move even higher.

The University of Michigan Survey

The University of Michigan conducts a separate, widely watched survey of consumer confidence and publishes several preliminary reports and one final report per month.

Key components of the University of Michigan Survey are

- ✔ Index of Consumer Sentiment
- ✔ Index of Consumer Expectations
- ✔ Index of Current Economic Conditions

In April 2008, the University of Michigan reported the lowest reading in consumer confidence since 1982. (Refer to Figure 5-2.) The stock market lost over 200 points. From a timing standpoint, it's very important to know when the report is coming out, and to be diligent about the potential effects that this report can have on the markets. The report cited general concerns on the part of the public over rising fuel prices and unemployment as the major reasons for the low reading.

Markets often anticipate data. Figure 5-4 shows how U.S. bond market interest rates dropped as bond traders correctly noted that economic weakness was coming way ahead of consumers, and even stock traders. The rates started their decline in June 2007, as the market was getting wind of potential problems in the subprime mortgage market; the overall trend toward lower interest rates continued as unemployment started to rise.

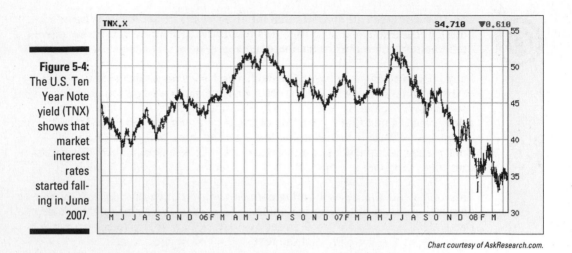

Figure 5-4:
The U.S. Ten Year Note yield (TNX) shows that market interest rates started falling in June 2007.

Chart courtesy of AskResearch.com.

Poring over the Beige Book

The *Beige Book* is one of my favorite reports and is released by the Federal Reserve eight times per year. In each installment, the Fed delivers a thorough summary of current economic activity in each of its districts, based on anecdotal information from Fed researchers and data gleaned from key businesses, economists, and market experts.

The Beige Book is made available to the members of the Federal Open Market Committee (FOMC) before each of its meetings on interest rates and is widely seen as a significant source of information for the committee members as they're deciding what direction to take interest rates.

On March 5, 2008, the Federal Reserve district in Boston had its turn to publish the Beige Book and summarized its findings as follows:

> *Reports from the twelve Federal Reserve Districts suggest that economic growth has slowed since the beginning of the year. Two-thirds of the Districts cited softening or weakening in the pace of business activity, while the others referred to subdued, slow, or modest growth. Retail activity in most Districts was reported to be weak or softening, although tourism generally continued to expand. Services industries in many Districts, including staffing services in Boston, port activity in New York, and truck freight volume in Cleveland, appeared to be slowing, but activity in services provided some positive news in Richmond and Dallas. Manufacturing was said to be sluggish or to have slowed in about half the Districts, while several others indicated manufacturing results were mixed or trends were steady.*

Look for language that suggests that inflation or severe weakness is being noted. In the example above, the news was mixed, and there was no big move in the markets over the intermediate term.

I pay special attention to what the Beige Book says about individual sectors of the economy or any language that seems a little more dramatic than the usual description of the economy. One thing caught my eye in this report, aside from the fact that most areas of the economy were showing signs of sluggishness. Deeply buried in the text was this sentence: "Boston and New York mentioned that some manufacturers are experiencing slower payments from their customers."

This was a clue that the upcoming earnings season might be rocky, as businesses were starting to delay payments to manufacturers. On April 11, 2008, General Electric shocked Wall Street by missing its earnings expectations. It pays to read the fine print and the text of the Fed's Beige Book.

The Beige Book usually is released in the afternoon, one or two hours before the stock market closes. The overall trend of all markets can reverse late in the day when the data in the report surprise traders.

You can read through the Beige Book report on the Internet. Links to the report are on the Fed's Web site, www.federalreserve.gov.

Focusing on housing starts

The housing starts report is a good one to follow because housing is central to the U.S. economy. It gives you indirect but useful data about the status of demand for raw materials, the state of lending and banking, manufacturing, and the real estate market. This report often leads to big moves in the bond market.

The U.S. Department of Commerce releases this report every month, and traders focus on three parts of it:

- ✔ Building permits
- ✔ Housing starts
- ✔ Housing completions

Traders look for changes in the rise and fall of these three numbers from the previous month. For example, in 2005, the housing market was steady despite a long growth phase. (Refer to Figure 5-2.)

But things change: Building permit numbers in February 2008 showed a 7.8 percent decrease since January 2008, and a 37 percent decrease compared to a year earlier, while housing starts were 0.6 percent below the previous month's data and 28 percent below the year earlier levels.

Housing stocks had been trying to rally around this time in the markets, as traders were betting on a bottom being in place due to the small decrease in housing starts but sold off once the consumer confidence data was released.

Housing data is a volatile series of numbers and can be significantly affected by changes in the weather. The data is also seasonally adjusted and includes a significant amount of revised data within each of the internal components.

For example, if you don't know that winter stalls construction projects, and that it's normal to see a decline in activity during the winter, you can be fooled by the data, and make trading mistakes by betting that interest rates are going to fall in response to a weak market. By the same token, when the weather improves, the numbers seem to show an explosion of new activity, and you can make trading mistakes in the other direction. Experienced traders look at the seasonally adjusted, smoothed-out numbers in order to prevent mistakes.

Still, this is a tricky series of numbers, and the Commerce Department lets you know that it can take up to four months of data to come up with a reliable set of numbers. That means that it's important to know when the data is released, what the data says, and then it's most important to see how the market reacts.

Taking in the Index of Leading Economic Indicators

The Conference Board compiles ten key indicators in calculating the Index of Leading Economic Indicators, including

- Index of consumer expectations
- Real money supply
- Interest rate spread
- Stock prices
- Vendor performance
- Average weekly initial claims for unemployment insurance
- Building permits
- Average weekly manufacturing hours

✔ Manufacturers' new orders for nondefense capital goods

✔ Manufacturers' new orders for consumer goods and materials

In March 2008, the overall index dropped for the fifth straight month and was falling at a 3 percent annual rate. The report noted that although money supply was rising and interest rates were falling, other components such as weekly jobless claims were rising, and consumer confidence, building permits, and stock prices were falling. In other words, the forward-looking indicators weren't responding to lower interest rates and more money in circulation. That's a very negative report. Thus, it was no surprise that bond prices continued to hold up, keeping interest rates low, and that stock prices, having perhaps bottomed, were quite in rally mode.

Timers had no reason to aggressively buy stocks at this point, as the markets had yet to show that they believed that the worst was over. (Refer to Figure 5-3.)

The Index of Leading Economic Indicators is a lukewarm indicator that sometimes moves the markets and other times doesn't. It's more likely to move the markets whenever it clearly is divergent from data provided by other indicators. For example, if this indicator had shown that strength was building in some areas of the economy, stock prices might have begun to rally more convincingly.

Grasping Gross Domestic Product

The report on Gross Domestic Product (GDP) is a big-picture report that measures the sum of all the goods and services produced in the United States. This report can lead to significant volatility in the markets, and it can be a big market mover whenever it's above or below what the markets are expecting it to be. At other times, GDP is not much of a mover. Multiple revisions of previous GDP data accompany the monthly release of the GDP and tend to dampen the effect of the report. Although the GDP is not a report to ignore, by any means, it usually isn't as important as the PPI, CPI, and the employment report.

And more importantly, it can be very volatile, making its use in timing decisions unreliable some of the time. Your best bet is to use this report in the context of other reports. If it trends along with others, such as the ISM data, it can be supportive of the overall trend.

GDP does have a fairly important component called the *deflator,* which is a measure of inflation. The deflator can move the markets if it surprises traders with its data.

Trading the Big Reports

The important reports are most likely to influence bonds, stocks, and currencies. Thus, the best strategies for trading based on these reports are found in those markets, which can be traded directly, or via exchange-traded mutual funds (ETFs).

Any report can make the market move up or down if traders in that market find something in the report to justify the move. But some general tendencies to keep in mind include the following:

- ✔ Reports that show a strengthening economy are less friendly to the bond market and tend to be friendlier toward stock-index futures and the dollar. As always, trade what's happening, not what you think ought to happen.

- ✔ Signs of slowing growth or a weak economy tend to be *bullish,* or positive, for bonds and less friendly toward stock indexes and the dollar.

- ✔ Short-term interest rate futures, such as in Eurodollars, may move in the opposite direction of the 10-year Treasury note (T-note) or long-term (30-year) bond futures.

- ✔ Gold, silver, and oil markets may respond aggressively to these reports. (To find out more about the markets in these commodities, see Chapters 13 and 14.)

- ✔ The Federal Reserve may make comments that accelerate or reverse the reactions and responses to economic reports.

Chapter 6

The Seasons and Cycles That Influence the Markets

"Sell in May and go away." The stock market is full of sayings like that, as well as conventional wisdom about "the summer rally," the "Santa Claus rally," the "dark days of autumn," "the presidential cycle," and so on. The real question is whether any of these so-called "traditions" or "seasonal tendencies" can actually help you time the markets.

The answer? Sometimes.

The market is no longer the province of a handful of wealthy bankers moving money around. It's about a lot of big banks, insurance companies, hedge funds, sovereign funds and governments, mutual funds, and individual investors creating a very diverse and dynamic battlefield, and it's always changing. Money moves in and out of stocks, bonds, currencies, and commodities with the stroke of a mouse and at the speed of light millions of times per day. Reliable news and top-of-the-line analytical tools are available to anyone who can pay for them and access the Internet.

Still, a certain amount of seasonality to the markets remains in place, and is worth exploring. In this chapter, I give you the lowdown on what's still out there that works.

Getting the Big Seasonal Picture

In the past, the markets were a whole lot less complicated because they were mostly moved by money coming from the United States and Europe. But as globalization took hold and the ability to communicate in real time became accessible to a broader cross section of the global population, money started to move in a less predictable pattern.

In the 1960s, when Wall Street's big players took the summer off, volume dried up, and the market tended to have a slight upward bias, as the B-team of underlings was left running the shop. Now, with satellites and high-speed Internet everywhere, any money manager with a laptop or a souped-up mobile phone can stay in touch with the markets and make transactions even as she lounges in Tahiti.

That immediacy has altered well-ingrained trading patterns. And further change is inevitable. What works today may not work tomorrow, and that means that you shouldn't rely on seasonal analysis as your main method of deciding when to buy or sell stocks, bonds, or anything else. At the same time, it's important to understand that this is a widely discussed phenomenon, and that there are times when the market does respond to seasonal tendencies.

Here are some basic facts about seasonality to keep in mind:

- **The market is no longer static, thus seasonal tendencies may be interrupted by events.** More people and institutions have real-time access to information and larger amounts of capital than at any time in the past. That means that there is more volatility at any one time, which could derail a perfectly good presidential cycle, for example

- **Institutions have taken over the daily action in the markets.** This is particularly evident in the large-cap stock sectors. Indexes such as the Dow Jones Industrial Average and the S&P 500 are almost exclusively the province of mutual funds, hedge funds, and insurance companies. Individual investors give these giants the control of their money and have essentially stepped out of this arena.

  In a relatively event-free environment, seasonal trends may hold up fairly well. This is especially true at the end of any year, in which institutions want to make their year's results look as good as possible for shareholders and tend to buy stocks to do so.

- **Long-term investing is dead.** Fairly frequent market crashes have taught investors that investing for the long term is a risky business, so there is more short-term trading going on. And with fewer people willing to hold stocks for longer periods, it's increasingly difficult to predict seasonality.

✔ **Derivatives and outside the market trading activities are increasingly prominent in the daily action of markets.** Wall Street has established a network of "off the book" institutions called *dark pools*. These are nothing more than secret stock exchanges where big traders make transactions directly with other big traders and where the price action is reflected only at the end of the deal. Big traders do this so that they can get one price for any stock instead of having to watch the price of their stock rise or fall as you and I piggyback on their moves. The net effect has been a rise in volatility, especially during difficult times when big traders have to deal with margin calls.

✔ **Changes in demographics are afoot.** As the population ages, the overall trend will be more toward income-producing investments. That means that interest is on the rise for owning bonds, money market funds, and preferred stocks that pay high dividends. At the same time, investors looking to switch to these investments are likely to sell, again adding a new wrinkle to what were once well-ingrained seasonal patterns.

✔ **Everyone knows about seasonal tendencies in the stock market.** After a large number of investors acknowledge the existence of any phenomenon, it loses its appeal and thus becomes less effective. And with the media attention to the more popular seasonal tendencies of the market rising over the past few years, this previously reliable factor is not as dependable as it once was.

Glimpsing the Monthly Tendencies

The stock market has a tendency to move in certain directions during certain months of the year, and this general seasonal trend is a good one to keep in mind as part of the background of your timing decisions.

Here are some general tendencies you find as the calendar pages flip:

✔ **September tends to be the toughest month of the year.** According to the Stock Trader's Almanac (STA), the average return for the S&P 500 for the month of September from 1950 to April 2007 was 0.6 percent. The Dow Jones Industrial Average has had a worse time of it, having lost an average of 1 percent during the period.

✔ **November tends to be a good month for the bulls.** The S&P 500 has a general tendency to rise during November. Several important market bottoms have occurred in November. In 1990, the market started the first leg of a multiyear bull market in November. That particular rally picked up steam as the United States invaded Iraq, in Gulf War I.

✔ **December is another typically strong month.** The general good cheer of the holiday season and the need for money managers to have good results at the end of the year in order to make themselves look good tend to move prices higher.

The party in December often extends into January, although the action tends to be a bit more tentative in January. There can be a bit of a December hangover taking its toll in the new year.

✓ **October has had its share of crashes.** The most dramatic ones were in 1929 and 1987. Other Octobers, such as 1990 and 2007, were moderately nasty as well. The latter was essentially the month where the subprime mortgage crisis became a prime-time event in the stock market.

If you want to time the stock market using a very broad seasonal system based on this analysis, here are your best bets:

✓ Own an S&P 500 or Dow Jones Industrial Average index fund during November, December, and January. For more on which funds to use, see Chapter 11.

✓ Sell at the end of January and stay out of the market in February altogether.

✓ Buy back into the market in March and April.

✓ Take a vacation May and June; the market tends to be flat during those months.

✓ Buy your index fund back in July, and based on the way things look you can take it or leave it in August.

✓ Get out by September, though, as things are likely to get ugly.

The January effect

TV commentators love to pontificate on whether stocks experience a *January effect* — a significant rally during the start of a new year — and whether the first week of January actually sets the tone for the rest of the month and even the rest of the year.

The January effect can be quite a rally, but much depends on the overall economy, how good December was, and whether there is any significant catalyst to move prices. (The 1991 U.S. invasion of Iraq is one such example.) Keep these basics in mind when looking for a January effect:

✓ The January effect actually starts in mid-December.

✓ This seasonal trend tends to favor smaller stocks.

✓ The most profitable period of time that includes January, on average, starts on December 31, and extends until February 28, with the average return, as measured by the Russell 2000 index of small stocks being 6.6 percent during that time. If you sell by February 15, you don't lose much, though, as the average gain is about 6.5 percent.

There is some fine print, as the January effect is not guaranteed. One example came in December 2007, as the market topped out and moved aggressively into a bear market that didn't start to look to bottom out until March 2008. The Nasdaq also topped out in December of 1999, and the market got off to a rough start in January 2000.

The turn of the month

The last day of the month and the first five days of a new month — the *turn of the month* — is a very good seasonal pattern that actually holds up more often than not. If you buy stocks on the last trading day of the month and hold them for the first five trading days of the new month, your chances of making money aren't too bad. At the end of the period you move your money back to money market funds and leave it there until the end of the month.

The only other wrinkle is that you do the same with all holidays — move your money in on the day before and sell it at the close of the market on the day after the holiday. This system works in theory because pension funds tend to put new money to work during this time period, and the overall tendency of the market to rise improves.

The system was developed by Norman Fosback, a financial newsletter writer and author of *Stock Market Logic* (Dearborn Trade), and the results are pretty good, especially if you adjust for risk aversion because of decreased exposure to the market. If you had followed this system for 25 years, as of November 24, 2006, you would have made 13.7 percent annualized returns, versus 12.9 percent if you bought and held the Wilshire 5000 index.

Timing Summers, Holidays, and Santa Claus

The holidays and those times when people traditionally take vacations often lead to higher prices: Fewer traders leads to lower trading volume, which in turn tends to exaggerate price moves. Wall Street hypes up the seasons quite loudly, with the summer rally, certain holidays, and especially the Santa Claus rallies getting a lot of print and television time. If it sounds like they're trying to drum up business during slow times, you're probably right. Still, if you're not on vacation (and if you keep your head on straight and get your charts together), you may make some money during these periods.

Summer folly

The Wall Street hypesters start trumpeting the so-called summer rally every year around late May. But in fact there is no such thing; most traders can't even agree on what the summer rally is.

Some say that the official definition is the market period from Memorial Day to Labor Day, while others measure the rally starting at the lows of May, and call the end at the highest point in June, July, August, or September.

No matter how you measure it, a summer rally isn't much more likely than a fall or spring rally. In fact, if you were to measure from the lows to the highs of any season, your best chances of making money would be in winter. (Read more about the winter bump in the earlier section "The January effect.") Why this notion of a summer rally persists is beyond me, other than it's become a Wall Street marketing ploy.

Holiday fun

People start to feel positive when holidays approach and buy stocks before they run off to celebrate Christmas, the Fourth of July, Labor Day, and so on. After the party, reality sets in, and the stocks are sold.

Here are a few holiday trends to watch for:

- The three days before New Year's Eve and the first three trading days of the New Year are your best holiday bet for making money. That's because these days fall within the most bullish time period of the year, winter.

- The next best bets are Labor Day and Memorial Day because they often fall before the first days of trading in September and June, respectively.

- The day before President's Day is the worst pre-holiday period, and the day after Easter is the worst day after a holiday.

As in other seasonally influenced periods of trading, a lot of factors come into play, and you have a lot of room for error.

Santa Claus is coming to town

The best time of the year to own stocks, on average, is during the *Santa Claus rally,* which for all practical purposes is the 17-day stretch from December 21 to January 7.

This is a great time of the year, as most of the time folks are feeling fairly good about themselves. There is also low trading volume, which exaggerates the trend. Most interesting is that if the economy is slowing, the Federal Reserve tends to lower interest rates during the holidays in order to go into the new year with less to worry about.

Cycling with the Presidents

One of the most widely followed cycles on Wall Street is the *presidential cycle* — the notion that the stock market responds in certain ways to the particular part of the term at any given time. The basic tenet of the cycle is that the stock market tends to be down or flat during the first two years of any administration but has a tendency to rally in the last two years. This cycle has a lot to do with the Federal Reserve, which tends to raise interest rates early on in the cycle and lower them as the president seeks re-election.

Much of the presidential cycle stuff started with Yale and Jeffrey Hirsch's *Stock Trader's Almanac,* which essentially put forth the theory. Those who rail against it point out that we've had only 43 presidents and therefore not enough opportunity to get a real statistically significant picture of the issue. Of course, that doesn't really matter to you and me, because by the time there are enough observations, we'll be dead and buried.

I first became interested in the presidential cycle in 1992 when I read an article by the late master technician Arthur Merrill in the March issue *Technical Analysis of Stocks and Commodities* magazine. Merrill looked at the Dow Jones Industrial average from 1898 onward and found that the Dow Jones Industrials tended to start rallying in December of the third year of the presidential term and to rally into the autumn of the third year, then forming a base and starting to rally again after bottoming in the summer of the fourth year.

The theory tends to hold up fairly well, at least in a macro sense, as you look at things over long periods of time. In a micro sense, where you're actually trading the markets, the presidential cycle isn't a good substitute for daily portfolio evaluation and good, nose-to-the-grindstone trading discipline. Still, it can help point you in the right direction.

Examining the cycles during two presidents' terms

Both George W. Bush terms (shown in Figure 6-1) followed the general tendencies of the presidential cycle as measured by the Dow Jones Industrial average (DJIA):

✔ The first years of each term were mostly flat.

✔ Year two in term one was fairly good, as was year three — until the sub-prime crisis hit.

✔ Year four in the second Bush term, at least as of August, went against the grain. The market was in a very bearish trend.

Year three was quite good in both terms as stocks moved higher.

Figure 6-1:
A look at the Dow Jones Industrial Average during George W. Bush's two terms.

Charts courtesy of DecisionPoint.com.

A look at both Clinton terms (Figure 6-2) tells you that

✔ Both first years were pretty good years, which goes against the expectations of the cycle.

✔ The second year for Clinton was fairly flat in both terms.

✔ The third year was quite good.

✔ The fourth year was flat in both terms.

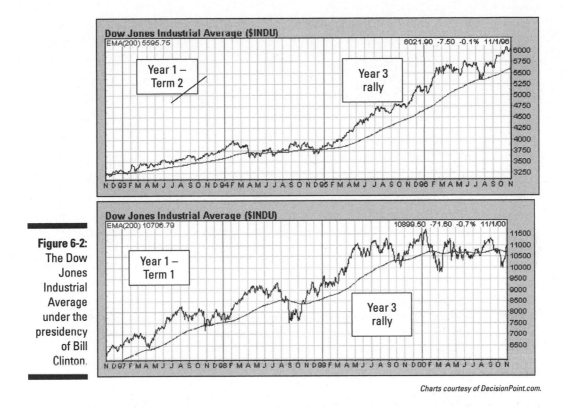

Figure 6-2:
The Dow
Jones
Industrial
Average
under the
presidency
of Bill
Clinton.

Charts courtesy of DecisionPoint.com.

Using the cycle cautiously

In the past ten years, the cycle has played out with a good deal of variability. Some extraordinary reasons contribute to the way things have worked out and add an asterisk to any cycles that existed in the past:

✔ The September 11, 2001, terrorist attack came in the first year of the presidential cycle for President Bush and ushered in a major and aggressive recession that prompted the Federal Reserve to lower interest rates and eventually led to the invasion of Iraq.

✔ Scandals in Washington were rampant over the decade from 1998 to 2008. President Clinton's second term was marred by the Monica Lewinski story, and Bush's two terms were scandal-ridden, as well, with the war in Iraq and its aftermath and the Scooter Libby/Valerie Plame scandal.

The Bush years came in with a great deal of drama with the terrorist attacks of September 11, 2001, and continued with the further implosion of the Internet bubble. Then the tumult of Enron and WorldCom bloomed to its fullest expression during the first term, only to be followed by the subprime mortgage crisis. All of these significant developments had their effects on the stock market.

✔ Globalization grew during the 1998 to 2008 decade, with China, India, Brazil, and other emerging markets moving their economies toward the upper tier of both production and consumerism, leading to a major boom in resource demand and sparking global inflation.

Perhaps at the center of the whole dynamic is how rapidly information now travels. The Internet has revolutionized the way information travels around the world, with the 24-hour news cycle expanding beyond television into formal news on the Web, as well as the explosion of opinion and factual news in the blogosphere.

We do live in a different world now, where events beyond Washington, D.C., can affect the markets more often and more rapidly than they used to. And of these events, along with more normal (for lack of a better word) developments such as regional conflicts, religious wars, the rise and fall of tyrants and the ascension of new ones to take their place, as well as the normal amount of ebb and flow of money and information, added a whole new set of twists to the behavior of the financial markets around the world.

The presidential cycle is still an important guideline, especially in year three where the odds of the stock market rising remain quite favorable. Otherwise, anything else you can say about the cycle is highly variable and most likely, in the present, will be influenced by the political tone of the world at the time. What I found most useful during the research for this chapter are these three points:

✔ Stocks tend to do better with Democrat administrations than with Republicans in the White House.

✔ Small stocks tend to outperform large stocks during Democrat administrations.

✔ Most interesting, though, is the consistency of year three as a profitable year for stock investors. Even during the tumultuous presidencies of Bill Clinton and George W. Bush, the third years were profitable.

Chapter 7

Digging In to Trends, Momentum, and Results

In This Chapter

▶ Identifying and utilizing trends

▶ Spotting trend changes

▶ Introducing important trend indicators

*I*n practice, market timing is 95 percent pure boredom and 5 percent total excitement. It's kind of like hunting or being part of a police stakeout — a long period of vigilance that at some point leads to precise action with little room for error.

Successful market timing is about many things: analysis, preparation, discipline, and agility. The centerpiece of actual trading is the ability to be on the right side of the trend, whether that trend is up or down. You also need to be able to identify the momentum of the trend and to identify whether the trend is at the beginning, the middle, or the end.

The most successful market timers are the ones who can spot the trend changes early on, recognize the general direction of the trend, and gear their timing strategies to go with that primary trend. In this chapter, I show you the key steps and indicators that get you in on the dominant market trend as early as possible and keep you on the right side of the curve.

Trending with the Times

A trend in prices is something like an ocean current. Waves move toward the shore, but they don't do so in straight lines. Wind currents, gravity, and the rotational force of the earth push and pull at them.

Price trends function in the same fashion, governed by the ebb and flow of information and the way the market interprets the information. Here are some general characteristics of all trends:

✓ **All trends start somewhere and end somewhere.** There is always a beginning, a middle, and an end. From a timing standpoint, you don't have to catch the precise start of the final endpoint of any trend. Your goal is to spot the trend and trade with it for as long as it stays in place. Trying to catch the perfect wave in timing is nearly impossible. If you can capture intermediate-term pieces of the dominant long-term trend, and do it consistently, you'll be very satisfied with your trading results.

✓ **Trends are influenced by external and internal events.** External events, such as politics, changes in interest rates, wars, and the execution of corporate strategies — buyouts, takeovers, innovation and new products, and asset sales — are part of what create and nurture trends.

✓ **Trends tend to seed and feed new trends.** Just as the PC-software-Internet trend had its heyday, its existence led to the emergence of new trends. As technology became faster, more efficient, and more readily available, so did the information revolution start to spread beyond the United States and Europe. Asia, Africa, and South America became participants, and innovation in those markets led to significant improvement in the lifestyle and aspirations of the inhabitants of those areas. As a result, energy demand rose in those countries, and the era of tight oil supplies arrived.

Read on to find out how to spot these key dynamics from multiple points of view, always focusing on their effects on the markets — the key to timing opportunities.

Looking for trends by time

Keep an eye out for three major kinds of trends in the stock market:

✓ The *overall price trend* — the major direction of prices — is what stock indexes and related indicators express.

✓ The *secular trend* has nothing to do with whether you're religious or not, but whether a trend is large and significant enough to last for years and give you a chance to make big money if you identify it early enough and stick with it.

✓ The *niche trend* is one wherein a single theme moves a particular stock or a sector of the market higher or lower despite the dominant trend of the market.

The most significant trend is the secular trend, because that one lasts for years or even decades and defines all of the others. I think of the secular trend in two ways: It's a price trend that lasts for a very long time, and it's a social phenomenon that changes the way people live and do business. It becomes ingrained in the way society acts, and at some point, it becomes so common that it's no longer a novelty.

As a timer, you want to note when a trend becomes a given, because at some point beyond that instant, the investment aspects of the trend cease to be important, and the market turns.

The best example of such a trend in recent times is the PC revolution, which evolved into the Internet boom, and eventually gave way to the oil boom, which was partially fueled by the technology explosion that preceded it and catalyzed by the September 11, 2001, attacks.

Trends also fall into three categories according to their duration:

- The *short-term trend* for most market timers is one that lasts for days to weeks. For day traders, this is a trend measured in minutes.

- The *intermediate-term trend* is one that lasts for weeks to months. This is the major trend of interest for market timers. It's the one that gives you plenty of time to get in and usually plenty of time to get out without missing the fat portion of the move.

- The *long-term trend* is one that lasts for months to years. The long-term trend is beneficial for timers because it's composed of many intermediate periods. And so even though as a timer you aren't likely to hold any specific assets for the entire duration of the long-term trend, the length of the trend gives you ample opportunity to trade for the intermediate term.

Secularizing the trend

Secular trends at some point become self-evident but are hard to spot — sometimes for months and even years. In fact, secular trends in markets are identified mostly in retrospect, but they're important because as long as they are in place, investors, traders, and money managers are willing to keep moving prices in the direction of the trend. As long as a secular trend is in place, the rest of us should be looking to time the market with a bias toward the direction that the big money is moving.

Figure 7-1 shows a multi-decade period of trading in the Nasdaq Composite. A secular trend started in 1982 and was interrupted in the year 2000 but still in place as of 2008, based on the multi-decade rising trend line. Within this multi-decade bull market in technology stocks were several bull markets and several bear markets of normal duration, but the overall trend remained up.

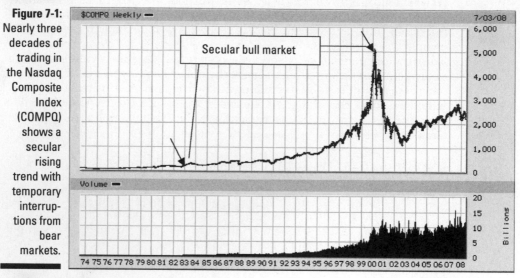

Figure 7-1:
Nearly three decades of trading in the Nasdaq Composite Index (COMPQ) shows a secular rising trend with temporary interruptions from bear markets.

Chart courtesy of Prophet.net.

Most noticeable bearish periods during this secular bull run were the

- Crash of 1987
- Bear market of the summer of 1990, preceding the first war in Iraq
- Sideways bear market of 2004
- Enron-WorldCom bear raid of 1999

Other big stories during that time include

- The attempted assassination of President Reagan
- The Iran-Contra affair
- The fall of the Berlin Wall
- The Monica Lewinski scandal
- The first attack on the World Trade Center
- Major hurricanes
- Wars in Bosnia and Iraq
- The start of the boom of the Internet and wireless communications

None of these events was able to derail the secular trend, which kept moving higher until it finally ran out of gas in 2001, only to find support at the rising trend line.

So what made it run out of gas? At some point, all trends end, or at least take a break. And the one common point that ties them all together is the feeling among investors that the trend is so well entrenched that it can never change. The hint that the end or that at least a significant disruption is near is usually when the common, everyday guy is bragging about how well he's doing in the market, as was evident at the end of the dot-com boom when taxi drivers with laptops were selling advice to their passengers and getting interviewed on CNBC. Similarly, the end of the housing boom (which wasn't a secular trend but a very long-term trend) became clear as house-flipping shows proliferated.

Important points about secular trends include the following:

- ✔ They last for decades, and at their peak seem as if they can never be broken. That impression is usually the key sign that the end of the trend is near.

- ✔ When they finally break, no one believes that this is truly the end. That's when you see the volatility start and when the real damage to investors done, as they try to hang on to a good thing.

- ✔ Knowing when you're in a secular trend is very difficult until you've been in one for quite a while; that's why intermediate-term trading is suitable for maneuvering during run-of–the-mill long-term trends as well as extraordinary secular trends.

As a timer, your only concern is to be on the right side of the intermediate-term trend. Yes, recognizing the prevalent, secular, and long-term trends is important, but that kind of analysis is for background information — not for formatting your primary trading strategy.

Using the short-term trend properly

The secular trend is the mega-trend that governs investor behavior over very long periods of time. But inside the secular trend are other important trends.

The short-term trend is about minute-by-minute volatility. And that's stuff for a day trader, who sweats out the minutes, and makes trades based on short-term trend analysis. Timers are looking to make large percentage gains over longer periods of time, often weeks to months. That means that timers have to be more patient and — contrary to popular belief — make fewer trades.

Use short-term charts to view entry and exit points for intermediate-term timing. View the short-term trend through the prism of charts that feature 15-minute ticks to put it in its proper context with regard to timing. I've found that if I use short-term charts that feature 1-minute or 5-minute ticks I end up making bad decisions much more often for the intermediate term.

Figure 7-2 shows you a ten-day period of trading of the U.S. Oil Fund (USO) featuring 15-minute bars. If you compare Figure 7-2 to 7-3, which shows a 12-month view of USO, you see two different views of the same trading activity. Figure 7-2 shows a market that has been weak in the short term, and Figure 7-3 puts that weakness within a longer-term context, that of a market that is looking a bit tired and that could fall farther. The X in each figure is a reference point to align both charts.

The trend line in Figure 7-3 shows that the fund is still in a long-term up trend, but the magnified trading action in the ten-day view shows that the short-term trend line has been tested twice during the time period featured in the chart. That means that a break below that trend line would be significant. As a timer, this is a time to be very careful, because the market is clearly trying to make a decision that will affect your trading.

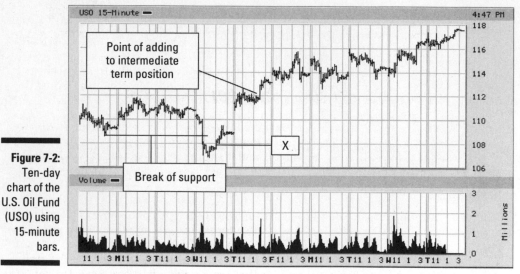

Figure 7-2:
Ten-day chart of the U.S. Oil Fund (USO) using 15-minute bars.

Chart courtesy of Prophet.net.

Use short-term charts only to help magnify the action — to get a better look at what's going on before making decisions and to help pinpoint entry and exit points. For example, you could have used the short-term chart in Figure 7-2 to figure out where you could add money to a long position in USO if the trend line held, or to sell — or sell short — USO if the ETF broke below the key support level.

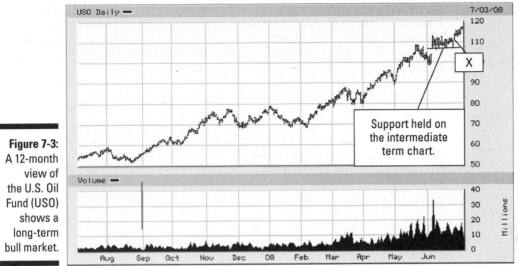

USO Daily —   7/03/08

X

Support held on
the intermediate
term chart.

Volume —

Millions

Aug   Sep   Oct   Nov   Dec   08   Feb   Mar   Apr   May   Jun

Figure 7-3:
A 12-month
view of
the U.S. Oil
Fund (USO)
shows a
long-term
bull market.

Chart courtesy of Prophet.net.

Looking at the long-term trend

In this section, I concentrate on the long-term trend, that which unfolds over
months to years. Identifying the long-term trend is the first step in the analysis required for accurate timing, and it's where the real trading decisions
start for timers because it's where you get more specific by using indicators
and oscillators. (See Chapter 4.)

The long-term trend is about getting your bearings so that you can start
making trading decisions about the intermediate-term trend. When prices are
above the 200-day moving average, the long-term trend is up; prices below
this line signal a long-term down trend. When prices are above the 200-day
line, look to trade stocks or ETFs that are moving higher, or breaking out of
bases and getting set to move higher. When prices are below the 200-day line,
protect your portfolio by selling weak stocks and ETFs; if you're an aggressive
trader, look for stocks and ETFs to sell short.

Get started by looking at a two-year chart. If that doesn't really give you what
you want, then add a year, and another year, and so on.

I like to use the S&P 500 for my benchmark of the stock market. It's where the
big mutual fund managers put their money. And because I want to go with the
big money, that's where I start my analysis.

Figure 7-4 shows the S&P 500 for two years and gives me what I want to know as I start to work my way down to making timing decisions. Look over the chart as from left to right, and you see a market that was heading nicely higher until it ran into trouble, began to struggle, and finally turned over and started heading lower.

Figure 7-4:
A Two-year view of the S&P 500 Index shows a market slowly topping out.

Chart courtesy of Prophet.net.

The labels in Figure 7-4 illustrate the first important point, that the long-term trend in the S&P was tested at its 200-day moving average and failed. The line going across the chart, the 200-day moving average, was important support — a place where prices held — throughout the time period in which the S&P 500 was rising. Note how the buyers came in at the 200-day moving average, on the left of the chart, but sellers gain the upper hand in the middle and reassert themselves on the right.

These three chart points are clearly the transition from a bull market to a bear market, and they show that it takes time for markets to change trends. Initially the S&P 500 recovered slightly (August 2007) and then broke below the key long-term support, the 200-day moving average, in the January to February 2008 time frame. The market failed to rise above the 200-day line and is a classic illustration of the transition from bull market to bear market, with the breakdown having started in October 2007, and the first leg of the bear moving down until March 2008. Next came the snapback rally and the failure.

Buyers and sellers tend to line up just above and below key support and resistance levels such as the 200-day moving average. That's why the success or failure of a move often depends on what happens at these key chart points.

Support is a chart point above which prices hold. *Resistance* is the opposite — a chart point above which prices fail to rise.

Spotting trend changes in the intermediate term

The intermediate-term trend is the Goldilocks "just right" time frame for market timing because it usually gives you enough time at the start to get into the market without missing too much and enough time at the end to get out of the market with some sort of profit — if you play your cards right. The intermediate-term trend also is the easiest to spot and the easiest to keep tabs on with indicators.

In the next few sections, I dissect an important 12-month period in the stock market as measured by the S&P 500 Index. I show you how to spot important changes in the trend and how to time a sideways market, a rising market, and a falling market.

Timing sideways markets

Sideways-moving markets are among the most difficult markets for timers, but they're a fact of life. Sideways markets are the periods between up trends and down trends, where the market forms what technical analysts call *bases*. Prices eventually move above or below the bases embarking on the next trend.

Figure 7-5 shows what I call a "fully loaded" chart with Bollinger bands, the 20-, 50-, and 200-day moving average, and three oscillators: stochastics, RSI, and MACD histogram, which enable you to confirm what the ticks on the chart are telling you. (Chapter 4 gives you the details about these indicators.)

Your first look at any chart is the most important. Figure 7-5 shows you the S&P 500 index moving through a period of rallying (left), consolidation (middle), and eventually breaking through support and starting a bear market (right).

If you concentrate on the time period from August 2007 to December 2008, you see a grinding trading range market. That is a tough market to time, although it could be done depending on your risk tolerance and your ability to pick tops and bottoms of trading ranges. But here's where Bollinger bands come in handy, as they frame the trading range and give you entry and exit points.

I marked both the bands (upper and lower) in the figure, at several good entry and exit points. The lower band is marked at points where you can enter the market on the long side (buy point). The upper band is marked where you can exit your long position (sell points) or sell short if you're more aggressive.

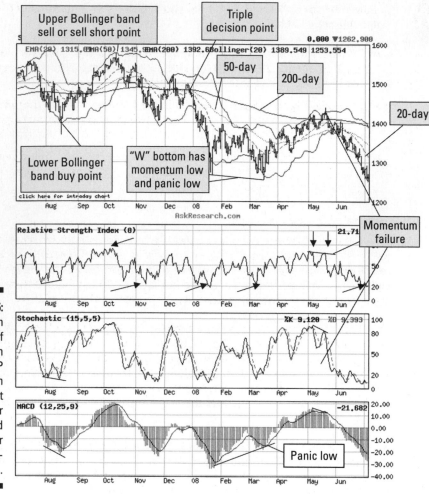

Figure 7-5:
A 24-month view of trading in the S&P 500 with important Bollinger band and oscillator top and bottom signals.

Chart courtesy of AskResearch.com.

The key to using Bollinger bands to time a trading range market is to spot when prices move outside the band and come back inside. Prices outside of the band are a sign that the trend has gone too far in that direction and that you're going to have some sort of consolidation or a change in direction. In both of these cases — March and August 2007, and October and November of the same year — a change in the trend came after the move outside the band.

Look at the oscillators for confirmation of what the Bollinger bands signal. As a general rule, you want to see the oscillators peak and trough along with the market. If you're in an up trend, then the oscillators should rise with the market and rise to a new peak each time the market makes a new high. When the market makes a new high and the oscillator doesn't, the rally is losing momentum. The opposite is true at market bottoms. I've marked these important areas as "loss of rally momentum" and "loss of selling momentum" in Figure 7-5.

Bollinger bands and oscillators help you spot tops and bottoms of trading range markets. Look for

✔ Prices rising above the top Bollinger band as a sign that the market has gone too far too fast to the up side. That's the signal to sell your long position and to consider short selling.

✔ Prices falling below the lower Bollinger band as a signal that prices have gone too far to the down side. That's when you look for an opportunity to buy.

✔ MACD and RSI oscillators giving buy and sell signals when momentum changes, even in sideways markets. Look to those indicators to confirm moves above or below the Bollinger bands.

Beyond sideways markets

The one thing that always holds true about trading ranges is that they eventually end, and the market will move higher or lower. Even as the trading range in the last half of 2007 was developing, the market was clearly giving signs that it was getting tired, as the MACD and RSI oscillators were showing signs of weakness, and the market itself was increasingly volatile.

The whole thing came to a head when the charts gave us what I call a *Triple Decision Point (TDP)*, when the 20-, 50-, and 200-day moving averages cluster together and become a major hinge or pivot point for prices. In Figure 7-5, the TDP came in late January 2008, when the S&P 500 was hovering just below 1500. This, in retrospect, was really the tipping point wherein the bear market became fully engaged as the major trend when the market failed at the key chart point.

A failure at a TDP means that the market has failed at three significant trends — the short-, intermediate-, and long-term trends. That means that the path of least resistance, until proven otherwise, is in the direction from which prices break at the TDP. In January 2008, it was clearly to the down side.

A price break above a TDP is a buy signal, and a break below a TDP is a sell signal or a signal to sell the market short.

Timing market bottoms

Although it's not an exact science, getting in as close to the bottom of any rally is an important part of market timing and enables you to participate in the new up trend for longer — assuming that the bottom turns into a good intermediate-term rally. That's not guaranteed during any bottom, but if you get used to looking for these events, you'll get enough of them right to make your timing efforts worthwhile.

The next opportunity to trade the intermediate-term trend during the 12-month period shown in Figure 7-5 came in February and March of 2008. After the October 2007 top and the December-January failure at the TDP, the market sold off quite aggressively until March, when it bottomed near the S&P 500's 1260 area. This was a classic *W* bottom, which is made up of two *V* configurations. The *V* on the left is what is known as the *momentum bottom* — when the first wave of selling is exhausted. A second bottom usually follows it, as it did in this case. The second bottom is called the *panic bottom,* and it washes out the rest of the sellers that come in after the first bounce.

The best oscillator with which to spot the bullish *W* bottoms is the MACD histogram. (See Chapter 4.) Look for two important signs of a *W* bottom: First, the momentum bottom causes a deep trough on the MACD histogram; the second *V* causes a much higher trough on the MACD histogram — the sign that the market is about to rally, as it did in Figure 7-5, because even though the market made a lower bottom, the selling had a lot less force behind it, making the market vulnerable to buyers.

The key to being accurate in diagnosing the *W* bottom is that the second bottom is often a lower bottom than the first. When a shallower trough accompanies the second bottom on the MACD, then you have the true buy signal. When you spot this kind of chart bottom, be ready to trade on the long side, as prices are likely to rise.

The momentum failure

All trends have momentum — the tendency of prices to move up or down for an extended period of time. As long as prices are moving higher, they have upward momentum, a sign that buyers have the upper hand. During down trends, the sellers have the upper hand because prices are moving lower, and momentum is to the down side. This section shows you how to spot the clear warning signs that momentum is shifting from buyers to sellers, or vice versa.

The final stage of the 24-month period in the market that Figure 7-5 shows was the momentum failure that came in May, as the market rolled over, once again pointing out the importance of key moving average support and resistance levels.

As the market bounced back in March, it started moving higher, first crossing above the 20-day moving average, and then the 50-day moving average. Those were positive signals that the short-term and the intermediate-term trends had turned higher. The real test, though, was the 200-day moving average. During similar periods, look for signs similar to those in this example:

✔ **A good solid bottom was in place:** The MACD lighter trough was a good entry point for a small long position. You could have bought an index ETF. Or you could have picked some individual stocks. See chapters 10 and 11 for good ETF and individual stock timing ideas for the stock market.

Any timer worth his salt will go long when a bottom is in place.

✔ **The short- and intermediate-term trends turned up:** The positive cross-overs of the 20- and 50-day moving averages illustrated that the trend had changed. Periods where prices cross above key technical levels, such as moving averages, are good places to enter the market or add to positions.

✔ **The big test is the 200-day moving average:** As Figure 7-5 shows, a significant momentum failure occurred at the 200-day moving average. Several things were evident at that point:

- • The S&P 500 moved outside of the upper Bollinger band — a sign that the market was going to slow its rate of ascent.

- • The RSI and stochastics showed the reverse of what the MACD showed at the March bottom, as the S&P 500 made a marginal new high for the move, but the oscillators made a lower peak than the previous peak. Refer to Figure 7-5 to see the momentum failure in the oscillators. This is a classic loss of momentum to the upside, as it shows that the buyers are exhausted. That it came at the 200-day moving average made it even more important, especially because that was the point where the market broke in December and January.

WARNING!

Before making a move, you need to know where you are in terms of the trend. In Figure 7-5, the bottom was made below the 200-day moving average, which is by definition bear market territory, meaning that the market has a higher burden of proof with regard to its ability to deliver a significant rally. It's your job as a timer during these periods to be wary of every important resistance level along the way. In this case, the 20-, 50-, and 200-day moving averages were opportunities for the market to fail. Clearing the first two hurdles is no guarantee that the third, and most important hurdle, the 200-day moving average, would be just as easy for the buyers to overcome. In order to have been successful during this period in the market, as prices approached each important chart point, your level of caution needed to rise, and you should have been ready for a price reversal, which is exactly what happened at the 200-day line. During that period of time, I spent a lot of time going over the possibility of a failure at the 200-day moving average at www.joe-duarte.com. And it paid off both for me and for my subscribers as we unwound long positions and put on some short positions that did well in the period that followed.

Examining Market Breadth

Market breadth is one of the most important components of intermediate-term market timing. *Market breadth* refers to how many stocks are advancing versus those that are declining.

Two important indicators are very useful in giving you the overall trend of the market: the New York Stock Exchange advance decline line (NYSE A-D line) and the McClellan Summation Index (MCSI).

The *NYSE A-D line* is constructed by plotting the difference between the number of advancing stocks on the NYSE on a daily basis. As the points add up, the line starts moving higher, lower, or sideways. A line that's moving higher indicates a rising trend, and vice versa. The A-D line is at its best when it diverges from the major indexes, such as the S&P 500 — a signal that the market is starting to weaken and that some kind of price correction is likely in the future.

The *McClellan Summation Index* is a trend and momentum indicator for the stock market. It's derived by plugging several different parameters into a formula that the average investor really doesn't need to know. (And why tax yourself unnecessarily?) What you do need to know is that the MCSI is an excellent indicator and very useful to market timers. I give you more details in the section "Analyzing the McClellan Summation Index" later in this chapter.

Greg Morris (www.pmfm.com), a good friend of mine, profiles important market breadth indicators in a book called *The Complete Guide to Market Breadth Indicators* (McGraw-Hill). Check it out if you want to delve deeply into this critical concept.

Consulting the NYSE advance-decline line

The NYSE A-D line is one of my favorite indicators. I think of it as blood pressure monitor for the markets, and I look at it almost every day, and after every week of trading.

In a well-functioning market, you want the broad market to keep up or in some cases to lead the indexes — a signal that the bulls are in charge. More important from a timing and trading standpoint, when the A-D line is acting well, your chances of buying winning stocks increase, making it a better environment for being long.

Figure 7-6 shows you the S&P 500 Index and the NYSE advance-decline line over a period of three years.

Note that the overall upward slope of the chart is very similar to the upward slope of the S&P 500. The sign that you're looking for is when the index makes a new high, as it did in the September to October period in 2007. The A-D line does not match it. This is called a *divergence,* and it means that the underlying market is starting to weaken, even though the major indexes are still showing some strength. Divergences of this kind usually lead to weakness in the market, as in this case. Similar failures of the A-D line to confirm new highs in major indexes preceded the crash of 1987, as well as the major summer 1990 bear market and the 2000 break of the dot-com boom.

Figure 7-6:
The S&P
500 Index
(above) and
the NYSE
Advance
Decline
Line, weekly
(below).

Charts courtesy of BigCharts.com (upper) and Stockcharts.com (lower).

The NYSE A-D line is calculated on a weekly and a daily basis. Some technical analysts prefer one version over the other. I like to use them both in case one of them misses something important. In Figure 7-6 the weekly A-D line caught the divergence quite well.

After you notice the failure of the A-D line, review your portfolio and look for winners and losers. Consider taking profits or tightening your sell stops on the winners and sell any laggards. The object is to raise cash and prepare for a significant decline. The worst that could happen is that you're wrong and the market takes off. If you are, you can always re-establish new positions. If you had been riding the huge up trend for any length of time you had some nice profits. Don't be greedy; this indicator has an excellent record and if you ignore it the odds are high in favor of your losing.

To calculate your own advance-decline (A-D) line for any index or sector, subtract the number of declining stocks from the number of advancing stocks on any given day or week. Then you plot the number on a chart. The line develops over a few points. In a healthy bull market, the advance-decline line has an upward slope.

Analyzing the McClellan Summation Index

The McClellan Summation Index is one of the greatest contributions to technical analysis in the history of the stock market. It is the sum of the readings of all the McClellan oscillators for any given day. The *McClellan oscillator* is based on a moderately complex formula that calculates the difference between two moving averages of the daily advance-decline numbers and is often useful as a short- and an intermediate-term indicator. You can get more information on it at the McClellan Web site (www.mcoscillator.com).

Most big-time trading software enables you to calculate the MSCI and the McClellan oscillators. They're also available at technical Web sites such as www.decisionpoint.com and stockcharts.com.

Interpreting the index is fairly straightforward. According to Tom McClellan, the son of its inventors Sherman and Marion, who now does most of the work with the McClellan indicators:

- The MCSI normally oscillates between zero and +2000. Moves above +2000 are considered very bullish and are a sign of significant strength in the market.

  Extremes in the MCSI, according to data from DecisionPoint.com, are +4000 to –2000. According to data in Greg Morris's book *The Complete Guide to Market Breadth Indicators,* the Summation index fell to nearly –3500 in 1998 and rose above +6000 in 2003. Market drops followed all the four drops below zero in the time frame depicted in Figure 7-7.

- A move below the zero line by the MCSI is a precursor to a bear market. Figure 7-7 shows four such occurrences. (Look for the arrows.) Each was followed by a fairly impressive decline in prices of the NYSE Composite Index.

✔ The bounce after a significant decline is also important. When the MCSI moves from a very low level to a very high level in a period of months, it's a sign that the market is in a strong up trend. But if the indicator fails to achieve a high enough level, the bear market is still in place. In 2002, when the market first bottomed after the bear market that followed the dot-com bubble, the bottom for the MCSI came at –2000. The subsequent high, +6500, came in 2003, nearly at the time of the third bottom in the S&P 500, from which the bull market that ended in 2008 rose.

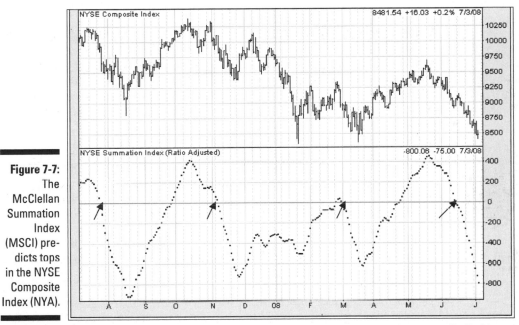

Figure 7-7: The McClellan Summation Index (MSCI) predicts tops in the NYSE Composite Index (NYA).

Chapter 8

Timing with Feeling: Making Market Sentiment Work for You

*F*inancial markets function within a spectrum of emotion defined by greed and fear. You see greed when trading is completely out of control on the up side and fear during those periods when it feels as if there will never be an up day again. When the markets are at either extreme, it makes sense to look for a potential change in the prevailing trend.

Market timers are at their best during extremes; they're the ones looking to exit the market as close to a market top as possible and enter as close to the bottom as possible.

In this chapter, I show you how to spot greed and fear and how to avoid getting hurt too badly by extreme market behavior — how to get in touch with the market's feelings.

Getting in Touch with Your Contrarian Self

Being a *contrarian investor* (someone who knows when to trade against a prevailing trend) is a popular topic, but going against the grain isn't always easy, especially when you're early in making your move. If you sell too early you could lose big gains that could make your returns for months or even years, depending on what part of the cycle the market is in. On the other side of the market, if you buy too soon, you'll almost certainly feel some pain.

You can't completely avoid selling too early, or getting in before it's time to buy. It's just part of the game when you're a contrarian. Here are some other important things to remember when you're going against the grain:

✔ Look for key turning points when shifts in market sentiment become noticeable. Understand that picking the absolute top and bottom is nearly impossible, so one good way to avoid trouble is to build small positions at times when the market is starting to bottom and to expect to make some mistakes in the early going.

✔ When markets start looking *frothy,* or out of control on the up side, look for reasons to sell, especially when everyone else is bullish.

✔ Trading on sentiment — making timing decisions solely based on sentiment indicators like the ones I describe in this chapter — is inexact and can lead to losses whenever you pull the trigger too early during the cycle. Your best bet is to combine sentiment analysis with other analytical methods.

Contrarian trading requires that you develop a sixth sense about the markets. You want to question every piece of news, and every market move, and put it in the proper context. For example, if the news is generally bad and the market is no longer falling, that's a sign that a buying opportunity is developing. If the news is good and the market is no longer rising, that's usually a sign that a decline could be near. The only way to develop this sixth sense is to study prior market cycles and to experience them in the present and the future by both studying and trading the markets. The upcoming sections "Identifying greed cycles" and "Identifying fear cycles" tell you more.

Going with Your Gut — and Your Charts

One of the most common tenets of timing and trading is that you should never make trading decisions based on emotion. I readily agree. But — (there's always a *but*) — if you ignore your gut, you'll probably be sorry.

I'm not suggesting that you go out and try to make money solely based on your instincts. I'm saying that your gut has a certain role to play in your trading, and that the better you tune into it, the better off you are. Just don't give your gut more credit than your charts.

Here's what I mean: When you walk into a room of people you've never seen, that first feeling you get is probably the most important. If the crowd creeps you out, you know that you'll probably head for the door early. You don't really know why, but you know that it's the right thing to do.

It's the same thing with market timing. After a market has been in a steep decline, the news is usually terrible. At some point, though, you note that the market first stops falling to new lows, and then starts to move higher — slowly at first, and then with gathering steam. That's when you raise your antenna, acknowledge what your gut and your sixth sense are telling you, turn to your charts, and start looking for signs that a trend change may be near.

Figure 8-1 shows you a good example of the greed-fear spectrum as it took place in the 2000 to 2003 time period. In it you see what happens when total insanity takes over on both ends, as the Internet stocks took off in the middle of the year and didn't stop running until early 2001. Here's the rundown:

- **Greed rears its head:** In 2000, the Internet-led bull market was at its peak. The prevailing wisdom was that a company didn't need to make money as long as it had a good concept and its Web site had traffic. Analysts were tripping over each other to raise price targets on companies that had no earnings. And anyone who tried to point out how silly the whole thing was and that a bear market was coming was laughed at.

  When the market collapsed, everyone called it a correction and said that it would come back. And the more that stocks fell, the more that the same analysts would keep telling everyone that things would improve any day. The whole thing unraveled and the selling gathered steam after September 11, 2001.

- **Fear takes over:** By late 2002, the headlines were ominous. Analysts had lost their jobs and had been proven to be frauds as some were e-mailing each other pointing out the truth about companies that they covered while hyping them to the public. Most investors felt as if the market could never rally again. By 2003 a new bull market was on the run. See the sections "Identifying greed cycles" and "Identifying fear cycles" later in this chapter for more details.

Identifying greed cycles

Extremely greedy behavior in the markets is usually the prelude to a market top and what can turn out to be a severe bear market where prices fall for extended periods of time. Here are some signals that indicate greed cycles:

✔ **The market can't seem to be stopped.** Every day prices go higher and higher, and when a pullback (decline in prices) occurs, it doesn't last very long; buyers step in to buy stocks with every price dip in shares.

✔ **The prevailing sentiment is that this time is different, that you're in a new era.** In the *blow off* (price behavior that goes straight up) that Figure 8-1 shows, the biggest story from TV pundits and experts everywhere was that Internet companies didn't need to make money because the concept that Internet stocks would never fall was so endearing that many truly believed that buyers would always be around to support the price of the stocks.

When have companies *not* needed to eventually make money in order to keep up their stock prices? In other words, if it's too good to be true, it is.

✔ **Charts develop parabolic patterns.** Prices go straight up, such as you see in Figure 8-1, where I marked "blow-off phase," and when prices crack, they go down fast and hard. Figure 8-1 clearly shows that even though the Internet bubble burst in the year 2000, by 2008 prices hadn't recovered even 50 percent of their all-time highs.

Blow-off phases are rallies that you can't afford to miss, even though your gut and your charts should be telling you to be careful. Still, you're a market timer, and you should be able to recognize these price patterns, as well as the fact that blow-offs can make you a lot of money. But blow-offs are periods of totally insane behavior. Be careful and disciplined; follow your trading rules and follow the advice of the indicators that I describe in Chapter 7.

Figure 8-1:
Historic extremes of greed and fear were evident as the Internet bubble burst and the Nasdaq Composite ($COMPQ) collapsed in the year 2000 and recovered in 2003.

Chart courtesy of Prophet.net

Identifying fear cycles

If greed is all about feeling as if stocks will never fall, the opposite is true of fear cycles, as eventually the sellers get exhausted and markets begin to recover.

In 2003, when the stock market bottomed, the news was so dark that many were predicting the end of the United States as a superpower. It was two years after the events of September 11, 2001, and the Federal Reserve had lowered interest rates to nearly 1 percent. The U.S. economy was in a deep recession, with job losses mounting and the U.S. dollar weakening. And sure as heck, the stock market bottomed and nearly doubled, as measured by the S&P 500 over the next five years, before the next crisis finally hit, the subprime mortgage crisis. Stocks topped out in late 2007 as the housing market collapsed, and the S&P fell nearly 20 percent — a very aggressive decline — by March 2008.

The news was dire: Investment banks were writing off billions of dollars worth of bad loans from their balance sheets, the home foreclosure rate skyrocketed, and the U.S. labor market topped out. Inflation was on the rise in China, the dollar was falling, and oil prices were rocketing past $100 per barrel. So what happened? The stock market bottomed and began to rally, as you see in Figure 8-2.

Figure 8-2: The S&P 500 bottoms in 2003 and in 2008 amid high amounts of fear and bad news.

Chart courtesy of Prophet.net

Use the following earmarks to identify fear cycles:

- **The news is bad.** It seems as if everything is wrong. The headlines feature stories about society's ills and how the current financial mess worsened them. You see interviews with people who have lost everything and with public servants who are at wits' end trying to figure out how to help the rising numbers who are in trouble. Companies that you've never heard of, such as mortgage counseling firms, are doing booming business.

- **Public opinion is uniformly negative.** In 2008, at the bottom of the stock market's decline in March, the majority of Americans polled said that the market was heading in the wrong direction, and consumer confidence had fallen to record low levels.

- **Politicians scramble to appear to be helpful.** You see all kinds of bills being debated in Congress aimed at fixing the problem and a lot of money being pumped into the economy. In 2008, tax rebate checks were mailed to taxpayers so that they could spend money and "revive" the economy. The House and Senate, along with the president, put forth multiple initiatives in order to prop up the housing market. And chief executives of Wall Street investment banks and mortgage lenders were paraded and berated before Congress.

When you see the earmarks of a fear cycle, take a look at what the market is doing. If prices seem to have bottomed, it's a good time to start nibbling at stocks.

Using Bellwether Stocks

One of my favorite sentiment indicators is *bellwether stocks* — key stocks that are leaders in their fields. When investors buy or sell these shares, it's usually a good sign of confidence or the lack of it in that sector of the market and sometimes even the economy.

Each bull market has a new group of bellwethers. They are the stocks that start moving higher and whose developments are seen as a sign of what's likely to happen to all other companies in their sector. Previous bellwethers have been companies like IBM, Intel, General Motors, and Citigroup. A recent one that was still fairly popular when I wrote this book was Google.

My favorite bellwether stock from the bull market that ended in 2007 was Goldman Sachs (NYSE: GS), the king of investment banks in the 21st century. Goldman's businesses span the entire world and include not just traditional investment banking functions of advising on and underwriting takeovers and initial public offerings (IPOs), but running hedge funds, trading aggressively in all markets, and actually owning and operating businesses. This diversified business model makes Goldman an excellent bellwether for the market.

Here's how I looked at Goldman during that period:

- ✔ When Goldman shares were on the rise, I saw at it as a positive for the entire market, and I looked at the market as a bull market.

- ✔ When Goldman shares were in decline, it was either because the company itself was having problems or because big money players were starting to lose confidence in the market. Either way, it was not a good thing: If Goldman was having problems, you can bet that other big banks were having trouble because they were likely to be involved in deals with Goldman. And when the investment banks have problems, it's just a matter of time before the market has problems, as these big trading houses unload assets aggressively when they have problems, and the markets usually fall hard.

Goldman went public in early 1999, and as you can see in Figure 8-3, even as the Nasdaq was going crazy (refer to Figure 8-1), shares of the investment bank were fairly sedate. In retrospect, this might have been a clue about what the big money was expecting as the Internet blow-off was in full swing.

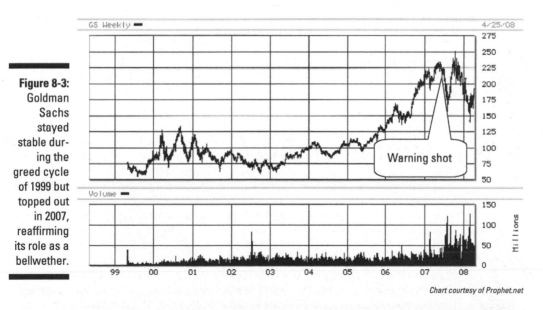

Figure 8-3: Goldman Sachs stayed stable during the greed cycle of 1999 but topped out in 2007, reaffirming its role as a bellwether.

Chart courtesy of Prophet.net

As the market went down until 2003, Goldman shares didn't do much, again suggesting that the big money wasn't particularly interested in the market's prospects. In 2003, Goldman started to rally along with the market, buoyed by two dynamics: one was the overall bull market, as it spawned deals and its traders made money trading. The other was that by 2007, Goldman was into everything, including the oil markets, not just on the trading side of the business but also as an operator of storage tanks for crude and heating oil on the New York harbor and as a major deal maker and obtainer of financing for private equity deals.

However, in early 2007, the stock fell, and it fell hard, as higher interest rates that had been on the rise from the Fed finally took a bite out of the private equity side of the business. That's the area labeled "Warning shot" in Figure 8-3. Shares recovered but again crumbled as the market began to factor in the effects of the subprime crisis on Wall Street. Ironically, Goldman made money on the subprime market mess by short-selling mortgage-backed securities.

In 2008, Goldman shares started to rally along with the market, a sign that some confidence was returning. For more on other bellwether stocks, check out the chapters on sector timing in Part IV.

Gauging Feeling with Sentiment Surveys

Sentiment surveys are opinion polls produced by advisory services that specialize in this branch of stock market analysis based on their review of newsletters and other publications. The results of these surveys are best used as background indicators for the overall opinion of market participants about the direction of prices.

The most commonly cited weekly investor sentiment surveys are

- Market Vane's Bullish Consensus (www.marketvane.net)
- Consensus Inc. (www.consensus-inc.com)
- Investor's Intelligence (www.investorsintelligence.com)

The American Association of Individual Investors (AAII, www.aaii.com) also offers a weekly sentiment survey, one that measures individual investor sentiment instead of the sentiment of professionals. If the advisors are leaning one way and the individuals another, the market may be more volatile.

You get access to these surveys by buying subscriptions to them, but you can get the results through the media a short while after they're released to subscribers. *Barron's* prints results from Consensus Inc., Market Vane, and the AAII surveys every weekend.

Each of these sentiment surveys is basically a poll of a subsection of market participants: Market Vane, Investor's Intelligence and Consensus monitor newsletter writers; Market Vane and Investor's Intelligence lean more toward the stock market, and Consensus covers the futures markets but does include sentiment readings on stock index futures. AAII surveys its members, individual investors, which gives you a glimpse into the thoughts of the general investing public.

When you read a sentiment survey, you generally want to see the following:

- ✔ The number of bulls, or those investors that are expecting the market to rise, to be below 40 to 45 percent in at least one or two surveys, as a sign of pessimism in the markets high enough to be consistent with a bottom and a potential buying opportunity.

- ✔ The number of bulls to be above 65 to 70 percent or higher in at least one or two of the surveys in order to consider that the market is near some kind of top.

- ✔ A higher number of bears usually means that fear is on the rise, and that you may be near an important market bottom.

So how good are sentiment surveys for market timing? Not as good as they used to be. They're now well known and understood by the markets. In other words, they're no longer a secret, which means that even though traders look at them, the surveys no longer have the impact that they used to.

Sentiment analysis is important, but some see it as akin to voodoo, as these numbers could be at extremely low or extremely high numbers for extended periods of time before anything happens. They're important background information, however. Think of them as a warning system: Sometimes, it's an early warning, and other times they start forecasting things that take a long time to develop. The only thing that these surveys tell you when they reach extremes is that the market is potentially near a bottom or a top. The market eventually signals what it's going to do when it's ready, and you need to be ready to anticipate and react accordingly. Major tops can take a long time to build. As Figure 8-1 shows, the number of bulls was consistently high for a long time in 1999 and 2000 before the Nasdaq finally broke down.

Using Trading Volume As a Sentiment Tool

Trading volume, or the number of shares that trade on any given day, is a little more tangible than sentiment surveys, but it can also be seen as a sentiment indicator. Generally, higher volume in a rising trend is positive and is called *accumulation,* and rising volume in a falling trend is called *distribution,* a negative. Here are some other things to remember about trading volume:

- ✔ Rallies in weak volume are suspect; they signal low levels of conviction from the market's big players — mutual funds, hedge funds, and rich speculators.

- ✔ Declines with low volume tend to be a sign that the big-money guys aren't dumping stocks.

✔ When volume starts to rise significantly as the market rises, it could be a sign that things are getting a bit too speculative. That's a good time to start looking at other indicators such as sentiment surveys and index charts to see if prices are keeping up with volume. If the market isn't keeping up with volume, it's *churning,* or spinning its wheels, and mostly going nowhere as sellers are starting to increase.

✔ Volume can be very high at market bottoms, as panic selling reaches a crescendo. This is often as good a sign as any that the market is sold out and that a rally is coming.

Figure 8-4 shows some key points about volume. On the left side of the chart of the S&P 500 SPDR exchange-traded fund, you see three major sell-offs. Note that each of them was pushed further by rising volume — a sign that sellers are in control. Notice also that the March to June rally failed. Volume was much lower during this rally than it was on the selling that preceded.

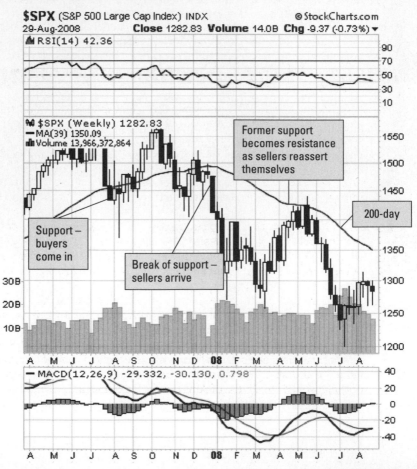

Figure 8-4:
A two-year view of the S&P 500 Index shows key turning points in prices.

Chart courtesy of StockCharts.com

Any trend that's in place needs to have support behind it or it will fail. Volume, thus, is a measure of the support of the trend. Weak volume usually leads to a failure of the trend.

Volume tends to precede price. If volume is on the rise and the market isn't moving, it's just a matter of time before the market responds, and you need to be prepared for the direction of the move by paying close attention to the market and lining up stocks or ETFs to buy, sell, or sell short. By the same token, if volume stalls but the market keeps moving in one direction, you need to prepare for a trend change.

Here's another way to think about it: When prices advance along with rising volume, it's a sign that traders have conviction in the direction of prices. This is what you want to see. By the same token, if you're still in an up trend, volume should contract when the market declines in price. That's a sign that the selling is due only to partial profit-taking, and that the up trend remains intact. If volume starts to rise when prices fall, sellers are becoming more aggressive and the up trend may be in trouble.

Finessing "Soft" Sentiment Indicators

Soft sentiment indicators are signs that most people wouldn't notice, such as magazine covers, the amount of traffic at a department store, how many cars are out driving, and so on, and they're the most inexact of all sentiment indicators. Yet, they can be helpful, as sometimes they signal that something is going to happen immediately, and quite often they have no apparent effect on the market. Keep your eyes open for them because they may tip you off to upcoming changes in the market's trend before other indicators turn.

The Drudge Report (www.drudgereport.com) is a popular soft indicator. Drudge is always full of gossipy and sensationalist headlines. But once in a while the Web site starts paying attention to the stock market. You can almost bet that if the Drudge report is hyping up the market's trend, some kind of trend change is coming.

Here are some examples of soft sentiment indicators at work. In April 2007, Drudge was all excited about the fact that Europe had surpassed the United States in market capitalization. The Drudge report had a link to a *Financial Times* headline that blared: "Europe has eclipsed the U.S. in stock market value for the first time since the first world war in another sign of the slipping of the global dominance of American capital markets."

By August, the Drudge headline bore out: The FTSE 100 had begun to fall, only to rebound long enough to fall again when the subprime mortgage crisis began to emerge as a significant issue.

Here's an even better example: A *Time* magazine from June 16, 2006 shows a man hugging his home, signifying that it's his piggy bank. At the time, the housing market was starting to top out after a multi-year run; television shows were spending hours showing average folks how to renovate dumpy old homes and sell them for huge profits, a practice dubbed *flipping*. And in the stock market, the housing stocks were the darling sector delivering stellar earnings reports.

But, as Figure 8-5 shows, as early as 2005, the housing index (HGX) was starting to struggle, finally breaking down in 2006 and failing to recover fully in 2007, as the subprime mortgage crisis finally accelerated what had been going on for some time.

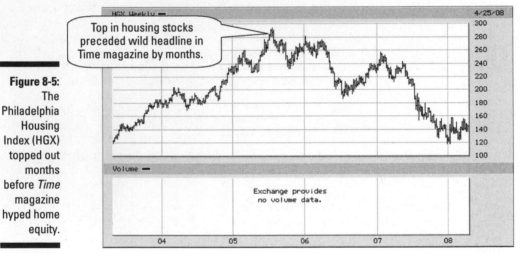

Figure 8-5:
The Philadelphia Housing Index (HGX) topped out months before *Time* magazine hyped home equity.

Chart courtesy of Prophet.net.

You can always count on the mainstream media being too late to the party. By the time the evening news hypes a market-related story, you're near the end of the trend from the market's standpoint. When the reality shows pick up on the trend, and your neighbors start dabbling in it, start looking at the stock market's reaction to the situation.

When the real estate boom was on the rise, a good friend of mine started borrowing money to buy rental houses and even upgraded his own already large home for a monstrous country estate. He told me on multiple occasions that the market was never going to fall because people in the know had told him that this time was different.

I talked to him about this a few days before writing this chapter, and now he's having a hard time unloading his rental houses. Although he still has tenants, he can't raise their rent enough to cover his costs since the houses were old when he bought them and the tenants are fearful of losing their jobs

So what's he got left? A lot of debt, and a lot of worrying. He could've gotten out but instead got greedy and decided to ignore the warning signs.

Watch for these important soft signs of extreme market sentiment:

- **Cold calls from creepy brokers offering you a chance to get in on the ground floor of the next Microsoft:** As the market heats up, you'll start to get calls from boiler room con artists, and the volume of spam in your e-mail box will rise. These intrusions will increase as the stock market goes to new highs and the media hype increases, and they'll disappear when the market topples. Funny, no one ever seems to call when the market is making a bottom and you can buy Microsoft cheap.

- **Stock tips from co-workers at the water cooler or from the grocery store kid that's helping you take your stuff to the car:** When your friends — especially the ones who have never invested in stocks — start telling you about the latest and greatest tech stocks, pay special attention to the markets. Sometimes the unwary actually take the advice offered in magazines, and respond to the cold calls and spam.

- **Local news channels hyping the market:** When the local news at 6 team starts featuring stories about taxi drivers making millions with their laptops as they drive clients across town, it's time to run for the hills.

Finally, my all-time favorite: When I start bragging to my wife about how well I'm doing in the markets, it's always a warning sign.

Pay attention to sentiment indicators. When you see something outrageous, look at the market, check out what your non-market savvy friends are doing, and beware.

Part III
Applying Timing to the Markets

The 5th Wave   By Rich Tennant

"I'm a market timer, Doug. This keeps me sharp."

In this part . . .

In this part you find the nuts and bolts of executing trades like a pro. I give you the specifics of turning market analysis techniques into trades that give you the best chance to make profits. You discover how to time the stock and bond markets and to explore profit opportunities in foreign markets as well as in gold, metals, and commodities.

Chapter 9

Timing in the Real World: Examining a Sample Trade

. . . .

In This Chapter

▶ Preparing to place a trade by observing a full range of details

▶ Executing and analyzing a sample trade

▶ Evaluating your trade so you can benefit from your mistakes

. . . .

*I*n this chapter I take you from theory and concept to the real world of market timing. You go blow by blow through a real-life, profitable timing trade that I made during June and July of 2008, in the midst of a very dramatic stage of a bear market in stocks.

In previous chapters, I've discussed the thought process that you need to be a market timer, how Wall Street really works, what tools to use, how to anticipate and prepare for timing the markets, different analytical and trading methods, as well as how to identify trends, seasonal patterns in the markets, and how to use market sentiment to your advantage.

This chapter is all about putting together the analysis, the execution, and the management of a trade — in real time.

Setting the Stage for a Sample Trade

On June 6, 2008, the stock market fell apart: oil prices skyrocketed to $11 per barrel as news reports quoted Israel's transport minister saying that an Israeli attack on Iran's nuclear program was unavoidable. On the same day, the U.S. Department of Labor released its May employment report, which delivered an unexpected twist to the view that the U.S. economy was significantly weak; the unemployment rate had risen 0.5 points, the highest one-month jump in 22 years.

The combination of soaring oil prices and significant job losses, coupled with the fact that the average retail price of gasoline in the United States hit $4 during the same week was enough to push the stock market over the edge.

The sell-off was significant enough to take me out of the few long positions that I had in place. But, to be honest, I wasn't quite sure about selling the market short on June 6, as the selling was rampant. A 400-point down day in the Dow Jones Industrial on a Friday might lead to a 200-point open on Monday because the politicians and the cheerleaders might come out over the weekend and pump things up on Monday.

I decided just to clean up any messes that I had, count and review any losses that had come about, and to spend some time over the weekend looking at the technical aspects of the situation, and develop a trading plan for Monday.

I sold some shares of Apple and Research in Motion that I had bought a few weeks earlier. I still had some small profits. And I kept a position in natural gas and gasoline that I had open. I kept a couple of technology-related ETFs that had held up. I put some sell stops under then, and I started to figure out what to do next.

Sorting through a major mess

Before you make any decisions about what to do next, you need to assess your current situation. In this case, I had a lot of cash available, and a few open long positions in the stock market, in the form of exchange traded funds. They were sporting small paper losses after that Friday, but not enough to sell them without reason.

The key to what I was going to do next was to figure out whether the Friday hit was going to be something that lasted or that would blow over. After all, it was mostly due to a big jump in oil prices, based on a news report from comments made by a little-known Israeli cabinet minister — hard telling whether his words would have any lasting impact.

Because I had time, I did a little research on the transportation minister of Israel. I found a bit more than I expected: The minister was Shaul Mofaz, a former defense minister and someone who might succeed the current Israeli Prime Minister, Ehud Ohlmert, who was involved in a bribery scandal. So, the oil market was properly rocked by the comments, and Monday wouldn't necessarily be a day where prices would fall back too rapidly without something happening.

The other big news of the day, the employment report, was also worth looking at and turned out to bear significant news: The number of people looking for work had risen significantly, and the United States had had its fifth straight month of job losses.

It was looking as if the economy was starting to buckle under the weight of the higher oil prices. This was significantly important because every U.S. recession since the 1970s had been preceded by an oil shock. And oil prices at $138 per barrel and retail gasoline at $4 per gallon surely could be called an oil shock. There was clearly a connection between the stock market's negative action and the economic data.

Following any sell-off, such as the one on June 6, three possible scenarios exist:

✔ A major break in the prevalent trend is near, or has already happened.

✔ The market can move sideways.

✔ A short-term correction in the primary trend is unfolding, and by being patient you may be able to establish a position in the dominant trend at a better price.

The problem is that you really don't know which way things are going to go. In this case, the dominant trend prior to the sell-off was up. Knowing the trend that was in place prior to the selling, and with these three possibilities in mind, I started to look at some charts in order to formulate a plan.

Charting your way to the next step

Pay close attention to your charts when you notice a clear connection between economic data and price action in the stock market. Your three major goals are

✔ **Analyzing the situation.** Combine your knowledge of technical and fundamental analyses with the psychology of a market in the midst of what's happening in the market.

✔ **Designing a trading strategy.** Based on your analyses, design a well-crafted, step-by-step, careful plan that either makes you some money or gets you out of the position with as little damage as possible if you're wrong or the market turns against you.

✔ **Putting the plan into action.** Make the trade, establish the position, and then manage it as you take the plunge into chaos.

Getting the long-term picture

When doing your technical homework, start with a long-term view of the market. Figure 9-1 gives you a good long-term picture of the market. This is a weekly chart, which means that the action is compressed more than you'd see in a daily chart. This is the kind of chart that I looked at over the weekend after June 6. And here's what the chart in figure told me:

✔ **The S&P 500 had been in a bear market since October 2007.** That made sense from both the fundamental and technical standpoints. The subprime mortgage crisis was just a few months old in June, and economic time bombs were going off everywhere, with bank earnings falling and housing foreclosures mounting. The U.S. employment picture was getting worse, and the Federal Reserve had its hands tied with regard to lowering interest rates because the dollar was very weak.

✔ **The rally in the S&P 500 that started in March was clearly a bear-market rally that had failed in late May.** The rally started as the S&P 500 found support at its 200-period moving average after losing some 20 percent of its value in about five months. After the media got all excited about the S&P 500 falling 20 percent and being in a bear market, the market rallied in March, but only long enough to grab headlines and get the hype going about the end of the bear market. All that added up to the S&P 500 failing to rally above its 50-period moving average.

Weekly charts use different parameters for moving averages. In this section, I describe them generically by using the term *period*. What's important is that the S&P 500 found support and resistance at these key moving averages on a long-term chart. The longer the support and resistance level, the more important the break above or below this area.

My first analysis was that the market's long-term trend was still down and that the Friday sell-off was more than likely a reassertion of the down trend. My first impression was that I should look to go short at the earliest opportunity, unless the market could convince me otherwise.

Viewing the intermediate term

As I moved along in my analysis, I wanted to prove or disprove my initial impression. In Figure 9-2, I was looking to see whether I was right or wrong in my first run through the charts. Fundamental aspects of the economy (rising levels of unemployment and rising oil prices) were less than rosy during this period. So I had two votes for going short.

I dove into more coffee and looked at a four-month chart. This one showed me a failure at the 200-day moving average by the S&P 500 in May. The failure was fully confirmed by weakness in the RSI and MACD oscillators. (Turn to Chapter 7 to find out more about RSI and MACD oscillators.)

After the May failure, the S&P drifted lower (Figure 9-2) as oil prices continued to climb. Yet the circled area in Figure 9-3 shows that two days of panic in the oil market, combined with bad economic data, was enough to trip the S&P 500 below its 200-day moving average. That was another vote for selling the market short. And now I had three, which meant that I had enough evidence to move on to the next step, executing the trade.

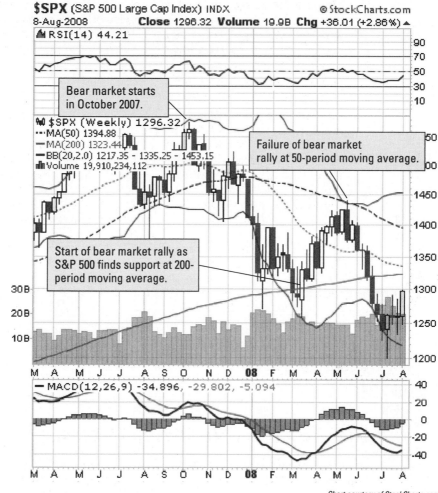

$SPX (S&P 500 Large Cap Index) INDX © StockCharts.com
8-Aug-2008 **Close** 1296.32 **Volume** 19.9B **Chg** +36.01 (+2.86%) ▲
RSI(14) 44.21

Bear market starts in October 2007.

$SPX (Weekly) 1296.32
MA(50) 1394.88
MA(200) 1323.44
BB(20,2.0) 1217.35 - 1335.25 - 1453.15
Volume 19,910,234,112

Failure of bear market rally at 50-period moving average.

Start of bear market rally as S&P 500 finds support at 200-period moving average.

MACD(12,26,9) -34.896, -29.802, -5.094

Figure 9-1:
The S&P 500 bear market started in October 2007.

Make sure that reliable oscillators confirm your moving average and trend analysis. I used the RSI and MACD oscillators. For more on these two useful oscillators visit Chapter 7. The RSI and MACD oscillators are important indicators that can be both early warning systems as well as confirmatory evidence. In this case, they both came in handy by helping me to spot the overall negative trend in the S&P 500, in both my long- and my intermediate-term analysis.

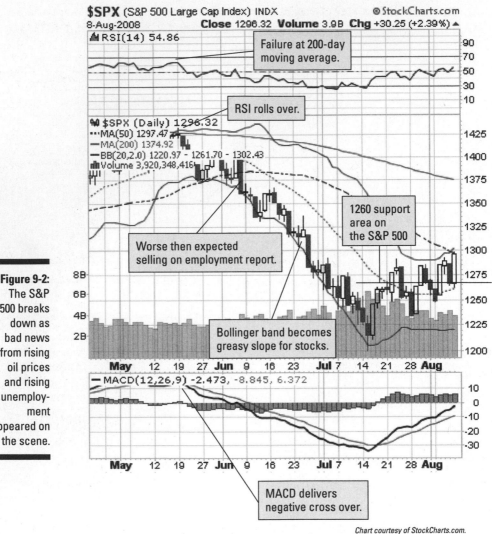

$SPX (S&P 500 Large Cap Index) INDX   © StockCharts.com

8-Aug-2008   **Close** 1296.32 **Volume** 3.9B **Chg** +30.25 (+2.39%) ▲

RSI(14) 54.86

Failure at 200-day moving average.

RSI rolls over.

$SPX (Daily) 1296.32
MA(50) 1297.47
MA(200) 1374.92
BB(20,2.0) 1220.97 - 1261.70 - 1302.43
Volume 3,920,348,416

Worse then expected selling on employment report.

1260 support area on the S&P 500

Bollinger band becomes greasy slope for stocks.

MACD(12,26,9) -2.473, -8.845, 6.372

MACD delivers negative cross over.

Figure 9-2:
The S&P 500 breaks down as bad news from rising oil prices and rising unemployment appeared on the scene.

Chart courtesy of StockCharts.com.

Two days of panic in the oil market.

Figure 9-3: The S&P 500 dips below its 200-day moving average.

Chart courtesy of StockCharts.com

Getting Ready to Trade

By Monday morning, June 9, I was ready to short the market. I had taken a big chunk of money out of the market on Friday and had secured the other long positions by placing sell stops under them. And I had some money in energy, in a gasoline futures ETF. I felt as if I were in fairly good shape, all things considered.

Now I was looking for the setup, the right opportunity to pull the trigger and make the trade.

I like to use the ProShares Ultra Short S&P 500 ETF to short the market, because it gives me twice as much of a move as the Short S&P 500 Shares (SH), the one-to-one ratio ETF that also shorts the S&P 500. Although I'm not flawless in picking when to short sell the market, it's a totally different experience than going long, and I've found, that for me, using the leverage works better.

Short selling is more volatile than going long. Instead of trying to hold on for a long period of time, I go for as much of a gain as possible in the shortest term possible. This is a high-risk strategy and one that sometimes leads me to sell too early. But I really don't mind, because if I have a 20 percent paper profit that turns into a 5 percent loss in two days because I got greedy, I'm going to be very upset.

When I sell short, I'm looking to use leverage, as that lets me get more of a down market in a short period of time.

Looking for the right opportunity

A big part of timing the markets is the trading plan. I recommend the following three major aspects of a trading plan that have worked well for me:

- ✔ **Define the major trend.** The trend in Figure 9-2 was clearly to the down side, and I had decided to sell the market short.

- ✔ **Use the right timing vehicle.** You want the path of least resistance and the most chance at a good return in as short a time as possible.

- ✔ **Manage the trade well.** Find a good entry point to the market and set up some rules as to what you'll do if things go right (or wrong). Make sure you have an exit strategy.

Following my trading plan, I went into Monday looking to short the S&P 500. I had my trading vehicle picked out — the ProShares Ultra Short ETF (SDS) — and I had a fairly good idea that I wanted to enter early in the day, especially if the market was quiet.

I had also decided that I would stay on the short side as long as the overall trend was fairly smooth but that I would look to get out if volatility picked up, and that I would use a fairly tight trend line to keep me in line. See Figure 9-4 for my trend line on SDS.

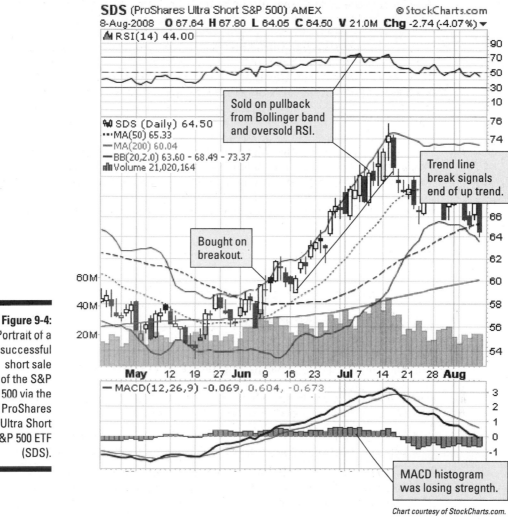

SDS (ProShares Ultra Short S&P 500) AMEX   © StockCharts.com
8-Aug-2008 O 67.64 H 67.80 L 64.05 C 64.50 V 21.0M Chg -2.74 (-4.07%) ▼

RSI(14) 44.00

Sold on pullback from Bollinger band and oversold RSI.

SDS (Daily) 64.50
MA(50) 65.33
MA(200) 60.04
BB(20,2.0) 63.60 - 68.49 - 73.37
Volume 21,020,164

Trend line break signals end of up trend.

Bought on breakout.

Figure 9-4: Portrait of a successful short sale of the S&P 500 via the ProShares Ultra Short S&P 500 ETF (SDS).

MACD(12,26,9) -0.069, 0.604, -0.673

MACD histogram was losing strength.

Chart courtesy of StockCharts.com.

Tracking the trade

The stock market was fairly quiet on June 9, at least in the early going, as oil prices pulled back and the stock market took a wait-and-see attitude. That oil was quiet was no surprise; it had moved quite a long way in a very short time.

Things were developing according to my plan, so I bought SDS at $60.45 (the buy point shown in Figure 9-4). I bought in on a quiet Monday but above the breakout point on SDS. I was looking for strength; by buying SDS, which sells the market short, I was actually betting against the market rising.

By June 10, oil started moving higher and became more volatile. A key economic report, the IBD/Tripp consumer confidence poll, which doesn't get as much publicity as other polls but can move the market, showed more weakness. The S&P started to move lower and gathered steam, falling farther below its 200-day moving average.

There was nothing to do but watch. That can be the toughest part of timing, that after you establish your position you become a spectator. The trade is now out of your hands, and your money is at the mercy of the market until you decide to do something about it. This spectator period is why you want to have some rules in place to help you manage the situation and to prevent you from getting antsy and making ill-advised moves such as selling too early.

Fine-tuning your exit point as things progress

By June 11, the S&P 500 had broken below 1350, and I started to look for the bump in the road because things were getting a little too comfortable. Whenever I get too cozy in a trade, I get uneasy. And I was starting to get uneasy with this one just two days into it. The market was slicing through support levels like the proverbial hot knife through butter.

I started looking at the charts and found that the 1260 area in the S&P 500 had been support and resistance in the past and therefore was a point to watch: Markets retrace prior moves, which is what was happening here. The S&P 500 wasn't going to hit 1260 anytime soon — it was down the road about 90 points from where the market had closed on the previous day — but this number became my make-or-break target. The market clearly was going to test it at some point in the future, and it was close enough to the bottom of the trading range that volatility would likely start as prices neared the price area. In other words, I was going to probably start selling this position as the market closed in on it.

The trade progressed well, as Figures 9-2 and 9-3 show. And, just as I expected, when the S&P 500 got to the 1260 area, it started to show some volatility. Instead of going straight down, it started to jump up and down, and in fact, started to act as if it were forming a base.

The media was going crazy, and so was the price of oil. During this period, the oil market was so volatile that I appeared on CNBC twice — on June 4 and again on July 23. For them to call me back so often meant that they were looking for a bit of an "outside the box" presence as they tried to help viewers make sense of things. I'm not quite a Wall Street guy, as you've probably figured out by now. CNBC's interest told me that this might be an extraordinary period of time and that caution was the best policy.

The more the market moved up and down near 1260, the more uncomfortable I became. And on July 8, I sold my position in SDS at $70.06, for a nice 15.89 percent profit. I continued to watch the market, in case I had made a mistake.

Because the market seemed to be starting to break below the 1260 area, I thought I *had* made a mistake, and I bought back in a couple of days later, with a smaller amount of money. But I put a very tight stop on my position and when the market finally turned, a few days after my original sale of SDS, I was stopped out, with a small — less than 1 percent — loss, still netting me about a 15 percent profit for the whole trade.

When prices fall below key support, such as the 50- or 200-day line, the former support level then becomes resistance. After July 10, the S&P 500 started to move lower, seeming to use the lower Bollinger band (Figure 9-2) as a greasy slope. When you're short the market, you want to see prices walking down the Bollinger band — a sign that sellers have an easy time, and that to go against the grain is a bad idea. As long as this was evident, I stayed short.

Reviewing your timing endeavor

In this trade, I bought an ETF that specializes in short selling the S&P 500 for a month. I made a 15 percent profit during this period. And I did it by paying attention to both the fundamental and technical aspects of the market.

Successful timing doesn't happen because you do what you want to do. It happens when you find answers in the charts and in the fundamental data, and then act on the information with a well-crafted trading plan.

Here are some key questions to ask yourself after a trade, whether you make money or not:

> ✔ **Was my pre-trade analysis sound?** Three important aspects of pre-trade analysis make good guidelines for all your trades:
>
>   • Look at long-term charts to get a good idea where the major trend is headed.

- Shorten your time horizon to pick an ideal entry point into the trade.

- Match the fundamentals to the charts so you can confirm that your trade has the best chance of succeeding.

✔ **Was my trading plan sound?** Any trading plan worth keeping holds up in real time, so keep these points in mind:

- Take care of any open positions that may suffer when the market turns against you.

- If you have time to make decisions, use it — after you've protected your open positions. A weekend can be useful.

- When you've had a good opportunity to look at the situation and you know that you're leaving as little as possible to chance, execute the trade.

✔ **Was the trade well executed and managed?** You always want to give yourself the best chance to succeed. Thus, if you can enter the market during a pause that doesn't change the overall trend, take the opportunity. If you enter a trade well, you're already feeling positive about the situation, and your state of mind is relaxed. This allows you to think clearly and continue to manage the trade.

If you start to become uncomfortable with the trade, and you have a decent profit, it's a sign that some profit-taking is the right thing to do.

 A trading plan is a part of any timing strategy. After you come up with a plan, you need to review it every time you make a trade. That's how you get better at timing. Turn to Chapters 2 and 3 to find out more about building and revising your trading plan.

Finding a Sequence for Successful Trading

The trade that I outline in this chapter is a good representation of what you should be able to accomplish if you follow the methods outlined in this book.

Yet, note that analyzing and executing successful trades follows a definite sequence:

1. **Address potential problems.**

   Review any open positions that you have that may be harmed by market events.

2. **Analyze the market's trend and your options for capitalizing on it.**

Look into buying stocks if the trend is up, short selling if the trend is down, or staying in cash and not trading at all if there is too much volatility.

3. **Make sure that the fundamentals and the technical aspects of the market are pointing in the same direction.**

   Ask questions, such as, "Is the economy sending bad signals at the same time that the market is selling off?" If the answer is yes, then the economic data and the charts are telling the same story, and your chances for success improve significantly.

In other words, timing is as much preparation, recognition, and the execution and management of the trade as it is about the tools that you use. You can make trading as simple or as sophisticated as you want, but in the end, the only thing that counts is whether you make or lose money. And if you lose and *don't* learn from the experience, you pay for it over and over again.

Chapter 10

Timing the Stock Market

· ·

In This Chapter

▶ Working the stock market as a whole

▶ Applying your timing skills to individual stocks

▶ Buying stocks at the bottom

▶ Buying before a second stock rally

· ·

*W*all Street wants you to believe that you can't time the stock market successfully. I'm here to tell you that you can. And in this chapter, I'm going to show you how.

But first I want to make sure that you have your expectations in check. Even for money managers who have access to the best information possible and staffs of several people to do their research, timing the market is not about beating the market, which is a very difficult thing to do year after year. Instead of being about performance that's a few percentage points higher than the market over 12 months, which is what professional money managers try to do, market timing is about making money when the market rises, and preserving your gains or even making money when the market falls.

A good market timer rarely beats the market in the short term but may actually do so over longer periods of time. Here's why:

✔ Picking the absolute top and bottom in any one market is virtually impossible in general, let alone in every bull to bear cycle. Anyone who tries to tell you otherwise is not telling you the entire truth. Those ads that promise 1,000 percent returns in three months? Not worth the ink they're printed on.

✔ Although it's a nice idea, beating the market is not the goal of market timing. The goal is to trade with the dominant trend, up or down, every time the market makes an intermediate-term turn. That means that you gear your trading method toward discerning the trend and going with it, rather than toward delivering spectacular results.

So, why do I bother to time the market? Because I don't like to see my hard-earned bull-market gains disappear when the big money players decide that they want to sell. I'd rather keep my 7 or 8 percent profits in my pocket than watch it disappear into the abyss. And more important, I'd like to make money when the market goes down as well as when the market goes up, which is where you increase your chances of beating the market — or coming close to it — if you remain disciplined.

In this chapter, I show you how to be a consistent and reliable deliverer of profits to your portfolio by timing the stock market whether it's rising or falling.

Timing the Whole Enchilada

Timing the entire stock market sounds a whole lot harder and a whole lot spicier than it actually is. Exchange-traded funds (ETFs) have made the whole process of timing the entire stock market, via index trading, the province of every investor.

The key is to sort out which ETFs are best suited for timing each of the major indexes, and then applying sound buy, sell, and sell-short rules to the process. The following sections show you how.

Starting with the S&P 500

The S&P 500 is a fairly balanced index of large-capitalization stocks. These companies are essentially the 500 most well known on Wall Street, and they're the ones that most analysts follow and most mutual fund managers invest in. That makes them liquid — and attractive to timers looking for an index play, such as the S&P 500 linked ETFs or stock index futures.

Here are some general principles about using the S&P 500 (SPX) as a timing vehicle:

- ✔ **SPX is a good placeholder.** You will encounter times when finding individual stocks is difficult, although the trend remains up. You can participate in the trend by owning the S&P 500 via ETFs or futures.

- ✔ **You can use SPX as a hedge.** Say for example that you've got some great profits in a stock that you want to hold onto for a while, but the market looks as if it's going to pull back slightly. You can short the S&P via a "short S&P" ETF in order to protect the gains in your stock without necessarily having to sell them.

✔ **Use ETFs when you don't have the capital to diversify a big portfolio.** Timing the S&P 500 via ETFs is perfect for smaller portfolios, especially those with $20,000 or less because they enable you to participate in the overall trend of the market with one position.

If you're interested in more details about the futures markets and how to use stock index futures as your market timing tools, pick up a copy of my book *Trading Futures For Dummies*. I do recommend that you get familiar with the techniques that you'd use with ETFs first.

Here's a good cross-section of ETFs that track the S&P 500, both in rising and falling trends:

✔ **SPDR S&P 500 (SPY)** is the most commonly traded S&P 500 ETF. It's very liquid and is accessible through any broker or online trading account. SPY trades at one-tenth the value of the S&P 500 cash index, so if the S&P 500 is at 1400, SPY trades at 140. SPY works well when you want to trade the overall trend of the broad stock market. It's my favorite ETF for going long the SPX. The next section gives you an example of how to use SPY.

✔ **Ultra S&P 500 ProShares (SSO)** is a leveraged ETF that rises and falls at twice the rate of the daily performance of the S&P 500. For example, if the S&P 500 rises or falls 3 percent, this ETF would rise or fall 6 percent in the same direction of the index. This is an excellent fund when the market is starting to come out of a significant decline. The potential risk of losing twice the drop of the S&P 500 on any given day, though, makes it a tough one to use until a rising trend is clearly in progress.

✔ **Short S&P 500 ProShares (SH)** moves in the opposite direction of the S&P 500. When you buy this ETF you're hoping that the S&P 500 falls in price so that the ETF rises in price. In other words, if the S&P 500 lost 1 percent at any given time, SH would rise 1 percent.

✔ **UltraShort S&P 500 ProShares (SDS)** is my favorite way to sell the stock market short, because it follows the trend of the S&P 500 quite closely and gives me the opportunity to leverage my gains. The investment goal of this fund is to deliver twice the opposite performance of the S&P 500 (200 percent), before fees and expenses. So if the S&P falls 2 percent, this ETF rises 4 percent.

Figure 10-1 shows you a perfect example of when to use these ETFs. The chart covers the period of time between April 2007 and May 2008 where the stock market began to show significant volatility, partially because the sub-prime mortgage crisis began to unfold in this time frame, and also because the stock market had been in a bull market since 2003.

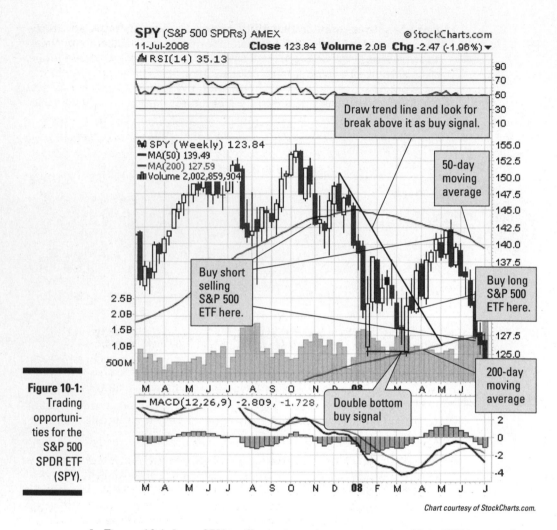

Figure 10-1:
Trading
opportuni-
ties for the
S&P 500
SPDR ETF
(SPY).

In Figure 10-1, I use SPY to illustrate an important point: This ETF is an index
unto itself and can be used as its own indicator to generate buy, sell, and sell
short signals.

Note the following important points about Figure 10-1:

 ✔ **SPY is trading between its 20- and 50-day moving averages.** The chart
    shows a period of transition for the market, which means that traders
    aren't sure about the long-term direction of the market. This in turn
    means that you should be cautious, and that an ETF where you are
    concentrating on the market's trend is the appropriate trading vehicle.

✔ **Periods of transition and volatility come in two basic forms.** One is the type pictured in Figure 10-1, in which the market's swings are very tradable because they last for several weeks to months, and it's a perfect environment for market timing. Another type of transitional period for the market is where the trend changes are too frequent to be worth trading. During those times you want to stand aside.

✔ **Figure 10-1 shows four timing signals.** Three of them are short timing signals, which are good opportunities for using SH and SDS. The area of the chart labeled "Double bottom buy signal" is an excellent buying opportunity and a good time to use SPY and SSO.

Trend lines are very useful indicators when you see the technical configuration in Figure 10-1 — when the 50- and 200-day lines are the bookends of a market's trading range. Trend lines can help you decide whether to go long, go short, or just stand aside. In this case, the down trend line served as a great indicator and clearly pointed to a period where you could go long and do well. The 200-day moving averages served as support (double bottom) and the 50-day moving average served as resistance in June 2008.

Timing and taming the Nasdaq 100

The Nasdaq 100 Index (NDX) is a growth-stock blue-chip index that houses the largest 100 stocks (excluding banking stocks) that trade on the Nasdaq Composite Index.

Here are some of the general facts to keep in mind about NDX:

✔ **The Nasdaq 100 Index is heavily weighted toward large technology stocks:** Intel (INTC), Cisco Systems (CSCO), Microsoft (MSFT), Google (GOOG), Apple Inc. (AAPL), and Research in Motion (RIMM) are very heavily weighted components of the index. Any news or activity in any of these stocks exerts a fair amount of influence in the index and the ETFs that trade along with it.

✔ **You might want to look at the individual heavily weighted stocks in the Nasdaq 100 as potential stand-alone investments despite the overall trend of the index or of the market.** Some of these large companies will be rising or falling on their own despite the market's trend because of their product cycles, their earnings, or the whim of big money players who want to believe that the stock can move against the prevailing trend.

Figure 10-2 shows an example. In 2008, Apple Inc. showed significant amounts of relative strength during a very difficult period for the overall market and was worth considering as an individual investment during that period of time. Other big stocks such as Research in Motion and Google also presented excellent opportunities on the long and short side during this period. See the section "Timing Individual Stocks" later in this chapter for more details.

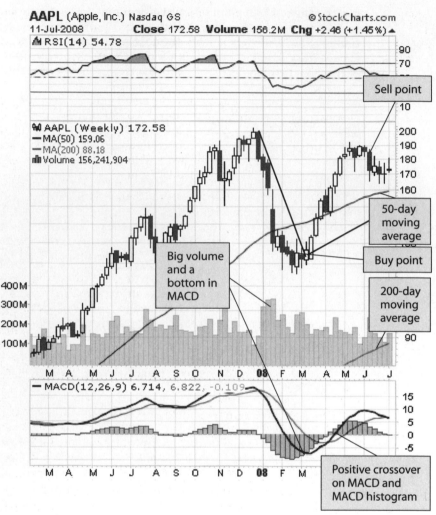

Figure 10-2:
Apple Inc.
(AAPL)
shows rela-
tive strength
by rising in
an other-
wise down
market.

Chart courtesy of StockCharts.com.

Relative strength means that certain stocks hold up during difficult times for the market. Sometimes relative strength stems from a company's products. Other times it arises because management has done a good job and the company has managed to make money during tough times while others are struggling. Figures 10-1 and 10-2 provide an example of relative strength. Figure 10-1 shows that the S&P 500 is in a bear market. Apple Inc. is clearly in a bull market during the same period. (Refer to Figure 10-2.) And even though Apple was off of its December 2007 highs, the stock was still in a long-term up trend, despite the overall bearish trend of the whole market.

Investing against the grain in relative-strength stocks during a bear market is risky. You have no guarantee that those companies won't eventually fall at some point. Although staying with those stocks that show relative strength may be a good strategy, it's only good as long as the trend lasts. Watch whatever stocks you keep during bear markets very closely.

As with the S&P 500, four basic ETFs enable you to time both the up and the downtrend in the Nasdaq 100 Index. Two of the ones I like to use are leveraged and the other two are not leveraged. You should decide which pair you like to use based on your own risk tolerance. For example if you're uncomfortable with the potential for two fold losses if the trend goes against you when you're using the leveraged ETFs, just stick to the one to one movers.

I use these four ETFs because they are widely used and thus getting orders filled for them is easy:

- **PowerShares Trust (QQQQ):** This highly popular and liquid ETF contains the largest 100 stocks that trade on the Nasdaq and is a good trading vehicle for more conservative timers. It moves in a one-to-one ratio with the Nasdaq 100 index and is an excellent ETF for bull markets in the Nasdaq 100. You can sell short and buy and sell options on this ETF.

- **Ultra QQQ ProShares (QLD):** Designed to double the returns of the Nasdaq 100 Index, this ETF is a good vehicle to use when you're expecting a significant rally and want to get more bang for your return. Just remember that what goes up twofold also falls twofold. This ETF is better for aggressive timers.

- **Short QQQ ProShares (PSQ):** This ETF shorts the Nasdaq 100 Index on a one-to-one basis; that is, a 1 percent drop in the index leads roughly to a 1 percent rise in the price of PSQ. This fund is ideal if you want to sell NDX short but aren't willing to get too leveraged. I use this ETF in most of my Nasdaq short-sale trades.

- **UltraShort QQQ ProShares (QID):** As with all Ultra funds, this one gives you a twofold return on the trend of the index that it mirrors. In this case, QID rises twice the amount of the Nasdaq 100 when the index falls. This is an excellent fund to use when large technology stocks are having difficulties and you're looking to leverage your short positions. The down side is that the volatility can be costly if the market is indecisive.

Timing the Dow Jones Industrial Average

The Dow Jones Industrial Average is the most famous stock index in the world, but it has only 30 stocks and therefore isn't a very broad-based index. You can argue that those 30 stocks are a good representation of the U.S. economy and perhaps the market. But if you're a purist, then it's not really a broad market index.

What it is, though, is very liquid. Money moves in and out of those 30 stocks, and because timing is about movement of money and trends, the Dow Jones Industrial Average is another good timing vehicle.

You can use any of four ETFs for timing the Dow. Here they are, including key points about each of them:

- **Dow Diamond Trust (DIA):** Use this ETF to trade the general trend of the Dow Jones Industrial average. Its value is roughly one-tenth of the Dow Jones Industrial Average. This is a very popular way to trade the Dow Jones Industrial Average during rising trends, and it has an excellent correlation to the daily price movement of the index.

- **Ultra Dow30 ProShares (DDM):** This ETF tracks the performance of the Dow Jones Industrial average on a two-to-one basis. It's great when it's going up, but twice as bad on the way down. Use this one after you gain a bit of experience.

- **Short Dow30 ProShares (DOG):** To short the Dow Jones Industrial average on a one-to-one basis, use the Short Dow30 ProShares (DOG). You can use this one to short the Dow if you're not too aggressive but still want to participate in any down trend in the index.

- **UltraShort Dow30 ProShares (DXD):** If you're looking to leverage your return when the Dow is falling, use this fund. Leverage can be dangerous, but if you're a risk taker, this fund is made for you.

Timing Individual Stocks

Timing individual stocks can be as tricky or as straightforward as you want to make it. Your best bet is to stay with the prevalent trend (the direction of the 200-day moving average) and keep an open mind by looking for stocks that are bucking that trend and are worth taking the risk on.

You don't need to have open positions at all times: This is the hardest concept to get across to timers who are just starting out. Sometimes you just won't be able to find any stocks to time — on the long or the short side. Hold on to your cash and wait out those times. You may have to take a couple of days off and do something else, although I recommend that even on those days you at least check the market after it closes.

Develop a core list of stocks to time. You can use any stocks you like, but I recommend that you use large, liquid index stocks such as Apple, because those are the ones that the big money managers use and those are the ones that move, thus giving you timing opportunities. After a while, you'll get to know the stocks on your list as if they were your drive home. You'll start to see patterns that warn you of potential trend changes and problems that could develop down the road.

I also recommend that you become familiar with the three basic methods of timing individual stocks: bottom fishing, momentum investing, and short selling. Each has its own positive and negative aspects, which I cover in detail in the upcoming sections.

Rather than picking one method over the other, apply each method to the circumstances prevalent at the moment. Keeping an open mind gives you more opportunities to time stocks and to make profits.

No matter which method you choose, remember that going against the grain, except in special circumstances, such as when a stock is exhibiting relative strength during a bear market, is asking for trouble.

Bottom fishing

Bottom fishing means that you're looking for stocks to buy as they make a bottom, especially during periods after they've taken a very rapid and big loss, such as when a company misses an earnings report. Picking precise bottoms in the stock market is a very dangerous and nearly impossible endeavor. However, sometimes you can enter a position in a stock that has been highly oversold and make significant intermediate-term profits.

Refer to Figure 10-2, which shows that from February to December 2008, Apple Inc. stock more than doubled in price before entering a significant correction that brought prices to the 120 area, where the stock found support after losing 40 percent of its value.

Imagine that Apple is one of the stocks in your core list. You know its management; you know its product line; and you have a good idea about how the stock trades. A 40 percent decline in the stock's value as it starts moving sideways is probably a sign that a potential buying opportunity could be at hand. (Note the buy point in March 2008 in Figure 10-2.)

The following sequence of events supports that notion:

1. **The stock stopped falling.**

   Naturally, a bottom requires that the stock stops falling in price and that some sort of base starts to form.

2. **As selling accelerated, volume started to rise significantly.**

   Rising volume as a stock falls is often a sign that the selling is about to be exhausted as those trying to get out of the stock are in panic mode. Rising volume in a downtrend often means that a bottom is near. You get no guarantee that this is the way things are going to work out, but if you don't notice the rise in volume and start thinking about it, then you'll miss the turn.

3. **The stock started moving sideways, showing that the trend might reverse.**

   When the stock starts moving sideways, draw your trend line and start looking for the stock to move above the downtrend.

4. **In March, the market bottomed.**

   So did the stock, which moved above the down trend line. *That was the buy point.*

Look for signs to support your position. In Figure 10-2, you see several, including positive crossovers of the MACD oscillator as well as the stock moving back above its 50-day moving average, while remaining above its 200-day moving average the whole time. By the time May rolled around, the stock had delivered big gains and started moving sideways. That's when you draw your rising trend line. When the stock moves beyond the trend line, it's time to sell at least a portion of the position.

This trade would have yielded about $50 to $60 worth of profits if you took it and is an excellent example of a great opportunity to enter a trade after a significant decline in prices.

Riding the momentum roller coaster

Timing individual stocks by *momentum* means that you buy stocks that have already had a big rally but have paused and are looking to start the rally once again. You want to use this method in a bull market, especially in the early stages of such an event, as stocks that have been rallying in the early stages of a new bull run tend to be the strongest.

Part of my momentum timing method is based on the CAN SLIM method put forth by William O'Neill and Investor's Business Daily (IBD). Here's what the letters stand for:

- ✔ **Current quarterly earnings per share:** This method homes in on stocks that are delivering a minimum of 18 to 20 percent earnings per share growth and especially stocks whose earnings are accelerating beyond these growth rates.

- ✔ **Annual earnings growth:** The best momentum stocks are the ones that have had at least five to seven quarters of accelerating earnings growth and are showing earnings increases over the past five years.

- ✔ **New products, new management, and new highs:** You want to get into stocks where management has injected a dose of excitement into the mix and the market has responded by pushing prices higher.

✔ **Supply and demand:** You can buy any stock that meets CAN SLIM criteria, but the system is designed for smaller stocks, because smaller amounts of money can move the stock higher and increase the payoff for investors. The flip side is that stocks that trade under thinner volumes can also drop faster.

✔ **Leader of laggard:** The system is geared toward stocks at the top of the leader board. These are likely to pop faster and move higher at a faster rate, often for longer periods of time.

✔ **Institutional sponsorship:** If big money mutual funds don't like a stock, the chances of its moving higher are a lot smaller. You want to follow the big boys and their money in momentum investing.

✔ **Market direction:** The CAN SLIM system can be used regardless of the market's overall direction, but it does recognize that swimming upstream in a bear market can lead to higher rates of losing trades.

I agree with the CAN SLIM method's concept for momentum investing. And in a bull market, I look for stocks that are moving significantly higher after they've had a good run. I spend less time on earnings and product research for most of my trades, except on those stocks that I include in my core trading list (see the previous section for more on the core trading list).

Sifting through momentum trading's technical side

A mainstay of CAN SLIM is a chart formation called a *cup and handle,* which is a chart formation in which the stock traces a pattern that resembles a cup, or a bowl, which is followed by a sideways pattern that often resembles a handle. It's another William O'Neill creation that is a hugely effective tool in momentum investing and market timing.

The chart in Figure 10-3 shows a cup and handle for Oil States International (OSI), an oil service and oil exploration company. You see a nice cup that lasted from November until March. The handle formed over the next several weeks, and then the breakout came.

Here are some key points about cups and handles:

✔ The best cups take several weeks to months to form. That gives enough time for all the sellers to be shaken out.

✔ Volume should rise as the left side of the cup is being formed. That sequence means that sellers are dumping all their shares in a panic.

✔ The right side of the handle often forms with moderate volume, with some sort of rise as the right side is being concluded. That's a sign of healthy buying interest, which is what you want to see at that point of the formation.

✔ The handle should form over several weeks and should have a downward slope, as the one in Figure 10-3 does.

✔ Volume should be low during the handle, as it shows that all sellers are now done but that few buyers are interested. A good period of quiet time is often a good sign, as it is usually followed by a rise in volume and the breakout. The cup and handle in Figure 10-3 is pretty much a textbook example.

✔ The buy point is as soon as the stock breaks out, above the handle. CAN SLIM rules say that you should have your total initial position in place within 10 percent of the buy point. For OSI, in the example in Figure 10-3, the buy point was somewhere above $45.

Figure 10-3:
Cup and handle formation in Oil States International (OIS).

Chart courtesy of StockCharts.com.

Over the years I've learned that cups and handles that don't meet the strict criteria outlined in the preceding bullet list are likely to fail. Make sure that you check off each of these criteria before you put your money to work with a cup-and-handle formation.

Cups without handles are also important CAN SLIM technical formations. A cup without a handle has all the same criteria as the cup and handle, except, of course that the breakout comes without the handle ever being formed.

Staying on top of your momentum trade

After you have your position in place the only thing to do is to monitor your position. Here's what you do:

- ✔ **Watch for opportunities to add shares.** This stock never pulled back to the breakout or the 50-day moving average. If you followed your plan, you never added shares. That's why I like to buy as much as I'm comfortable with at the beginning. A good momentum stock may not give you another chance to buy.

- ✔ **Pick a target or place a sell stop under the stock.** If you pick a target, you may get out too early. Figure 10-4 tracks European liquor distributor Central European Distribution. Say you bought the stock at $25 and decided that you were going to sell when it hit $40. That would have been a nice trade, but the stock was still moving higher at $50 and $60, and it got as high as $75. Think of all the money that you would have left on the table if you set your target too low.

  You have two ways to get around that. One is to take partial profits along the way. If you bought 500 shares, you could have taken profits on 100 shares at every 10- or 15-point interval in the rally. That would have kept you in the game a lot longer. You can also check your momentum indicators, such as MACD. When the MACD turns down, you can sell shares.

  The easier thing is to use a trailing sell stop. You could put your stop at 8 to 10 percent below your buy point and manually raise the stop periodically. I like to adjust my stops after any big gains, say 10 to 15 percent in any period, or place them a percentage point or two below a rising trend line or a key moving average.

  By raising your stop periodically you preserve more of your profits and stay with the trend longer.

Figure 10-4:
Central
European
Distribution
(CEDC) is
an excellent
portrait of a
momentum
stock. Note
its steady
rise over a
16-month
period.

Chart courtesy of StockCharts.com.

Shorting the losers

The flip side of momentum buying is *momentum selling,* or selling stocks short when they're increasingly weak. This tactic is best for bear markets, but you can do it anytime you find a weak stock that looks as if it's getting weaker.

Figure 10-5 gives you a good example. In it, refiner Valero Energy (VLO) is a stock in a dismal state. The chart shows a classic short-selling opportunity for a momentum timer.

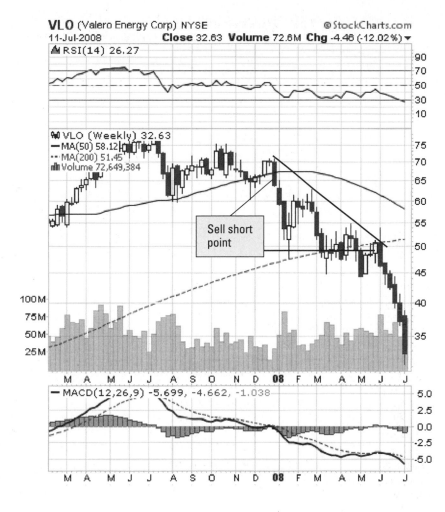

Figure 10-5:
Valero
Energy
(VLO)
breaks
below
50-day
moving
average,
providing a
short-selling
opportunity.

Chart courtesy of StockCharts.com.

Figure 10-5 shows an oil stock in the midst of the greatest bull market in oil in history. Yet, it's in a downtrend. This should come as no surprise, because this is a refinery company, and refiners' profit margins shrink if the price of oil rises faster than the company can pass the profits on to the customers, which is what happened in this case. As a result, the stock tanked and continued to fall dramatically.

I highlighted two great entry points for short sales, as the stock broke below the 50-day moving average and again as it broke below its 200-day moving average.

Short selling is a riskier strategy than going long, though, especially with individual stocks, because you can sell them only in a margin account. *Margin* is money that you borrow from your broker to buy stocks. You use other securities in your account as collateral. The problem is that if the position goes against you — the stock rises in price — you have to put up more margin. If you do this for an indefinite period of time you rack up big losses.

Here's how it works: You buy a share of ABC Inc. for $100 using $20 bucks of your own money and $80 bucks that you borrow from your broker. The net value of the trade is $20. The broker gets a minimum margin requirement of $10. If ABC falls to $85, the net value of the loan is $5. In order to meet your margin requirement you have to sell the share of ABC stock, sell other stocks, or add money to the account to that the margin requirement is back above $10.

In order to sell stocks short, you borrow shares from another investor in hopes of buying them back at a lower price. The other investor collects all the dividends during the period that you borrowed their shares and when you close out the trade, by covering (buying the shares back at a lower price), the other investor gets the shares.

I don't recommend that you use margin. It is however an integral part of selling stocks short, so it needs to be included in the discussion. I personally don't use margin because I don't like the thought of getting a margin call, which is what happens when the amount of money that you have in your margined positions falls below a certain price. When that happens, you have to either put up more money or sell other positions in your portfolio in order to raise cash.

Chapter 11

Timing the Bond Market

*B*onds aren't as sexy as stocks, but during some periods of time, such as recessions, they're a great way to make money. Contrary to popular belief, it's not the stock market but the bond and currency markets that rule the world. Everything and anything that anyone does in the financial markets anymore is based upon the effects of interest rates, and as globalization expands, the emphasis has expanded beyond the United States as the only benchmark.

As the credit crisis in 2007 and 2008 proved, when global bond markets seize up, so does everything else, including real estate, the stock markets, and the ability of the world to do business. Sure, it takes a near complete implosion of the global financial system to stop every single transaction and plunge the world into the dark ages, but a major seizing up of the bond market usually leads to a very difficult period in the global economy.

In this chapter, I show you how to make money where others fear to tread — the bond market.

Corporate bonds are a slightly different animal from treasury bonds; much of what affects them has to do not just with borrowing costs in the general economy but with the fate of the company that issues them. Unless I say otherwise, my remarks in this chapter refer to treasury bonds.

What Makes the Bond Market Tick

The bond market depends on and influences the action of central banks. Thus, from a trading standpoint, you need to understand the relationship between the bond markets, central banks, economic indicators, and real life, honest-to-goodness businesses. You also need to understand how that relationship is represented on a price chart so that you can make trading decisions about whether to go long or short bonds, or just to stay on the sidelines.

The give and take between Fed and bond market

Fail to get a grip on the key relationship between Federal Reserve and bond market and your trading takes a hit. Remember, though, that the only truth that matters from a timing standpoint is price action. What I mean is that if traditional relationships hold, the bond market and the Federal Reserve are two ends of the same spectrum, with current interest rates at the center. Yet during some periods of time what the Fed sees as the dominant economic picture and what the bond market perceives as the economic reality are different, and there is no agreement in the trend of interest rates. You may then see bond yields move in a different direction from what the Federal Reserve is trying to do. During those times, you should always yield to the action on the charts, as long as the trends remain in place.

Although I refer throughout this section to the Federal Reserve Bank of the United States, my comments apply to other global central banks except in cases where I say otherwise.

Here are some important points about how the Fed and the bond market work together:

- ✔ Long-term interest rates are generally more important to business planning than short-term rates, and thus are more sensitive to inflation.

  The Federal Reserve, and central banks in general, can't generally control long-term interest rates, and they rely on the bond markets to do so for them. In turn, central banks manipulate short-term interest rates by raising and lowering key central bank rates, such as the Fed funds rate, and sending the message to the bond market, usually through speeches and written communications such as press releases, about what they'd like to see with regard to long-term rates.

- ✔ Generally, as the Fed finds through analyzing key economic reports (see Chapter 4) that inflationary pressures are rising, it starts to raise interest rates.

In those instances, the Fed traditionally raises the Fed funds *target rate* — the rate that governs overnight deposits between banks. However, in 2007 and 2008, in response to the subprime mortgage crisis, the Fed began to use the *discount rate,* the rate that the Fed charges banks to borrow at its discount window, more aggressively and creatively. Traditionally, discount rate window borrowing was a loan of last resort for banks and a signal to the Fed that the individual bank was in trouble. During this unusual time period, the Fed made it clear that, at least in that particular instance, it didn't view discount window borrowing as a last resort measure. In fact, the Fed actually encouraged banks to borrow from the discount window, and also allowed investment banks to also use the facility, a significant change from previous Fed policy.

✔ Action from the Fed brings about some significant repercussions to the financial system.

When the central bank raises the Fed funds and/or the discount rates, banks usually raise the *prime rate,* the rate that targets their best customers. At the same time or soon thereafter, credit card companies raise their rates. Other rates, such as mortgages and car loans, also follow the general direction of the Fed. For example, most 30-year mortgages are tied to the interest rate for the U.S. one-year Treasury note.

✔ The bond market is often ahead of the Fed; bond traders also known as *bond vigilantes,* keep constant watch over inflation and sometimes respond to inflation indicators before the Fed does. In those situations, the bond market actually does influence the actions of the Federal Reserve.

For example, if there is a Federal Reserve Open Market Committee meeting in a few weeks, but the economic data on any given day shows inflation, bond traders respond immediately by selling bonds. Prices drop, yields rise, and market interest rates rise.

In other words, the bond market often sends the Fed a message. By the same token, the Fed often sends messages to the bond market, during member speeches or interviews with the media. If the Fed is convincing enough about its position in its statements, the bond market reacts to the Fed's statements — either by affirming the Fed's views or by retracing its own steps — and bond yields and market rates move to lower or higher levels, depending on the direction in which they were headed before the Fed made its intentions known.

Disagreements between the Fed and the bond market are an accepted part of the free-market system and tend to occur at the beginning or end of a trend in interest rates. For example, if the Fed has been raising interest rates for an extended period of time and wants to pause, it doesn't want the bond market to get ahead of it. So it will make it fairly clear that it's going to pause. At some point, long-term rates, which are controlled by the bond market, will begin to stabilize or drop.

The Fed wants the bond market to do the work that it can't do — to influence long-term interest rates, which in turn influence large business deals and mortgages. Be very aware of the general direction of both central bank and market interest rates or else you can get caught up in volatile trading and lose money.

Sometimes, however, the bond market will tell the Fed that the central bank may have gone too far in raising or lowering rates. During those times bond yields will start to drift away from the general direction of the Fed funds rate and the discount rate.

Finding general hints about bonds

Here are some concepts to keep in mind about bonds before you go throwing your money into the pit:

- **Rising bond prices mean falling yields.** The price you pay for a bond is in inverse proportion to the bond's *yield,* the interest rate that you collect as long as you hold the bond. As the price rises, the yield falls. Trends and events that are good for bonds, such as slowing economic growth or stable inflation, make the price rise and the yield fall.

- **Bonds hate inflation.** If you buy a bond that's supposed to pay you 5 percent for ten years, and inflation is running at 1 percent per year, you're getting a 4 percent return. If inflation climbs to 2 percent per year, your investment return has been cut by 20 percent.

- **Commodity prices affect the bond market.** Generally speaking, rising commodity prices are inflationary and lead to falling bond prices and rising yields. The most important commodity in this regard is oil, but other commodities, such as agricultural and industrial commodities, are also important to watch. Bond yields generally rise in response to higher commodity prices. Yet that relationship can sometimes change. The dip in bond yields evident in the latter part of the chart is due to the market expecting the global economy to slow in response to the burden placed upon it by higher commodity prices.

- **The effect of a weak currency is variable on bonds.** A weak currency can be negative for bonds, especially if it's weakened because of a rising money supply, in which case it's inflationary. However, a weak currency because of an underlying weak economy is not usually inflationary, at least not until the money supply reaches the critical stage at which it becomes inflationary. That tipping point is variable in every cycle.

- **Bond traders like slow growth or negative economic growth.** I think of bond traders as mini versions of Ebenezer Scrooge. They like misery. And the worse things get, the more bond prices rally and yields fall. A depression is, in theory, the best scenario for bonds — at least for treasury bonds — as long as the government is standing and meets its debt obligation.

✔ **The bond market can be volatile on a short-term trading basis.** However, as soon as it defines a trend in response to the economic data, the inflation outlook, and other factors that affect bond prices, it tends to stay in that trend for extended periods of time. It's not unusual to see the same general trend in bonds lasting for years.

Tying economic reports to the bond market

The bond market is very keen on monthly economic reports because the reports continue to update the state of the economy and inflation. (Chapter 5 tells you more about these reports.) Here is a list of the more important reports (in order of their influence, generally speaking) and how bond traders tend to respond to them:

✔ **The employment report:** Bond traders usually focus on the number of new jobs created and the general trend of wages. Big numbers in both of these categories of the report tend to be bearish (negative) for bonds and lead to lower prices and higher yields.

✔ **Consumer Price Index (CPI):** Big numbers are bearish; small numbers aren't always bullish but tend to be better.

✔ **Producer Price Index (PPI):** Especially if the number is way above or below expectations, this one can move the bond market.

✔ **Consumer confidence:** Consumer confidence can be a major mover if the market is at a significant juncture, and especially if the data falls in line with other data that's available at the time the numbers are released. In other cases, the bond market simply ignores it, no matter the number.

Figure 11-1 shows the U.S. Ten Year Treasury Note yield for 24 months, during a period when consumer confidence began to fall precipitously. Interest rates began to creep higher in the April to May period in 2008. Much of that rise in yields came in response to rising consumer and producer prices, which had been triggered by rising commodity prices, which preceded rising prices. Oil is central to the global economy, and as prices rallied to all-time highs repeatedly in the months following the April 2008 rally, the increase took its toll on the already shaky state of consumer confidence, a major driver of the economy.

✔ **Gross Domestic Product:** As they do with employment, bond traders look for strength here. Big numbers, especially in a component known as the GDP deflator, signal the potential for inflation. Weak numbers, or numbers that don't suggest big inflation, are generally benign.

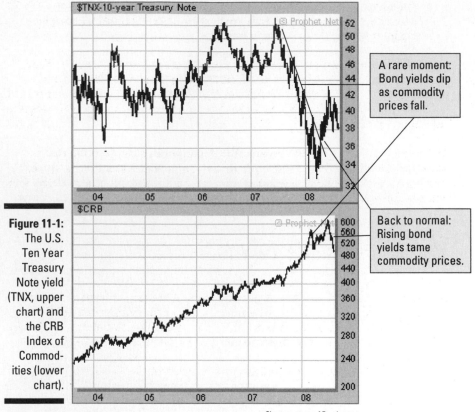

A rare moment: Bond yields dip as commodity prices fall.

Back to normal: Rising bond yields tame commodity prices.

Figure 11-1: The U.S. Ten Year Treasury Note yield (TNX, upper chart) and the CRB Index of Commodities (lower chart).

Chart courtesy of Prophet.net.

Globalization is here to stay. And at the center of the phenomenon is the entity known as the bond market. As a bond timer, you primarily deal with U.S. Treasury bonds. Yet, global events and the global economy will affect your trading. Over the next 10 or 20 years — or sooner — European, Middle Eastern, and Asian bond markets will play an increasingly important role.

Making Bond Timing Work

The major vehicles for trading bonds are futures and options, mutual funds, and exchange-traded funds (ETFs).

For my money, ETFs are ultimate timing vehicles for bonds because

- ✔ You can trade them anytime, anywhere, via your online stock account.
- ✔ You can find an ETF for just about any timing endeavor, including bonds, stocks, and commodities.

> ✔ The only thing that you have to get right to make money trading ETFs is the trend, which means that your knowledge of technical analysis (Chapter 4) is sure to come in handy.

Two ETFs in particular are excellent for bond timing: The I-shares 20+ Year Treasury Bond Fund (TLT) lets you time the long side, as prices rise and yields fall, and the ProShares UltraShort U.S. Trust ETF (TBT) lets you time the short side, as prices fall and yields rise. See the upcoming section "Finding the right time for bonds."

TBT is a leveraged ETF. That means that it exaggerates the trend in prices. More specifically, TBT is designed to deliver twice the amount of movement that you'd see in the bond market at any given time. Still, no other vehicle lets you bet on rising bond yields.

Reasons to time bonds

The bond market, also known as the credit market, is what makes the world go around, because a significant portion of global business transactions are conducted based on credit. If governments and corporations can't sell their bonds to the markets, and traders can't trade them, the global economy is in danger of collapse, as the subprime mortgage crisis showed in 2008.

The bond market is a central and very active market that's an excellent vehicle for timing — it has ample liquidity, gets plenty of opportunities to move in response to economic reports and news, and thanks to ETFs is easy to trade.

A good rule of thumb for timers is devote no more than 20 to 40 percent of your overall portfolio to timing bond ETFs, because the overall return potential and the volatility of the bond market make it less appealing overall than stocks for timing.

You may want to organize your allocation according to how well the stock market is doing. For example, when stocks are moving higher, limit your bond timing to 20 percent of your allocation. As things become more difficult in stocks, increase your bond-timing allocation.

Another common reason to time bonds is that the bond market, depending on the status of the global economy, can become the central focus of activity in the markets at any time. (In which case, as a timer, you're basically required to make that the focus of your trading.) Most of the time, when this is the case, it means that the economy is in pretty bad shape or that some sort of global crisis is under way. In either of those cases, you'd be short the stock market or out altogether, so that you'd have more capital to spare for bond timing.

The third case is that you've decided to become a bond ETF timing specialist. In that case that's what you'd do all the time, and you'd either go crazy, get bored, or become an excellent bond timer.

Buying bonds for hedging and diversification

Hedging, in the futures markets, is what big institutions do routinely. For an ETF timer in bonds, hedging means that you're trying to diminish the risk to other parts of your portfolio, such as stocks, by using a different class of assets. You can hedge against events or you can hedge against the action in other markets and the influence that such action could have on your major positions. Using bonds as a hedge for your stock portfolios comes in handy when the markets are starting to get volatile or when a specific set of data, such as the employment report, is due to be released.

Think of hedging as taking a position in the market that's in the opposite direction of a trading position you've already established. In other words, it's a form of insurance against a reversal of trends, such as what could happen if there is some sort of significant event.

Allocating time and money to bond timing

The amount of money you allocate to bond timing varies. As with anything else, the most appropriate answer is based on your risk tolerance and your ability to master the ins and outs of bond timing.

If you don't handle volatility well, you're better served by mutual funds that keep their bond maturities to less than two years. Short-term bonds tend to be less volatile. For timing, it's best to use trading vehicles that focus on bonds that are longer than ten years. The ETFs (TLT and TBT) that I mention in the section "Making Bond Timing Work" fit that bill.

As a timer, your focus will mostly be on the stock market, but I recommend that in general you allocate 20 to 40 percent of your timing asset allocation to bonds. If this sector of the financial markets doesn't make sense to you, then you shouldn't be dabbling in it. Although this applies to all markets, bonds are one of those areas that some people find particularly difficult to get excited about. If that's you, then find something else to trade.

Finding the right time for bonds

The two best opportunities to time bonds are when you see a clear trend, both in the economy and in the bond market, and when you see a decisive trend reversal.

A clear trend means that the economic data is trending in the same direction for a period of time, usually at least a few weeks, and especially after a trend line is broken — a sign that a new trend has begun. It doesn't really matter whether the economy is slowing or strengthening, as long as there is a fairly clear trend.

When the economy shows a clear trend, make sure that the bond market itself is in a clear trend, up or down. The bond market's trend doesn't necessarily have to match the trend of the economy. There just has to be a trend.

Furthermore, when there is a clear trend reversal, you want to catch it as early as possible and act upon it with vigor, meaning that you want to get your positions set up early enough to catch as much of the move as possible.

As a bond timer you have to be vigilant. Here are some key points to keep in mind:

- ✔ **The Ten-Year U.S. Treasury note is the benchmark for the U.S. Treasury market.** But TLT and TBT are very liquid ETFs whose action mirrors the action of the U.S. Ten Year note quite closely. That makes them the most ideal instruments for timing bonds, other than directly trading futures and options on futures.

- ✔ **TLT lets you go long the market.** Use this ETF when bond yields are falling and prices are rising.

- ✔ **TBT is essentially the mirror image of TLT.** Use this ETF when bond yields are rising and prices are falling.

- ✔ **Bonds can move significantly on any given day in response to events and economic reports.** Watch the market on a daily basis and look at the long-term trend in bonds as well as the response in the market to economic data and global events. Use charts that span more than one year to get the big picture. Figure 11-1 (upper chart) shows a five-year look at the U.S. Ten Year Note Yield (TNX). You can see that despite a rise in consumer and producer prices (Figure 11-2) that started in 2006, bond yields continued to fall. Yes, there was inflationary pressure building in the system. But the bond market didn't find it troubling enough to take yields higher.

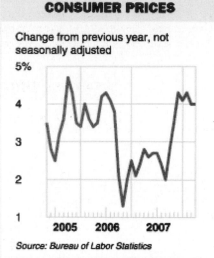

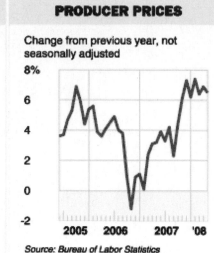

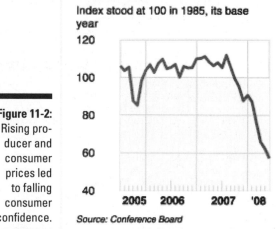

Figure 11-2:
Rising pro-
ducer and
consumer
prices led
to falling
consumer
confidence.

The bond market ignored rising oil and commodity prices for two important reasons:

- The bond market was betting that rising fuel prices would lead to a
  significant slowing of the U.S. economy, because most slow periods
  in the economy since the 1970s have been preceded by a rise in
  the price of oil.

• Some measures of the economy — industrial production and the Purchasing Manager's Index (ISM report) — were flattening out and started dropping during the period. Eventually the unemployment rate began to rise, and GDP was volatile. See Figure 11-3.

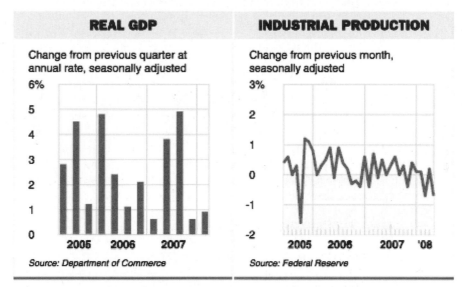

REAL GDP

Change from previous quarter at annual rate, seasonally adjusted

Source: Department of Commerce

INDUSTRIAL PRODUCTION

Change from previous month, seasonally adjusted

Source: Federal Reserve

Figure 11-3: Volatile GDP, flat to falling industrial production, rising unemployment, and falling purchasing managers' data suggest a flat to slowing economy.

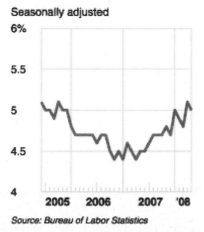

UNEMPLOYMENT RATE

Seasonally adjusted

Source: Bureau of Labor Statistics

PURCHASING MANAGERS' INDEX

Reading above 50 indicates expansion in manufacturing activity

Source: Institute for Supply Mgmt.

This mixture of data was enough to keep bond traders betting that eventually the economy would fall off a cliff. When the subprime mortgage crisis hit, the bond market rallied, once again betting on a slow economy.

But when the Federal Reserve eased interest rates aggressively in response to the subprime mortgage crisis and oil prices continued to rise, the U.S. dollar weakened significantly, and at a faster pace than in previous months. A weak dollar is usually the final straw for bond traders, because weak currencies are inflationary.

In this case, bond traders changed their perceptions, and instead of focusing on a flat to weakening economy, they decided that inflation was a bigger factor than a flat to weakening economy. And that's when bond yields broke above the long-term trend line in Figure 11-1 (upper chart).

✔ **Bonds tend to stay in trends for long periods of time.** That longevity means that a change in the trend is usually important. Figure 11-1 (upper chart) shows a nice trend in the long-term trend of the Ten Year Note Bond Yield. But, if you look at Figure 11-4, of the Lehman 20 year + ETF TLT, you can see a volatile market that broke through two important support levels, the 50-day moving average, and eventually the 200-day moving average. In a space of six weeks (roughly April 14 to May 27), the bond market's trend changed.

By watching the long-term trend chart and the U.S. Ten Year Note yield and monitoring the price action of your trading instrument, you can start to make plans for entering the market on the short side. Figure 11-4 shows you where you would enter the market — as the market is starting to show weakness — and where you would put your initial *buy stop* (exit point).

A quick look at the chart of TLT (Figure 11-4) shows you that this ETF's trading action usually clusters around 2 to 3 points before it makes a move above or below the cluster. That's the usual short-term trading range during this period. You want to put your stop just beyond that range, so that the odds are in your favor of getting out of a bad position that's about to get worse.

Figure 11-4:
The Lehman
20+ Year
Treasury
Bond Fund
breaks
below
support,
offering
timing
opportuni-
ties on the
short side.

Chart courtesy of StockCharts.com.

Chapter 12

Timing Foreign Markets

· ·

· ·

*T*he world is the timer's oyster. Money is changing hands somewhere in the world just about every minute of every weekday, and you could have your hand in the action with bonds, currencies, stocks, and commodities. Capture every single tick and news item through cable channels like Bloomberg and CNBC World and Web access to real-time quotes and news. Hot dog, what a wonderful world we live in!

But it wasn't always this marvelous. In the old days — the late 1980s — when I got started with market timing, most of us timing types would trade mutual funds, especially when timing foreign markets. That was all we had, and we made the best of it, but it was troublesome to say the least. For one thing, stock and bond funds were the only things we could trade. There was no market for other things. Currencies and commodities were for the "professionals" who could afford the fancy rigs and the real-time quotes.

Today, things are different; you can find an exchange-traded fund (ETF) for just about any kind of transaction you might want to make, short or long, leveraged or not. You can also trade foreign stocks, bonds, and currencies via the futures markets, or even by opening an offshore brokerage account that enables you to participate in these markets, although you may want to wait until you get fairly sophisticated before you move to that level of timing.

In this chapter, I tell you about timing international stock ETFs and how to use them for your own purposes, whether for pure gains or for hedging.

The Whole World Is One Market

In case you haven't figured it out yet, the world is essentially one big market-place. Trading anywhere can affect the activity of markets around the globe, as 24-hour cable news, international business channels, and the Internet have essentially connected all trading desks around the world to the action taking place at any one time.

As you sleep, things are happening in Tokyo, Shanghai, Amsterdam, and elsewhere. Traders everywhere have access to news about events, to economic reports, and to capital. That capital can move around the world at the speed of light and with the touch of a button.

Here are some general concepts to remember when trading international markets:

- ✔ **All markets are linked.** Volatility in one of the major markets — the United States, Europe, and Japan — can spread to other markets as they open. Trouble in one of the more prominent second-tier markets, such as Hong Kong, Shanghai, Singapore, Australia, or Brazil, can cause problems around the world. This kind of "contagion" was clearly evident as far back as 1987 when the U.S. market crashed. More recently, in the 1990s, the Asian currency crisis started a global market meltdown.

- ✔ **Events can trigger major global market problems.** Wars and terrorist attacks or other unexpected events (strikes, major weather events, and so on) can trigger market meltdowns. On the flip side, events such as surprising cuts in interest rates at important economic turning points, especially when the Federal Reserve cuts rates, can be very positive.

- ✔ **Economic reports can influence all markets.** An unexpected set of data, such as more or fewer jobs created than the markets expected, often sets off a chain reaction in which bonds, stocks, currencies, and commodities move.

- ✔ **Earnings surprises can be painful or gleeful.** If a major Japanese or Asian technology company or a major European bank delivers a positive or negative earnings report, it may be enough to spread to other markets — especially if the company is a key global player or a bellwether for its industry. Airlines, telecom companies, oil companies, and banks often set off a worldwide reaction.

Considering the Currency Effect

Whenever you invest in a foreign country, directly or indirectly, you should be aware of the effect of that country's currency on your investment. Generally, your foreign investments do better if the dollar is weak, as long as the investments are performing well, but the state of the currency of the country that you're investing in is most important.

Figure 12-1 shows you a good example — the Australian Dollar (FXA, Currency Shares ETF, left) and the Australian stock market ETF (AUS, the NETS S&P/ASX 200 Index ETF, right).

Figure 12-1: The connection between the Australian Dollar (left, FXA) and the Australia Index ETF (AUS, right).

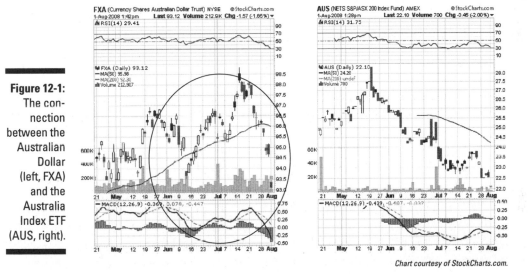

Chart courtesy of StockCharts.com.

The circled portion of the FXA chart roughly corresponds to the downtrend in the AUS chart. Note that when the volatility in FXA started to become apparent, around May 19, 2008, AUS began to weaken. And even though FXA managed to make a new high, AUS never did confirm it, creating a significant technical divergence. This is an excellent example of what could happen to your foreign investments if the currency starts to weaken, and why you should keep an eye on both the investments and the currency.

When you're timing foreign markets, watch for action in the underlying currency. If the currency starts to strengthen or weaken, watch what the activity is doing to your ETF, as it's going to have to work harder to give you potential gains because of the currency effects. If your ETF starts to weaken, either because the currency is too weak or too strong, it's likely a signal that things are getting worse and that you may want to consider selling the ETF.

Figure 12-2 gives you a slightly different take on the theme and throws in another variable — interest rates. On the left you see the Brazil iShares ETF (EWZ) and on the right, the WisdomTree Dreyfus Brazil Real ETF (BZF). The circled portion of the EWZ chart corresponds to the time period depicted in the chart on the right. Note that as the currency (the *real*) rose, the stock market, as represented by EWZ, fell. Brazilian investors feared higher interest rates from Brazil's central bank and sold stocks. But the currency rose because higher interest rates are generally positive for that country's currency. Watch both the stock market and the currency, and make your decisions based on the chart.

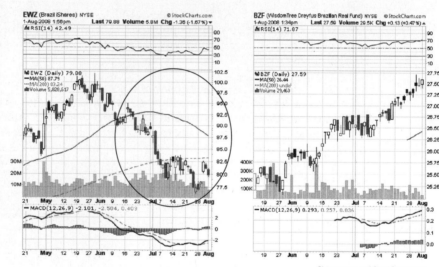

Chart courtesy of StockCharts.com.

Timing Foreign Markets

So what do you need to keep in mind when timing foreign markets? Aside from keeping tabs on the individual markets and the currencies, you need some timing vehicles. For most timers, ETFs and mutual funds are the best vehicles, although you can also own American Depository Receipts (ADRs) of individual stocks, or in some cases buy the listed shares of the company outright — many global companies are now listing their stocks on multiple exchanges simultaneously.

ADRs are bundles of shares of foreign companies that trade on American exchanges, valued in dollars. You can buy them and sell them as you would any share of stock via your broker or online account.

Getting started

I like ETFs because they let me time the region, and I don't have to worry about the particulars of any one stock. In most cases, an ETF that concentrates on any one region of the world or specific country is built based on an index. The ETF's price movements therefore represent the general action in that particular region of the world. You use it to trade the trend, not so much the details.

For the purposes of timing, I divide the world into a few separate regions and then subdivide them further into countries. You can mix and match, evaluating regions of the world or getting more specific, without any focus on one or the other approach.

Stay regional and you can get a little more diversification than if you just bought one particular country. The flip side is that if the region is not doing well, but one or two of the countries in it are, then you could miss out on making some money. The best thing to do is to put together a list of ETFs that is subdivided into two sections. One section should have ETFs that represent stocks according to regions of the world and the other should contain ETFs that represent stocks in individual countries.

Remain consistent in your trading strategy; rely on your chart analysis to determine which ETFs you want to own at any one time.

Dividing up your timing world

It's a pretty big world, and from a timing standpoint slicing it up into neat sections that you can analyze individually is a big help. You can divide it geographically, or you can divide it by market capitalization, meaning that you group large markets such as Europe and Japan in one category and smaller markets such as Southeast Asia and South America in another category. I prefer the former method, as it forces me to look at things via details.

In this section, I show you how to organize a handful of funds by market capitalization. The examples are some of the ETFs that I use on a regular basis. As you get better and figure out what regions of the world you like, you can develop your own relationships and apply this method to your own list. You can find lots of ETFs at the American Stock Exchange Web site (www.amex.com) and also at the New York Stock Exchange Web site (www.nyse.com).

Here are the most liquid and prominent global markets, and these ETFs are representative of the action that takes place in these markets:

- ✔ **Japan:** For Japan I use the iShares MSCI Japan ETF (EWJ). This fund is designed to follow the action in the MSCI Japan Index and concentrates on large cap stocks, such as Honda Motor, Sony, and Toyota. I combine EWJ with the Currency Shares Japanese Yen ETF (FXY) for a currency hedge when appropriate. (See the section "Considering the Currency Effect" earlier in this chapter to see how to use a currency ETF as a hedging mechanism for an international ETF.)

  Japan is an excellent region to time because it's a big liquid market, and the stock market in Japan can move in one direction for very long periods of time. That means that when a trend is in place, it may continue in the same direction, and you can make money just by staying with the trend.

- ✔ **The world without the United States:** For Europe and a diversified Pacific Basin and Asian exposure, I use the iShares MSCI EAFE Index Fund, which mirrors the action of the Europe Australasian and Far East Index.

  When the EAFE trend turns negative I use the Short EAFE ProShares ETF (EFZ). The EAFE can but does not always move in the same direction as the U.S. market. By investing in this ETF, you may get some diversification, and some currency benefit, if the dollar is weak.

- ✔ **Australia:** To trade Australia by its lonesome, you can use the NETS Trust Australia ETF. To hedge the exposure, you can use the Currency Shares Australian Dollar ETF (FXA). Australia tends to move higher when natural resources and commodities are in bull markets. That means that these ETFs can deliver gains when other markets don't.

- ✔ **China:** China is a growing market. Again, as with other ETFs that I like, China's market can trend in one direction for a long time. This makes the country and its stock market excellent timing targets.

- ✔ **Brazil:** Brazil is the largest economy in South America and its stock market is a big player that's frequently targeted by large mutual funds from the United States and Europe. That means that it's liquid. Its currency, the real, is also an excellent timing vehicle.

The New York Stock Exchange lists more than 20 international ETFs, and the American Stock Exchange over 50. You find single country ETFs, regional ETFs, strategy ETFs for growth, value, large and small stocks, and even international ETFs that offer the opportunity to invest in specific sectors such as oil, water, and consumer goods.

You can spend a lot of time figuring out the nuances of each and every single ETF, which is plausible but might be a difficult way to get started. Or you can do what I've found useful, to use a small sample of ETFs and to become very familiar with the way they behave. I use just a handful of ETFs for timing the international markets.

Choosing International ETFs

For me, trading international ETFs is all about simplicity, liquidity, and ease of hedging. Even if a market and an ETF are attractive from fundamental and technical standpoints, I won't trade them unless they provide the right answers to the following questions:

- **How easy is this ETF to follow?** Because of the time factors that govern my daily schedule, I have to do as much as I can with as little effort as possible. If I pick way-out-of-the-mainstream stuff to invest in, I have to spend a lot of time researching trivia, and that would lead me to miss something else. So I pick funds that are easy to follow and that are representative of where the big money moves. If I can't find a quote when I need it on my PDA, or via basic computer access, I just won't bother with it. The ability to know what your money is doing at any time is the key to success, especially as a market timer.

- **Can I short sell this sector of the market?** Because I generally use only a handful of ETFs, I want to know that I can sell short whatever each one represents if things turn down.

  You can sell most ETFs short by shorting the individual shares as you would with any stock. But that involves margin, and there is always the difficulty of finding ETF shares that you can borrow to sell short. Instead, as much as possible, I look for ETF pairs where one ETF goes long, and another does the opposite by shorting shares. That way I can just click one button and I'm on my way.

- **Can I hedge the exposure to this ETF?** You can hedge your exposure to country and region ETFs by using a good currency play. For more details, see the earlier section "Considering the Currency Effect." Another way to hedge ETFs is to buy another ETF that does the opposite. I show you how to do that in the next section.

The Chinese market is an excellent place to illustrate the concept of using a pair of ETFs — one that is long the underlying market, and one that is short the same market — and the simple but careful method of making your timing decision. Here are some important steps to take as you make your way into international timing via ETFs:

- ✔ **Identify the market that you want to time.** For this example, I want to time the Chinese stock market. Figure 12-3 shows the Shanghai Composite Index (SSEC).

- ✔ **Note the dominant trend.** Figure 12-3 shows the SSEC clearly in a bear market. It's well below its 200-day moving average, and it failed to reverse its intermediate term trend when it failed to rise above its 50-day moving average.

- ✔ **Choose the right ETF for the dominant trend.** Look to your list of ETFs and see what matches the market that you want to time. To time China I use the iShares FTSE/Xinhua 25 ETF (FXI) and the UltraShort FTSE/Xinhua China ETFs to time the Chinese stock market. FXI is a long ETF, and FXP is a short ETF.

- ✔ **Make your trade.** The chart on the left side of Figure 12-4 illustrates when to make your exit from a long ETF (FXI). It shows two exit points. The first is when the ETF fails to rally above the 200-day moving average. The second selling opportunity came when FXI fell below its 50-day moving average (50-day line). The MACD oscillator also gave a sell signal, confirming the negative price action.

  The chart on the right side of Figure 12-4 shows you the entry points for going long the FXP ETF, which sells the Chinese stock market short. Note how the action in FXP occurs nearly simultaneously with the action in FXI but neatly reverses. This kind of synergy between the two funds makes them an ideal trading pair.

You could waste a lot of time looking for something to time. But this trading pair, FXI and FXP, are nearly perfect, giving you the opportunity to time the Chinese market no matter what the trend.

You want to identify compatible ETFs even if they aren't from the same family. In this case, when the dominant trend is up, you should use FXI, and when the trend is down, you should use FXP. These funds illustrate well-designed inverse relationship ETFs, which means that when one rises, the other tends to fall. That's exactly what you're looking for when putting together your trading pairs.

Figure 12-3:
The
Shanghai
Composite
Index
(SSEC) dur-
ing a bear
market.

Chart courtesy of StockCharts.com.

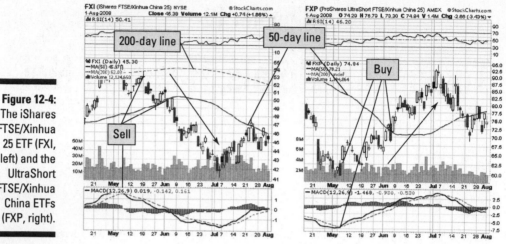

Figure 12-4:
The iShares
FTSE/Xinhua
25 ETF (FXI,
left) and the
UltraShort
FTSE/Xinhua
China ETFs
(FXP, right).

Chart courtesy of StockCharts.com.

Chapter 13

Timing the Metals, Heavy or Not

Not only has metal music been on the comeback trail of late but so have the real-life metals themselves: gold, silver, copper, iron, aluminum, and related products such as steel. Once again, world stages are featuring the likes of Judas Priest, The Scorpions, and Motorhead, just as companies such as U.S. Steel and Caterpillar found their way out of the cellars of the S&P 500 and into the mainstream of Wall Street in the first decade of the 21st century.

Just as music fans behind the Iron Curtain had never seen the metal music giants from the 1980s play live, or had the opportunity to buy their CDs or download their music, neither had many in the world's emerging economies ever have a real chance at owning appliances, automobiles, and perhaps even their own homes, not to mention cell phones, PCs, and just about every gadget that those of us who live in the Western world have had access to for some time now.

The goal of this chapter isn't to give you concert reviews but to help you to find the timing "sweet spot," or the perfect note, with regard to the metals sector.

The metal sector includes two basic groups: the industrial sector and the precious metals. Gold is the one that steals all the headlines, while the industrial metals do much of the work. Here's what I mean:

✔ Rising economic activity leads to increasing demand for industrial metals. When industrial activity reaches the point where demand starts to outstrip supply, inflationary pressures start to build in the system. At that point, or somewhere along the way, gold prices can start to rise.

✔ Industrial metal prices are sensitive to supply and demand, with supply being more important at some points along the cycle, especially if the cycle lasts a long time and there are disruptions, such as political upheaval or major labor strikes in producing countries.

> ✔ Copper prices tend to be a leading indicator of an increase in economic activity, because of its use in housing, electronics, and commercial construction. The flipside is that the copper market can be too early in giving signals about the fate of the global or even regional economies.

Getting the Golden Touch

Gold, aside from its use in jewelry, is viewed by many around the world as a storehouse of purchasing power, thus it is often seen as the currency of last resort. But it's difficult to pinpoint how much of the variation in the price of gold comes from market forces or the manipulation of the price by central banks, who look at gold as a constant competitor to paper money.

Therein lies the rub. Most of the world's supply of gold is in the hands of central banks, whose shared goal is fighting inflation. So here's how things often stack up: Central banks know that speculators see rising gold prices as a sign of inflation. That means that when gold rallies tend to get out of hand, central banks start selling the metal from their huge stockpiles, and prices eventually fall.

Here are some of the basics of the gold market:

✔ Most of the world's gold production — 25 percent or more and 50 percent of the accessible reserves — comes from South Africa. Russia, the United States, Canada, Australia, and Brazil make up the rest of the top-tier producers.

✔ The all-time high in gold prices was set in January 1980, when the price of the October contract hit $1,026 per ounce as the spot-market price rallied to $875. In Figure 13-1 you see that in 2007 gold touched $1,000 before backing off. The $1,000 price area is significant for gold. If the price ever moves significantly past that general area, the circumstances that accompany the development are likely to be extremely important.

✔ Political crises often lead gold prices to rise.

✔ Despite the view that global central banks sell gold to control the perception of inflation by global economies and markets, the rally in gold in 2007 and 2008 shows that this relationship is not always reliable, at least not in the short term — gold prices continued to rise along with consumer and producer price indexes around the world.

One of the most reliable characteristics of the gold market is the inverse relationship of the metal to the U.S. dollar: When the dollar falls, gold tends to rally, and vice versa. This relationship holds up fairly well in the long run, especially when trends are in place for several months and beyond. Find out more by turning to Chapter 15.

Figure 13-1 shows the action in gold since 1986 until the summer of 2008. From analytical and tactical standpoints, several things are important to note:

✔ Gold started an impressive bull market in 2001, and clearly the September 11, 2001, attacks contributed to the bull run. The outcome of the whole situation was of course inflation, as the economic dynamics spawned by the attacks led to an inflationary spiral.

✔ The bull market in gold was preceded by a multi-year *basing pattern* — a chart pattern in which a market moves sideways within a well-defined trading range — in which gold traded in a very wide trading range that lasted from 1987 to 2005 when the 1987 high price was finally taken out. This is classic behavior of a market before it begins a multi-year bull market. The basing pattern's function is to clear out all the bears. Whenever it succeeds — in this case it took 18 years — a new long-term bull market eventually appears.

✔ A parabolic rise started in 2007. Parabolic price patterns occur when the price of any asset rises huge percentages in short periods of time, giving the impression that prices can only go in one direction — up. Eventually parabolic rises lead to bear markets, often preceded by crashes. As of July 2008, gold was likely nearing the end of its yearlong advance. The other possibility is that this rally forms another consolidation pattern, such as the bullish or rising triangle pattern that preceded it.

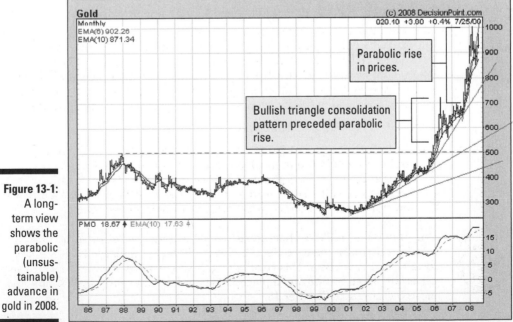

Figure 13-1:
A long-term view shows the parabolic (unsustainable) advance in gold in 2008.

Chart courtesy of DecisionPoint.com.

Treading carefully with gold stocks

Gold stocks are among the trickiest in the market to trade. Inherently volatile, these stocks tend to exaggerate the overall trend of the gold market and at the same time are subject to some degree to the major influences on all stocks: interest rates and the general supply-and-demand equation of the stock market. That, to me, makes them more trouble than they're worth, especially when you have a more direct way to time the gold market. (Check out the upcoming section "Choosing the best route for trading gold.")

The major benchmark for gold stocks is the Philadelphia Gold & Silver Index (XAU; see Figure 13-2). This chart shows a group of stocks whose performance closely correlates with the price of gold but has more volatility than the price of the metal. Also note that gold prices rose more in the seven years of the secular bull market, meaning that the metal, at least in this case was a better trade than the stocks.

Figure 13-2:
The Philadelphia Gold Index (XAU) generally follows the trend of gold prices, but its trajectory is usually more volatile.

Choosing the best route for trading gold

In my opinion, the best deal for making money in the gold market is the gold ETFs, with the StreetTracks Goldshares ETF (GLD) providing the best vehicle for timing. Like all ETFs, GLD is liquid, and you can sell it short as well as buy, sell, and create fairly sophisticated option strategies if you wish.

GLD holds gold futures and trades at one-tenth the value of the price of gold at any time (minus operating expenses for the fund) and closely follows the overall price trend of the gold market.

As with any other timing trade, determine the overall trend and know your exit strategy before entering into any position. You can apply any technical analysis technique described in this book to your timing of GLD.

As a rule, I avoid gold stocks because of their volatility. Instead I use GLD as my timing model and provide timing recommendations at Joe-Duarte.com based on GLD.

Rounding out the precious sector

Two other precious metals are worth mentioning: silver and platinum. The latter can be traded only in the futures markets and in my opinion is too volatile for most, other than the most experienced traders. If you want to know more about it, pick up a copy of my book *Trading Futures For Dummies* (Wiley).

That leaves silver, which like platinum is sort of a hybrid — both a precious and an industrial metal. Platinum is used as the key ingredient in catalytic converters for automobiles, while silver is still used in photography and other industrial processes.

Silver is much more volatile than gold but can be timed by using the iShares Silver Trust (SLV). This ETF follows the general price trend of silver and can be very useful if you decide to time this metal.

The Industrial Truth: Timing Copper and Other Metals

The industrial sector is where the real dirty work gets done, in copper, aluminum, zinc. In this section, I concentrate on copper, because it's the workhorse of industrial metals:

- Copper is the third most-used metal in the world, and it's found virtually everywhere around the globe. The most active copper mines are in the United States, Chile, Mexico, Australia, Indonesia, Zaire, and Zambia.

- Copper is most commonly used in the housing and industrial construction markets for wiring.

- It is also commonly used in the design and manufacture of semiconductor chips, as well as other electronic components.

Mining copper trades

To trade the copper complex successfully, look at the key relationships that affect its price. You can do that quite well by monitoring the action of three stock market sectors: copper, housing, and semiconductors. The following conditions generally ensure the best chance of success for timing copper:

- Look for strength in housing, construction, and the semiconductor and technology sector.

- Watch for other correlating signs, such as growth in housing starts and building permits, Gross Domestic Product, steady industrial production, and other signs of how the economy is performing. For more on economic reports, check out Chapter 5.

- Look to key sectors of the stock market for confirmation on how the big money is betting on copper. (Chapter 16 tells you about the key sectors.)

If you want to time copper, study the overall trend of interest rates and the dollar. These are important indicators in their own right. Usually, a weak dollar and falling interest rates in the United States are signs of traders betting on a weak U.S. economy. Stronger currencies, such as the euro, the yen, and even the Chinese yuan are signs that traders see those economies as being stronger. In the case of China and other economies, the key is to figure out whether demand from those economies is enough to offset any weakness in the U.S. or elsewhere.

Figures 13-3 and 13-4 provide a good illustration of the concept. The price of copper is on the left of Figure 13-3, with a decent bellwether stock for the sector, Southern Peru Copper (PCU), on the right. You see that the price of copper had been moving sideways in a volatile trading range for some time, forming what looks to be an ascending triangle, as the two trend lines suggest. At the same time, shares of PCU were showing significant weakness. This is a classic technical divergence, and the benefit of the doubt as a predictive tool goes to the stocks, not the commodities.

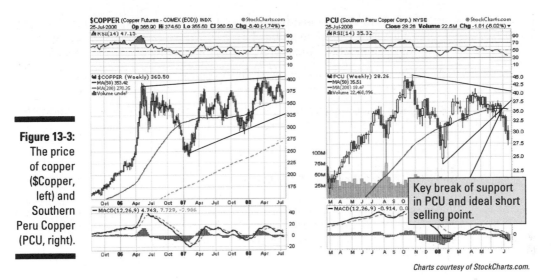

Figure 13-3:
The price of copper ($Copper, left) and Southern Peru Copper (PCU, right).

Key break of support in PCU and ideal short selling point.

Charts courtesy of StockCharts.com.

If you look at Figure 13-4, you see both the Homebuilders Index (HGX, left) and the Semiconductor Index (SOX, right). Both sectors were in the midst of forming some sort of consolidation pattern, and perhaps making a bottom.

Figure 13-4:
The Philadelphia Housing Index (HGX, left) and the Philadelphia Semi-conductor Index (SOX, right).

Charts courtesy of Stockcharts.com.

The bottom line for this complex is as follows:

- ✔ Copper prices were in a very volatile price pattern. Volatility makes for a difficult environment in which to follow trends.

- ✔ The sectors that measure investor opinion about the demand for copper were weak, suggesting that industrial demand for copper was low or at least reduced enough to warrant caution.

- ✔ The stock of a leading producer of copper and a sector bellwether was in the midst of a major technical breakdown. This was another warning sign, as weak commodity stocks usually signal the potential for weakness in related commodities.

When you trade commodity stocks, look at the price trend of the stock and the commodity with which it is associated. If the stock is weak, big investors likely are starting to sense the potential for future weakness in the commodity. Be very cautious about investing in that particular stock or that sector of the market.

Trading steel, ubiquitous steel

Steely Dan isn't a metal band, but it's still one of my favorites. (And the band has generated a lot of gold and platinum records throughout the years.) Global steel production has grown almost two-and-a-half times since the release of Steely Dan's first album, 1972's *Can't Buy a Thrill*.

The fundamentals that drive steel prices are similar to those of copper, except that steel is a much more diversified metal, having uses in just about all industries and especially in commercial construction, automobile and vehicle manufacturing, and the steadiest of all businesses — defense.

For timing purposes, use the same general methodology for steel as you would for copper. Keep an eye on the economic data and the chart(s) of the companies in the sector, which you can find in the Steel Index (AMEX: STEEL). For individual stocks, just see which one of the index components is showing the most strength, and overweigh your purchases to the top two or three stocks in the sector.

You can also find steel stocks with a lot of momentum in the "Stocks in the News" Section of *Investor's Business Daily* and apply the CAN SLIM method of momentum investing to this group. Chapter 10 tells you more about momentum investing and CAN SLIM.

Getting into aluminum

Aluminum is all about transportation, packaging and containers, and construction; a good portion of what you and I drink, drive, or open has something to do with aluminum. The highly flexible metal is also used in medicine and furniture construction.

Here are some key facts about aluminum:

- ✔ It's the second most-used metal in industry behind steel and just ahead of copper, as well as the third most-abundant element in the earth's crust, making it a big ol' workhorse and readily available.

- ✔ It's a better conductor of electricity than copper, making it ideal for transmission lines, especially above ground.

- ✔ More aluminum is produced than all the non-ferrous metals combined.

You can trade aluminum futures, although I wouldn't recommend it unless you're an experienced trader with a very good knowledge of what's going on in the industry and access to top-notch information. Unlike other futures contracts, such as gold and oil, aluminum futures are pretty much the province of big-time hedgers, such as the companies that produce the metal, and their professional trading desks.

Instead, you can participate by buying and selling the stock of Alcoa (NYSE: AA) or the other stocks listed in Table 13-1. Here are some other general thoughts on trading aluminum stocks:

- ✔ **As an industrial metal, aluminum will respond to the same general principles that affect steel and copper.** You should be able to correlate fundamental data on the economy as well as the technical aspects of each individual stock before buying, selling, or selling any of them short.

- ✔ **Alcoa is usually the first stock to report its earnings each quarter on Wall Street and will often, although not always, set the tone for earnings season.** Alcoa is the world's largest aluminum producer, and as a result, its results and its outlook are highly influential, given the central role that aluminum plays in the global economy. Many traders pay a good deal of attention to what the company reports with regard to its operations and earnings, and what it says about its expectations for the short- and long-term future. Thus it's a good idea to watch for the report, listen to details, and see how the market responds.

✔ **What Alcoa says about each segment of its business is worth special attention.** If the company cites overall weakness, you can bet other stock market sectors, such as automobile, aerospace, or technology stocks, might also get hit after the report. For example, if Alcoa says that its aerospace business is weak, have a look at Boeing (BA) shares and the airline sector. The flip side is also important, as demand from industry is what drives Alcoa's ability to raise prices and increase its profit margins. Both Alcoa and Boeing stocks are economically sensitive, and both depend on each other for a big chunk of their ability to execute their business models. When timing, you should make it a point to find such relationships between sectors, individual stocks, and even different markets.

After the earnings report, watch and see if what Alcoa says, and what the stock does, spreads to other metals, including gold, steel, and copper. This can be important, as the response to a good or bad report from Alcoa can be the start of a new trend, either up or down for the entire metals sector, depending on its content.

Table 13-1	Exchange-Listed Aluminum Companies
Stock	*Symbol*
Alcoa, Inc.	AA
Aluminum Corporation of China	ACH
Century Aluminum	CENX
Kaiser Aluminum	KALU
Quanex Corp.	NX
Superior Essex Inc.	SPSX
Tredegar Corp.	TG

Using ETFs to Trade the Metals

Knowing all you want to know about each individual company in the metals sector is cool, but if you don't have enough money to diversify your holdings among different companies, you can use an exchange-traded fund like the S&P SPDR Metals and Mining ETF (XME). This ETF holds a well-diversified metals and raw materials portfolio, composed of 26 different companies.

Alcoa is the largest component of the ETF but is worth only 3.81 percent of the total portfolio. AK Steel (AKS) is the stock with the largest weighing in the index, which means that a huge move in AKS could make the index move even if no other component can.

There are also other ETFs that you can use, especially if you want to trade gold and other mining stocks. You can find a huge selection of them at the American Stock Exchange Web site (`www.amex.com`). One example is the Market Vectors Gold Miners ETF (GDX).

If you want to trade the steel sector, you can use the Market Vector Steel ETF (SLX).

Chapter 14

Timing Commodities: Making Money Down on the Farm

*O*ld MacDonald had a farm, but he didn't have to deal with rising global demand for grains, fertilizer, raw materials, machinery, and the complexity of having to figure out how to make money from a trend that could be in place for years as the growth phase of globalization entrenches itself in the psyche of investors. *E-I-E-I-O!*

Several major factors have combined over the past decade to create a perfect storm of rising prices, inflation, and resource shortages. The world's population is growing, but more important, the population with means to a better life is growing, and therefore so is demand for better (and more) food, clean drinking water, farming equipment, automobiles, housing, fertilizer, seeds, the fuel with which to power expanding population centers, and the infrastructure needed to keep them moving.

Demand for food and resources has expanded beyond North America, Europe, and Japan — the traditional first tier of demand centers — to include other areas of the world, especially China, India, and large areas of South America, such as Brazil.

A market-wide squeeze has developed; producers have been forced to raise prices, and consumers have started to pay more, meaning that the inflation genie is out of the bottle, and the world's central banks are going to have to deal with it at some point by raising interest rates.

For investors, the changing landscape has brought the agricultural sector to the first tier of the markets and given market timers yet another venue to ply their skills.

In this chapter, I give you a taste of agricultural and related community markets, touching briefly on the data that futures traders key in on, and then I move on to the nuts and bolts of the more accessible exchange-traded mutual funds (ETFs) and individual stocks that may make it easier to profit from the trends in the agricultural markets without trading futures directly.

For a more thorough explanation of how to trade agricultural futures directly, see *Trading Futures For Dummies* (Wiley), where I cover the topic in significant detail.

Following the Farming Action

Supply and demand, weather, and the general state of the political season are all significant influences on the agriculture sector. Corn and soybeans are the most actively traded and quoted agriculture contracts and the focus of this chapter.

In the past, the lack of public participation in the commodities and related areas of the market led to a lack of liquidity, and the resulting thin trading conditions made the grain markets very volatile. They were the province of industry-related professionals, such as the traders who man the trading desks for major corporations. Yet, in the wake of the rise of ethanol as a leading fuel for vehicles in the Northern Hemisphere, the corn market has grown significantly. The soybean sector also has grown because of rising demand for the legume in China.

Getting a grip on the growing season

The *crop year* is the time from one crop to the next. It starts with planting and ends with harvesting. During that time, crops are going through what the U.S. Department of Agriculture and Joint Agricultural Weather facility call the moisture- and temperature-dependent stages of development — what you and I call the growing season.

What happens between planting and harvest most affects the prices of crops. Drought, floods, freezes, and hurricanes can lead to major disruptions such as shipping problems. Hurricane Katrina hit the port of New Orleans, for example, and created extreme turmoil where much of the Midwestern grain makes its way out of the United States.

Grains are used in the production of food and fuel year round, but most of them are replenished only one time during the year. That means that prices are affected by a combination of current supplies and future supply expectations, which in turn are affected by both internal (supply and demand) and external (weather, politics, and intangible events) factors. The way a grain market perceives future and current supplies and the way that traders predict the effect of internal and external factors on prices is a major set of variables to consider.

Volatility is inherent in the agricultural markets because of one major factor: the availability of information and the way traders react. The markets are efficient; they react to information instantaneously, which leads to short-term price volatility. If better information is available later, the markets can retrace their steps or move farther along their original direction.

These are some general guidelines to keep in mind when timing commodities:

- ✔ Extraordinary circumstances, such as dietary fads or major external, political, climactic, or geological events, usually affect the supply/demand equilibrium. Otherwise demand stays within a fairly predictable range.

- ✔ If under normal circumstances, demand fluctuates within certain bands based on the number of people and animals to be fed at any given time, the market focuses on anything that affects how much grain will be available to feed them from year to year.

- ✔ After 2007, the price of oil became a much more significant factor in the price of agricultural commodities. Farmers had to pass on the cost of fuel to wholesalers, and the chain of high prices began. Another significant effect of the rising cost of fuel was the need for farmers to buy more fuel-efficient equipment; fertilizer companies also saw their raw material prices rise and had to pass on those costs as well.

Weathering heights

Weather is usually the main influence on crops. And significant weather developments, or expectations, can and do affect crop markets. Globally, weather is important in both the grain and seed markets. Here's a rundown of the way weather affects the crop year:

- ✔ Spring weather affects planting season. Too much rain can delay planting.

- ✔ Summer weather affects crop development. Crops need rain to develop appropriately. Droughts play havoc with crop development.

> ✔ During the North American winter, agricultural market watchers and traders concentrate on the weather in South America, because it's summer there. Likewise, dormant winter wheat in North America needs enough snowfall to protect the crop from *winterkill*, or freezing, because not enough snow is on the ground to insulate the crop.

> ✔ A wet harvest in the fall can cause delays and decrease crop yields.

If you're going to get serious about trading agricultural products, you want access to the U.S. Department of Agriculture (USDA) Weather Bulletin, (www.usda.gov). This site is an excellent resource for information about weather trends and potential developments, and traders do react to it. You can subscribe to the report for $60 per year, or you can just wait for the markets to react and the news to hit the wires. The USDA releases its report on Wednesdays.

Turning to a commodity price resource

The most widely quoted barometer of commodity prices is the Reuters/Jefferies CRB Index (CRB), which is composed of 19 commodity futures contracts. Knowing the details of the index beyond its components isn't as important as knowing the general trend of commodities. Following that trend is the most important use of CRB.

The CRB Index, as Figure 14-1 shows, provides a consolidated picture of the general trend in commodity prices and is the first place to look for information on commodity prices, which in the first half of 2008 were still in the midst of a significant bull market.

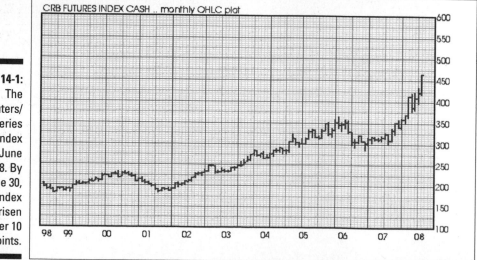

Figure 14-1: The Reuters/Jefferies CRB Index as of June 1, 2008. By June 30, the index had risen another 10 points.

Chart courtesy of BarChart.com

Table 14-1 shows the individual components of the CRB index. The index is most heavily weighted toward energy (39 percent) and food (36 percent), with the rest being made up of metals and fibers.

Table 14-1		Components of the CRB Index	
Commodity	*Index Weight*	*Contract Months*	*Exchange*
Group I			
WTI Crude Oil	23%	Jan-Dec	NYMEX
Heating Oil	5%	Jan-Dec	NYMEX
Unleaded Gas	5%	Jan-Dec	NYMEX
Total	**33%**		
Group II			
Natural Gas	6%	Jan-Dec	NYMEX
Corn	6%	Mar, May, Jul, Sep, Dec	CBOT
Soybeans	6%	Jan, Mar, May, Jul, Nov	CBOT
Live Cattle	6%	Feb, Apr, Jun, Aug, Oct, Dec	CME
Gold	6%	Feb, Apr, Jun, Aug, Dec	COMEX
Aluminum	6%	Mar, Jun, Sep, Dec	LME
Copper	6%	Mar, May, Jul, Sep, Dec	COMEX
Total	**42%**		
Group III			
Sugar	5%	Mar, May, Jul, Oct	NYBOT
Cotton	5%	Mar, May, Jul, Dec	NYBOT
Cocoa	5%	Mar, May, Jul, Sep, Dec	NYBOT
Coffee	5%	Mar, May, Jul, Sep, Dec	NYBOT
Total	**20%**		
Group IV			
Nickel	1%	Mar, Jun, Sep, Dec	LME
Wheat	1%	Mar, May, Jul, Sep, Dec	CBOT
Lean Hogs	1%	Feb, Apr, Jun, Jul, Aug, Oct, Dec	CME
Orange Juice	1%	Jan, Mar, May, Jul, Sep, Nov	NYBOT
Silver	1%	Mar, May, Jul, Sep, Dec	COMEX
Total	**5%**		

Looking for opportunities in corn and beans

Much of the commodity action takes place in the corn and soybean markets, and some soybean- and corn-related individual stocks are worth considering as trading vehicles and as bellwethers for the grains. One of them is Archer Daniels Midland (ADM, Figure 14-2). This company is one of the world's largest producers of seeds, oils, and a host of food-related products. It's also a major producer, processor, and exporter of corn, soybeans, and related products.

Its relationship to corn turned ADM into a bellwether when the ethanol boom started in the United States, as ethanol was seen as a way to decrease the U.S. dependence on Middle East oil to power gasoline-consuming vehicles. Figures 14-2 and 14-3 show how ADM and the price of corn moved along nearly in lockstep throughout the 1990s and the early part of the 21st century. In 2005, ADM shares started moving higher. About a year and a half later, the price of corn started its own climb. And for a period of time they both remained in a rising trend. This rally by ADM ahead of the price of corn is an example of how bellwether stocks tend to move ahead of the commodity that they're coupled with.

Figure 14-2:
Archer Daniels Midland (ADM) rallies ahead of corn.

Chart courtesy of BigCharts.com.

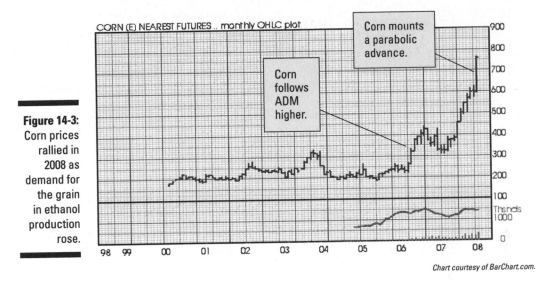

Figure 14-3:
Corn prices
rallied in
2008 as
demand for
the grain
in ethanol
production
rose.

Chart courtesy of BarChart.com.

Figure 14-4 shows that the timing of the rally wasn't accidental. Shares of
ADM started rallying in 2004, in expectation of ethanol becoming a major fuel.
Notice the close correlation of the price of ADM and the price of ethanol.
Also notice how the price of corn led the price of ethanol higher in 2008, even
as ADM started to fall.

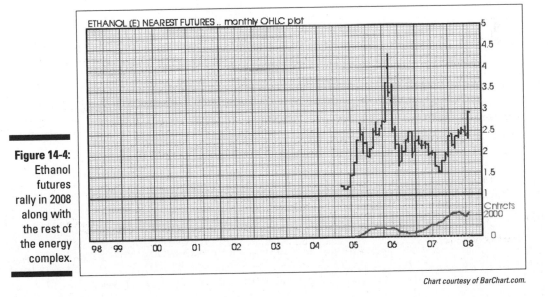

Figure 14-4:
Ethanol
futures
rally in 2008
along with
the rest of
the energy
complex.

Chart courtesy of BarChart.com.

Corn: Not necessarily on the cob

Corn is the most active commodity among grain contracts, and it is the major crop grown in the United States. American farmers grow about 50 percent of the world's corn supply, and 70 percent of U.S. production is consumed domestically.

Corn futures are known as *feed corn,* or corn that's fed to livestock and not the same stuff that you and I eat at summer picnics or find behind the Jolly Green Giant label.

Figure 14-5 depicts crude oil futures during the same period as the other figures. Note the overall similarity in the direction of the charts. In my opinion, this similarity is the key to the whole puzzle. In other words, the commodity story is linked to the price of crude oil, and the fact that corn became the major feedstock for ethanol in the United States drove things higher at a faster rate for the grains.

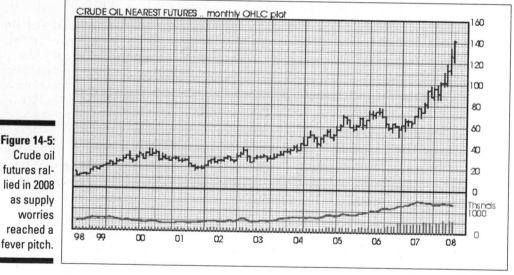

Figure 14-5: Crude oil futures rallied in 2008 as supply worries reached a fever pitch.

Chart courtesy of BarChart.com.

Take note of the following points that this example illustrates:

✔ **The market often starts to move before events become clear to the masses.** If you're a chart watcher, you can be in the market ahead of the news, and you can be well positioned ahead of the crowd.

ADM started to rally in 2005, a full year before President Bush high-lighted his intention to get behind ethanol as a major fuel source for U.S. gasoline-powered vehicles. When the president made the announcement in his State of the Union address in January 2006, corn prices started to move higher.

✔ **Stocks often lead commodities higher.** Money managers who trade stocks tend to have longer-term time horizons than futures traders who often time the markets based on events rather than on expectations or projections of future earnings. In this case, the adage proved true as ADM led the price of corn higher by a full year. More important, the price of ADM shares began to experience trouble, even as corn continued to move higher. Much of the reason for corn's continued advance was bad weather in the Midwest region of the United States, where flooding raised doubts about the ability of the U.S. to meet its corn demand, especially the portion meant to feed livestock. If the bellwether thesis is correct, then the price of corn eventually will fall in response to the fall in ADM.

✔ **There is always more to the story than meets the eye.** The price of crude oil was the centerpiece of the whole move in commodities. As crude oil prices rose, several things happened.

For one, the U.S. political apparatus, especially the White House and legislators from farm states, began to get behind ethanol as an alternative fuel. As time passed, though, it became clear that ethanol was not the panacea that many had hoped for. It's quite inefficient as a fuel, because it takes a lot more effort, cost, and raw material to produce one gallon of ethanol than many had hoped for. The United States had little of the transport and storage infrastructure it needed to deliver the amount of ethanol required to replace gasoline as the major fuel. When all this became apparent, the price of ADM started to fall.

As a timer, your primary focus is on prices and charts. After you saw the weakness in ADM, your job was to evaluate your position and sell the shares if the weakness continued, and then to ask questions later.

✔ **The markets can't rise forever.** Notice the parabolic advance in the charts of corn and crude oil (Figures 14-3 and 14-5). *Parabolic advances* are price moves that go straight up and seem to have the power to go on forever higher. Sensational headlines and a feeling of unbridled joy by those who own the underlying asset usually accompany parabolic advances. Unfortunately, parabolic advances usually turn into ugly disasters. The fact is that markets can't rise forever, no matter what the thinkers of the day seem to think. In other words, by the time this book is released, prices in the commodities may have cooled off significantly.

In this example, Archer Daniels Midland led the way for the corn/ethanol complex to move higher. The stock, barring any significant change in the months ahead of the snapshot pictured here also suggested that prices would eventually cool off.

Soybeans: The hardest working beans in the legume world

Soybeans are the most commonly used protein source by humans and animals around the world. There are three major ways to use soy: soybeans, soybean meal, and soybean oil. Soybeans and their major extracts are traded in the futures markets as three separate contracts.

Soybean meal is the sludgy substance left after the extraction of oil from soybeans. It's used for animal feed. *Soybean oil* is the third major soybean product for which futures contracts are bought and sold. A bushel of soybeans produces 11 pounds of oil, which is used very much as you'd use olive oil and other oils.

Until 2004, the United States was the largest soybean producer with about a 50 percent market share, which sounds impressive until you realize that in 1980 the United States held an 80-percent share. The drop in market share was the result of a grain embargo put on by the Carter administration in the 1980s. The U.S. farmer has yet to recover from this political maneuver. China and South America make up the rest of the world's soybean supply.

"ETFing" Your Commodities

Using bellwether stocks isn't practical for all commodities, especially if you're pressed for time or aren't getting paid to write books about the phenomenon. The next best thing is to get familiar with a few exchange-traded mutual funds that can help you participate in the overall trend of the commodity markets.

I love ETFs. These instruments have opened a world of possibilities to traders like me who are looking for an easier way to get in on futures markets without having to sweat every tick of every contract we own. You can trade just about anything in any direction through an ETF.

In this section I concentrate on commodity ETFs that are diversified and deal with agriculture. In Chapter 19, I go into specific details about using ETFs to trade oil, gasoline, natural gas, and heating oil.

Don't get cocky. Trading futures is not something to be taken lightly, even if you're using ETFs. I don't want to give you a false sense of security, as ETFs that use futures and commodities, as their underlying assets tend to follow the same basic trend of those markets.

For a comprehensive listing of ETFs, visit the American Stock Exchange's Web site, www.amex.com. Another great place to find commodity ETF information is the Deutsche Bank Web site for commodity ETFs, www.dbfunds.db.com. Also see Russell Wild's book *Exchange Traded Funds For Dummies* (Wiley) for a lot of good general pearls on ETFs.

There are several pure ETF plays for commodity futures and one for agricultural stocks. Several water-related ETFs also are worth looking at.

As with any other type of investment, the narrower the focus of the underlying investment, the greater is the potential for volatility. Thus, when timing these ETFs, you should have a good handle of what assets they're composed of and be very focused on keeping track of the price action while they're in your portfolio.

The PowerShares DB Commodity Index Tracking Fund

The PowerShares DB Commodity Index Tracking Fund (DBC) ETF has been around since 2006, and as Figure 14-6 shows has had an excellent run so far. DBC tracks a diversified commodity portfolio, including crude oil, heating oil, aluminum, corn, wheat, and gold. Its diversification is a good thing most of the time, unless of course one or two of the components are going against the grain (oops) and the index gets dragged down.

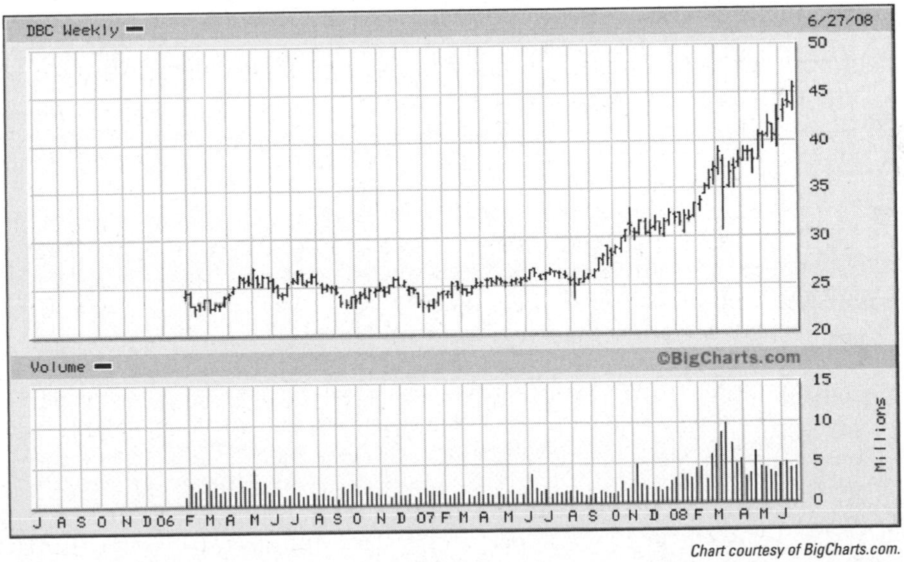

Figure 14-6:
The DB Commodity Index Tracking Fund (DBC) is an excellent vehicle to trade a basket of commodities.

![DBC Weekly chart from BigCharts.com showing price from around 25 rising to nearly 50 by 6/27/08, with volume bars below]

Chart courtesy of BigCharts.com.

Figure 14-6 shows that the fund nearly doubled in price since August 2007 following the general trend of all commodities in the CRB index. You want to see that an ETF follows the trend of the underlying assets that it owns; it then becomes a trustworthy vehicle for your timing.

But you always want to look under the hood. Although DBC generally tracks the overall price of the commodities it houses, it is heavily weighted toward energy with crude oil (35 percent) and heating oil (25 percent) together making up more than one half of the asset allocation. Aluminum accounts for 12.5 percent, while corn, wheat, and gold make up 11.25, 11.25, and 10 percent of the fund, respectively. Despite the diversification, this is no wall-flower of an ETF. And it hasn't really been tested during a period of time when its components weren't all headed in the same general direction.

As with many ETFs, you can also sell DBC short, and it offers options. That means that when it turns lower at some point in the future, you can make money by shorting it or via option strategies aimed at the short side.

The Greenhaven Continuous Commodity Index

The Greenhaven Continuous Commodity Index (GCC) is a more recent addition to the commodity ETF arena than DBC and is a fund to watch out for. GCC uses a combination of commodities and treasury bonds to meet its investment objectives. For its underlying index it uses the ninth revision of the CRB Index (circa 1995), which is an unweighted index of 17 commodities. Because the commodities are unweighted, a one-point move in crude oil is equal to a one-point move in soybeans. If you compare this strategy to that used in calculating the price for DBC (see previous section) you can see why Figure 14-7 (GCC) has a slightly different look than Figure 14-6 (DBC).

Figure 14-7: The Greenhaven Continuous Commodity Index (GCC) is not as clear a picture of raw commodity prices as DBC (Figure 14-6).

Chart courtesy of BigCharts.com.

Unweighted indexes that include large amounts of assets can be hazardous to own, as a bad day for a thinly traded component — orange juice, for example, or something that you've never heard of, like tallow — can take the price of the ETF down hard, even though the rest of the holdings are doing okay.

GCC is a managed ETF, and the fund's manager use a formula to prevent a one-point move in wheat from being the same as a one-point move in crude oil. That means that rather than reflecting the price of the commodities as they move, this ETF is always tweaking the weight of the components. According to the Greenhaven Funds Web site, www.greenhavenfunds.com, the use of the management formula "means the Index constantly decreases exposure to commodity markets gaining in value and increases exposure to those markets declining in value."

So now you have a fund with too many variables that have nothing to do with the market's price of the underlying assets that can influence the price. In other words, this fund doesn't represent a clear picture of what the market is doing and isn't as good for timing as DBC, which is just a straight picture of the trend of its components.

The PowerShares DB Agriculture Fund

The PowerShares DB Agriculture Fund (DBA) is a pure play on agriculture. Because DBA contains only agricultural commodities, the period of time shown in Figure 14-8, extending from February to June 2008, is quite similar to that of GCC (Figure 14-7).

Figure 14-8: The Power-Shares DB Agriculture Fund (DBA) closely tracks the agricultural commodities and is a useful ETF for timing that area of the futures markets.

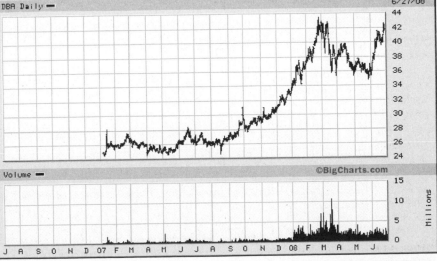

Chart courtesy of BigCharts.com.

Note that DBA's *expense ratio* (what the fund charges) is 0.91; the expense ratio for GCC is 1.09. Buy GCC and you're paying 0.18 more cents per share and not getting any better performance. How much money you put into a fund manager's pocket is an important aspect of timing ETFs, especially in volatile markets.

DBA is a good play on the agricultural commodities and is designed to track, before fees and expenses, the Deutsche Bank Liquid Commodity Index–Optimum Yield Agriculture Excess Return. DBA tracks the price of corn, wheat, soybeans, and sugar with each commodity getting a 25 percent weight in the ETF. It functions similarly to DBC, but is more volatile because it concentrates its assets on agriculture.

Market Vectors Agribusiness

Market Vectors Agribusiness has to have the best stock symbol in the world — MOO. This ETF tracks the Daxglobal Agribusiness Index (DXAG). The index and the fund have 43 component stocks.

Because MOO is a stock-based ETF, it's just as likely to move along with the stock market as it is with the commodities. Its whopping 43 components make it vulnerable to the issues of each individual company.

The index is heavily weighted toward a handful of companies, many of which are in the seed and fertilizer business, making the fund vulnerable to the cost structure of the component companies.

Still, if agriculture-related companies are doing well, this is a fund to own.

The rise of water ETFs

Common sense says that water will be a tradable commodity at some point. But so far the ETFs that concentrate on this particular sector are a bit disappointing.

Two of them that are liquid enough to consider are the PowerShares Global Water Portfolio (PIO) and the PowerShares Water Resource Portfolios (PHO).

Both funds are based on a pair of indexes called the Palisades Global Water Index and the Palisades Water Index. The idea is the same, but with a few twists.

The funds invest in the stocks of companies that have water-related businesses. But that's where the definition gets fuzzy, as the connection between water and the fund can be pretty loose. For example, as of June 27, 2008, the Global Water Portfolio's Web site showed that nearly 9 percent of the fund was invested in information technology companies and 64 percent of the fund was invested in industrial companies.

Buyer beware: The non-water focus of this supposed water-related ETF is another example of why you should do your homework before investing in any ETF.

Chapter 15

Timing Currencies and Related Markets

*T*he globalization of the economy has increased the links between bonds, stocks, currencies, and commodities and has given market timers opportunities to time multiple markets simultaneously. Doing so is not always an easy act to pull off. And it's certainly not for beginners, as it does require a good amount of knowledge about how markets work — independently and with one another.

Yet, as you gain experience, you start to see how intermarket analysis and cross-market trading can have a place in your strategic bag of tricks.

In this chapter, I show you how to time multiple markets at once and how to make it work for you. First, I go into details of the foreign exchange markets, and then I plug in some techniques that help you formulate strategies that involve bonds, stocks, and commodities.

As with much of this book, the focus is on timing via ETFs, although the analysis techniques can be applicable to any market.

Diving into the Currency Markets

The currency markets are among the fastest growing segments of the financial markets. In fact, the currency markets are as deep a set of markets as any on the planet and feature billions of dollars trading hands every few hours.

You can trade currencies via futures, the spot market, and — increasingly — by using ETFs and mutual funds. ETFs have become my favorite vehicle for currency trading, as they trade as easily as stocks through online brokers while still offering the opportunity to capture the overall trend of the currency markets. (I cover the spot market in great detail in the section "The spot market rules the roost" later in this chapter.) Thanks to ETFs, I can participate in a market that I truly love without having to suffer the hair-raising action that can go along with directly trading currencies and currency futures.

Don't fool yourself into thinking that by using ETFs or mutual funds you can stop being careful and vigilant. These trading vehicles can be just as treacherous as the real currencies if you're not on the ball.

What makes currencies move

Contrary to popular belief, currency markets don't move on the whim of some cabal that hides in a dark room and looks at crystal balls. Instead, currencies move based on the perception of traders about a handful of key factors, both internal and external to the markets, as well as factors related to the nation that the currency represents and the relationships between countries on multiple levels, both economic and political.

Internal factors are usually related to levels of control exerted by each country on its economy and currency. The most glaring example of a controlled currency that plays in the big leagues is the Chinese yuan, which the Chinese government maintains in a narrow trading band, although it's a band that has been expanding steadily for some time and may be abandoned altogether at some point in the future. The Chinese government began loosening the trading band on the yuan in July of 2005 by removing the currency's *peg* (link) to the U.S. dollar. Other global currencies, especially those from emerging markets and less developed countries, are controlled by their respective governments.

External factors have to do with trade issues or the market's perception of the political and economic situation in a given country. Of course, wars and natural disasters also qualify as potential market-moving events.

But aside from those hazy and nebulous-sounding factors, the most important influences on currency values are the following:

- **Interest rates *in* the country and *relative to* other countries in the world:** Higher interest rates attract traders. For example, if the Federal Reserve were to raise interest rates tomorrow, the U.S. dollar would likely rise in value, especially against currencies where rates were on the way down, or where they stayed the same.

- **Inflation rates across the world and in the issuing country:** Countries with higher inflation rates tend to have weaker currencies unless the central bank is raising interest rates to fight inflation.

- **Budget status:** The better any country's budget looks, the better the effect on the currency, although this isn't a hard and fast rule because you have to factor in traders' perceptions. Yes, the value of a currency can be that subjective.

- **Political stability:** Turmoil within governments can make turmoil for exchange rates. For example, the dollar suffered a good deal during the Clinton administration when the Monica Lewinsky scandal took place, even though the economy was in good shape. The same was true in the Bush years, where the U.S. economy was fairly strong for several stretches, but the dollar kept falling because of the unpopular Bush presidency and the Iraq war.

- **Foreign policy:** Trouble abroad can cause fluctuations in exchange rates. Unpopular events such as the war in Iraq were negative for the U.S. dollar.

- **Domestic policy:** National issues and the resulting taxation and health policies of the government, as well as other fiscal issues in a country, can cause currencies to gain or lose ground.

The spot market rules the roost

Before you start your currency timing adventure, you should know a bit about the basics that influence your ETF trades. Much of what happens in the currency markets starts in the spot market where most of the currency trading is done. (A fair amount of currency trading also is done in the futures markets, but for the context of this chapter, I talk mostly about the spot market.)

The *spot market* is a big market that is controlled nearly exclusively by large banks and corporations. And here are some of the key facts that you should take home before you time this potentially profitable market:

✔ Currency trading (spot and futures) happens continuously Monday through Friday, starting in New Zealand and following the sun to Sydney, Tokyo, Hong Kong, Singapore, Bahrain, Frankfurt, Geneva, Zurich, Paris, London, New York, Chicago, and Los Angeles before starting again.

✔ Over-the-counter trades are made directly between two individuals or institutions, usually by phone. They account for about one-third of all transactions in the foreign market. These are transactions that you and I can't see but that may have an effect on the market.

✔ The *interbank market,* where most of the transactions in the spot market take place between banks and corporations, is the action that you see when you look at a quote board for currency rates. This is a network of banks that serve as intermediaries, market makers, or wholesalers. Traders buy and sell currencies in this market, where trades are settled within two days. This two-day settlement is a tool of fairness to both parties because it allows enough time for both sides to put the money together and exchange it.

✔ The *retail market* is where you trade if you trade currencies directly — without using ETFs.

✔ ETF trades are based on the cumulative sum of trades that affect each currency the ETF owns. In other words, the prices and behavior of the ETFs that you choose mirror the trend of the underlying currencies.

ETFs are the best way for nonprofessionals to trade forex. These funds let you capture the overall trend of the markets without having to open new accounts or learn too many new procedural tricks. Direct trading is something to consider after you gain experience, but ETFs are the superior mode of transport for those with less experience. Among your options are

✔ **Currency Shares ETFs,** which invest directly in the underlying currencies and are designed to reflect the value of those currencies in U.S. dollars. They're managed by Rydex Investments, a well-known mutual fund company that specializes in providing vehicles for market timing.

✔ **WisdomTree Dreyfus Funds,** which aren't currency funds but ETFs that invest in money market funds; those funds hold foreign currencies in the denomination indicated by the fund's name (WisdomTree Dreyfus Indian Rupee Fund, for example). When you buy one of these ETFs, you're actually buying an income-producing fund in a foreign currency that's valued in U.S. dollars. In other words, these funds are direct plays on higher interest rates in foreign countries and actually give you the opportunity to make money when interest rates rise in those countries.

Finding the Nuts and Bolts of Foreign Exchange

As with any specialized field, foreign exchange (forex) has its own language, and the faster you learn the language, the more plentiful your chances for success. First, remember this guiding principle: Foreign exchange transactions are exchanges between two *pairings* of currencies, with each currency having its own International Standardization Organization (ISO) code.

The ISO code identifies the country and its currency using three letters, like a stock symbol on an exchange. The pairing uses the ISO codes for each participating currency. For example, USD/GBP pairs the U.S. dollar and the British pound. In this case, the dollar is the *base currency,* and the pound is the *secondary currency.* Displayed the other way, GBP/USD, the pound is the base currency, and the dollar is secondary.

My favorite term in the currency markets is the *pip,* the smallest move any currency can make. It means the same thing as a *tick* for other asset classes. Incidentally, whether Gladys Knight trades currencies anywhere, with or without The Pips, remains unknown.

There are four major currency pairings:

- EUR/USD = euro/U.S. dollar
- GBP/USD = British pound sterling/U.S. dollar (Another name for this pair is *cable,* from the days when a trans-Atlantic cable was used to coordinate and communicate exchange rates between the dollar and the pound.)
- USD/JPY = U.S. dollar/Japanese yen
- USD/CHF = U.S. dollar/Swiss franc

A foreign exchange quote tells you how much of one currency can be exchanged for another. A quote that reads GBP/USD = 1.7550, means you can exchange 1 British pound for 1.7550 dollars. The base currency in this case is the pound; it's the currency that you're either buying or selling.

When you trade currencies you're actually doing two things simultaneously: buying one currency and selling another. Currency trades in the spot market are based on lots of 100,000 units of the base currency. Whether you're buying or selling, you're required to deposit a margin, which usually is 1 to

5 percent of the entire value of the trade. If you buy 100,000 GBP/USD at 1.7550, your margin is in dollars, while the seller of sterling, the trader who is buying your dollars, reciprocates by putting down an appropriate margin in sterling.

Coring Down on Your Charts

Think of long-term charts as your guides to the prevailing trend in currencies. But remember that there can be trends within trends. You need to use charts that illustrate multiple time frames to help figure out the most tradable trend at any time. In this section, I give you tips for finding the tradable trend and the subtrends within it.

Finding the tradable trend

To find the most tradable trend, I use a technique I call the *zoom lens.* With the help of Figure 15-1, I take you through the steps of my zoom lens technique:

1. **Examine your longer-term chart.**

   Figure 15-1 gives you a roughly 18-month snapshot that shows the Euro in a rising trend and a nice consolidation pattern developing. But that's not the whole picture. Looking at the market in October 2007, you see that FXE delivered a nice chart breakout. I labeled that entry point "Buy here" in Figure 15-1. But if you weren't looking at the currencies during that time period and decided to look at FXE in May 2008, you found a different situation, a sideways market. That's when the Zoom Lens technique becomes most helpful.

2. **Take a closer snapshot of a smaller time frame.**

   On the right side of Figure 15-1, you see a totally different picture, that of a market moving sideways after a long rally that started in October 2007. What looks like a nice, smooth, consolidation is a disorderly trading range that — at best — would be difficult to trade, unless you magnified the picture and can see what's happening more closely.

3. **Use the information in the charts to formulate your strategy.**

   If you caught the rally early (October 2007) you could use the close-up chart on the right of figure 15-1 to figure out your next strategy. In this case, you have two choices. The easy one, for short-term traders, would be to avoid the Euro Currency Trust (FXE) until it makes up its mind. For long-term traders, who got in during the breakout in October, you can use the close-up picture to pick an exit point or to reduce your exposure. If you're looking to do some shorter-term trading, I added some buy and sell points based on the trading range that I defined with the horizontal trendlines.

Figure 15-1:
The
Currency
Shares Euro
Trust (FXE),
two views.

Chart courtesy of StockCharts.com.

Keeping your perspective

The currency market can be daunting, but one saving grace is that a long-term trend, once established, tends to stick around for a while. Even though you want to take advantage of every reasonable trading opportunity, including some short-term trading when the market pulls back on occasion, the long-term trend is really your number-one determinant of strategy and trading direction.

When a currency changes trend, such as when it breaks below a long rising trend line, you must consider that the long-term trend has changed direction. And even though the trend may not change every time this situation occurs, you have to take it seriously. In fact, some markets return to the original trend soon after a break, while others continue along the counter-trend for long periods. Figure 15-2 shows you two counter trend rallies along the very long down trend for the U.S. Dollar Index. These counter-trend rallies were both worth trading.

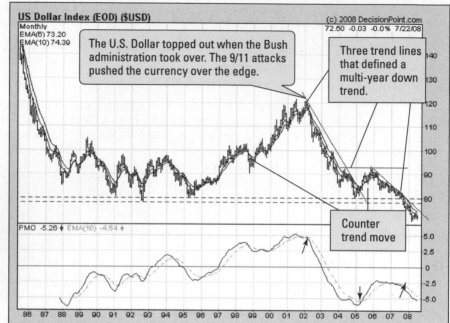

US Dollar Index (EOD) ($USD)   (c) 2008 DecisionPoint.com
Monthly   72.50 -0.03 -0.0% 7/22/08
EMA(6) 73.20
EMA(10) 74.39

The U.S. Dollar topped out when the Bush administration took over. The 9/11 attacks pushed the currency over the edge.

Three trend lines that defined a multi-year down trend.

PMO -5.26 ↓ EMA(10) -4.54 ↓

Counter trend move

Figure 15-2:
Long-term
view of the
U.S. Dollar
Index.

86 87 88 89 90 91 92 93 94 95 96 97 98 99 00 01 02 03 04 05 06 07 08

Chart courtesy of Decisionpoint.com.

Take your long-term charts seriously, and use your Zoom Lens technique but remain flexible. Markets can't go in one direction forever. If things have been moving in one direction for a while, expect a reversal. When you spot crossovers in indicators like the price momentum oscillator or the MACD (see Chapter 4), and you see a change in the general trend, the time is right to make decisions.

Currency markets are volatile by nature. Any reversal in the direction of prices can be big enough to change the long-term trend. Markets can also remain in trading ranges for years. Check out Figure 15-2 and note that the U.S. Dollar Index stayed in a trading range for 10 years (1988–1998). And if this sounds as if I'm saying that anything is possible, it's because that's the truth about these market, and it's why as a timer you need to be on your toes.

Pay attention to details. You give your timing a real boost if you understand the behavior of each currency. Check out the book *Currency Trading For Dummies* (Wiley) by Mark Galant to get a firm grasp on the currencies.

Timing the subtrends

Here are strategies you can use when you spot a trend within the big trend, especially when the overall long-term trend remains in one direction but a counter trend that lasts several months or longer develops:

✔ Go short when the long-term chart is pointing up but a counter trend move to the down side develops. Figure 15-2 highlights a counter trend move in the U.S. Dollar Index that lasted from 2004 to 2006. During that time, unless you had a very long term view of the market, and were very patient, which almost no one who times currencies does or is, you would have lost money by being short the dollar, or long another currency. During that time it would have been better to be long the dollar, short another currency, or both.

This works when your chart analysis includes long-term charts, such as Figure 15-1. If you don't see the big picture, you end up making short-term decisions that can be costly.

✔ Look for opportunities to go short when the long-term trend is up. This was possible for a short period of time during 1998, because the counter trend move lasted several months, as Figure 15-2 highlights.

Meeting the Major Currencies

Each currency has its own personality that reflects the general characteristics of the country that it represents and the market's perception of the amalgam of political, economical, and interactive characteristics of the country. For example, the trading patterns in the British pound and the Swiss franc are different from those of the euro and the U.S. dollar. So as you get more advanced in your trading, you can begin to factor in the specifics of each individual currency and how they can affect your trading. In this section, I introduce you to each individual foreign currency.

The U.S. dollar

The dollar, although much maligned as a major player after September 11, 2001, remains the world's reserve currency, meaning that the big deals around the world are done in dollars, and the major commodities still trade in terms of dollars. (The Euro has gained significant ground and in many places around the world is the currency of choice.)

The Federal Reserve Board introduced the U.S. dollar index in March 2003. As things stand in 2008, traders, politicians, and anyone interested in these things use the U.S. dollar index as the simplest way to gauge the overall trend of the dollar. The index is well recognized and is widely quoted in the press and on quote services.

The U.S. dollar index was modified at the inception of the euro and is weighted as follows:

- Euro: 57.6 percent
- Japanese yen: 13.6 percent
- British pound: 11.9 percent
- Canadian dollar: 9.1 percent
- Swedish krona: 4.2 percent
- Swiss franc: 3.6 percent

The euro

The euro is a good vehicle for trading from a timer's viewpoint because its direction closely follows the twists and turns of Europe's central bank policies, especially with regard to interest rates.

The general trend of the euro, in most instances, depends on the direction of the European central banks' intentions regarding interest rates. The tendency toward raising or lowering interest rates is based solely on the level of inflation in the European economy and includes an inflation target as the centerpiece for decision-making on whether to raise or lower rates. No matter what else happens in Europe, even in the midst of very slow economic growth, if inflation is rising above the central bank's inflation growth rate, the bank finds a way to raise interest rates to fight inflation.

This is in contrast to the United States, where the Federal Reserve has to fight inflation but seek full employment, making the dollar more vulnerable to the employment rate and the direction of the economy. In other words, if the European economy is weakening, the euro is likely to remain strong until the economy is so weak that the central bank is forced to lower interest rates.

During the time period shown in Figure 15-1, the European economy was starting to flounder, with consumer and business confidence falling on a fairly regular basis, budget deficits climbing, and joblessness on the rise. But the euro did little more than move sideways, albeit in a volatile range. This was because the European central bank continued to tell the markets that their number-one fight was against inflation and that their general tendency was toward raising interest rates.

The UK pound sterling

The pound moves actively against the dollar and the euro, which means that you have numerous opportunities to trade both pairs (GBP/USD and USD/GBP, if you're using the real currency). If you're trading ETFs, you should concentrate on the pound's action against the dollar by using the Currency Shares British Pound Sterling Trust ETF (FXB). Figure 15-3 shows that the pound sterling is somewhere between the strength of the U.S. dollar and the euro during the time period depicted. And this makes perfect sense, because the United Kingdom is a pivotal nation as it bridges the economical, geographical, and ideological divide between the United States and Europe.

Economically, the United Kingdom is more free-market oriented than Europe, and it tends to share a more common set of views with the United States on many issues. At the same time, the United Kingdom can't totally disassociate itself from Europe, given its history and its geography. The upshot is a currency affected by the economies and the politics of the two continents to which its destiny is so closely related.

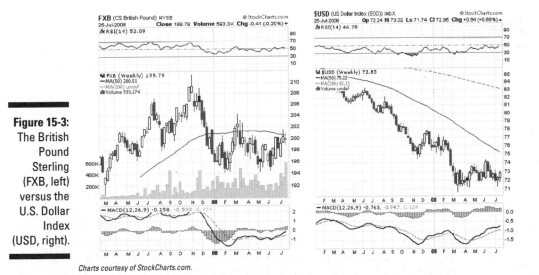

Figure 15-3:
The British
Pound
Sterling
(FXB, left)
versus the
U.S. Dollar
Index
(USD, right).

Charts courtesy of StockCharts.com.

The Australian dollar

The Australian dollar was among the strongest currencies in the world during the period shown in Figure 15-4. And its strength was quite sensible at the time, as the Australian economy has a strong dependency on natural resources, gold and iron ore, as well as oil. The Australian central bank was hinting at raising interest rates during this time as inflation was creeping into the system.

Figure 15-4:
The
Currency
Shares ETF
Japanese
Yen (FXY,
left) and the
Currency
Shares ETF
Australian
Dollar (FXA).

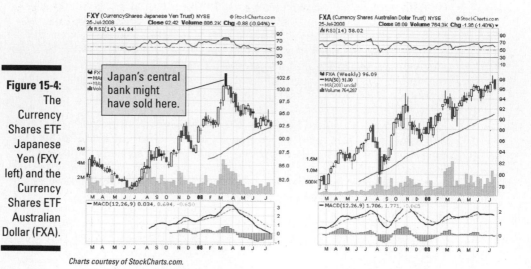

Charts courtesy of StockCharts.com.

The Japanese yen

The Japanese government manipulates the yen, keeping it at a low level in order to ensure that exports from Japan are attractive to foreign buyers. Any time the Yen strengthens, the government sells it on the open market. And that's quite evident in Figure 15-4, where the Yen strengthened against the dollar in March but ran into some heavy selling. The Japanese central bank may well have taken some part in the decline of the Yen into July.

Japan has not fully recovered from its economy's crash in 1989, and the lasting economic effects of that financial crisis have forced its government to keep the Yen's value low. The main purpose of maintaining a weak currency is to keep the Japanese export machinery operational. Over the long term, however, a weaker currency will hurt Japan's chance of achieving a lasting recovery.

The Swiss franc

Like the U.S. dollar, the Swiss franc is considered a *reserve currency* — one that's more reliable than other currencies and holds its value better during difficult times. It tends to attract traders and investors during periods of global crisis.

During some periods, the Swiss franc can move along with the price of gold as traders look for refuge. This correlation is clearly evident in Figure 15-5, where the action in the Swiss franc ETF (FXF) and the price of gold, as represented by the StreetTracks Gold shares ETF (GLD), are nearly identical.

Figure 15-5: The Currency Shares ETF Swiss Franc (FXF) and the Street-Tracks Gold Trust ETF (GLD) moving in the generally same direction.

Charts courtesy of StockCharts.com.

The strength of the Swiss franc is based on three traditional expectations in the market:

✔ **Reliable economic fundamentals:** Switzerland tends to have low inflation, balanced budgets, and stable trade, with no major deficits on the books. But what makes the franc most attractive is the Swiss banking system, well recognized for its service of wealthy clients and its secrecy.

✔ **Gold reserves:** The Swiss franc, unlike other global currencies, is still backed by gold, because Switzerland's gold reserves significantly exceed the amount of currency it has in circulation. That's one of the reasons that the franc often moves in a similar trend to gold; traders perceive both as safe havens.

✔ **Little political influence:** Switzerland's neutral politics enables the country and its central bank to operate in a near vacuum ruled only by the rate of inflation. Since December 1999, the Swiss National Bank changed; it now targets inflation as its main catalyst toward raising or lowering interest rates. The central bank's goal is to adjust interest rates so that inflation doesn't grow faster than 2 percent per year. In this way, the franc is similar to the euro. Note how currencies with inflation targets underlying policy seem to be stronger than the freewheeling U.S. dollar.

Part IV
Timing the Sectors

The 5th Wave   By Rich Tennant

In this part . . .

In this section, you dive into sectors of the stock market — everything from financial stocks to the drug and biotech area and beyond — and find out how to get the big picture for these smaller segments. I take you through the techniques that lead to profits in the sector arena.

Chapter 16

The Timer's Dream: Sector Investing

Sector investing — the practice of investing in one area of the market, such as health care — is to market timing as pitching is to winning baseball and defense is to capturing the NBA championship. In fact, sector investing was made for timers. The natural fit occurs because sectors are primarily trend-driven areas of the market, and market timing is all about identifying the major trend and trading with it until it reverses.

For example, the entire market could be in one of its worst bear runs of all time; even so, you can almost count on one or two sectors to be in rip-roaring bull markets. During those periods, timers are likely to be doing better than those who trade the whole market, as they're willing to be long the sector trend (own shares or ETFs with the expectations of higher prices) while monitoring the market, or even shorting the market (betting on falling prices).

You can't count on one area of the market bucking the overall trend, but in some bear markets for most stocks, areas such as metals, technology, and energy sometimes buck the overall negative trend and become excellent areas to trade separately from the overall trend.

In this chapter, I show you the basics of timing individual sectors of the market — without having to worry about how the rest of the market is acting.

Defining Sector Timing

Sector timing means that you're trading a single area of the market — basically, putting all your eggs in one basket. And although this practice seems to go directly against the conventional wisdom that preaches portfolio diversification, sector investing can be an excellent way of diversifying your portfolio: Your basket may be fairly broad, such as Chinese stocks, European stocks, or emerging markets. Or it can be something narrower in scope, such as health care, technology, or energy stocks.

You can further divide sector timing into subsector or industry timing. For example, sometimes health insurance stocks do well while drug and hospital stocks do not. In that case, owning broad assets in health care doesn't make sense. Concentrating on the area of health care that's doing well — health insurers, in this example — is a better option.

Sector timing requires your utmost attention as well as your active participation in the markets. If you like to look at your portfolio once a year, sector timing isn't for you. It's aggressive, interactive, and highly participatory trading. It can be very dangerous (or very profitable) in different circumstances.

The key to success is becoming familiar with the basic principles of sector investing, including

- **Technical analysis:** Chart reading and analysis of trends, momentum, and potential trend reversals are crucial.

- **Routine:** Get a good analysis routine and stick to it. You've got to get a groove in place and do it every day or as often as possible. The more charts you analyze, the better your chances of finding good timing opportunities.

- **Preparation:** Learn everything that you can about how individual sectors and the companies within them behave. Doing so helps you make better trading decisions, such as whether you should shotgun the whole sector (buy all the stocks in it, such as through an ETF or a mutual fund) or whether you should pick only the select few good-looking stocks in the area.

- **Vigilance:** Stay skeptical; never take anything for granted. A nasty surprise that can cost you big bucks and make your blood pressure rise could be right around the corner.

Be ready for a lot of volatility. Sector investing is very different from traditional diversified investing. When you invest in one single sector of the market, your risk rises. The chance that all asset classes will fall at the same time is slim, which makes a diversified portfolio more stable overall. But all the stocks in a single area can rise and fall on a piece of news that deals with only one or two stocks in the sector. Wall Street extends the net to others, and all the stocks in that sector hit the skids simultaneously. A killer for you if you aren't diversified.

When you time individual sectors, trading along with the market is less important than concentrating on the price action of the sector in which you're investing, because you're focusing only on the performance of that individual area. I'm not telling you to ignore the market. However, if the market is heading in one direction but a particular sector is heading in another, you might want to consider going along with the particular trend in that sector.

Here are some basic characteristics of sector investing:

- **There is always a "buzz."** A sector rally is almost always driven by new scientific, social, or financial trends specific to that sector and its underlying industries. Examples are the buzz in the 1990s that was created by the human genome as well as the breakout of the Internet sector. In the early 21st century we had the solar stocks and the ethanol sectors rally significantly along with the traditional energy sector because of the rising price of crude oil. Other amazing sector trends of the past two decades include Chinese stocks, emerging market stocks, and steel stocks. As a timer, you need to be aware of the emerging themes and stories as early as possible.

- **Wall Street always promotes the story.** If you're a cynic (Wall Street lingo describing an experienced investor), the buzz seems like more Wall Street nonsense — another promotion to entrap the unwary. You're right. That's probably how the story will end. But if enough people believe the story, there is probably a lot of money to be made along the way until they figure out that the story is either false or that it has run its course. And the truth is that a fair amount of the time, people believe a story and buy stock, which in turns increases volume. After enough people get on the train, the trend picks up a life of its own, and off you go.

- **Eventually the story that Wall Street has been hyping hits Main Street.** For example, Wall Street was excited about Apple's iPhone for a good while before Main Street finally got its hand on it. But the market didn't wait for the sales of the new hardware to hit records before buying Apple's shares. As the buzz built, the price of the stock rose. The same thing was evident in biotech when the human genome was being deciphered. As long as the genome deciphering was in process, investors stood a good chance of making money in biotech. After the human genome was deciphered, the selling in biotech stocks followed.

- **You can make money on the way up and on the way down.** Just as any bubble heats up, it eventually cools down. That means that you can make money when a particular sector rises by owning individual stocks, mutual funds, or ETFs that specialize in it, and as it falls, when you can short sell the sector, usually via ETFs or individual stocks.

Analyzing the Markets with a Sector Approach

I like to compartmentalize every aspect of my life and my trading. And I like to use the top-down approach, starting with a very broad picture and coning it down to the most elemental aspects. This approach works well for sector investing, too: Analyze the overall market first, and then examine individual sectors.

For example, when I look at the market, I look at the overall performance and trend of the Dow Jones Industrial Average, the S&P 500, The Nasdaq Composite Index, the Nasdaq 100 Index, and the Russell 2000 Index of small stocks. Each of these indexes tells me something different, which enables me to build a composite picture of the overall trend of the market. Here's what I mean:

- The **Dow Jones Industrial Average** gives me a glimpse into the largest blue-chip stocks in the market universe. I think of these as the market's generals, and I like to see them leading the charge, or at least keeping up with the overall trend of the market.

- The **S&P 500** is like a larger version of the Dow Jones Industrials and a good composite picture of how the broad market of blue-chip stocks is performing. I use the performance of the S&P 500 as a confirmation of the action in the Dow Jones Industrial average.

- The **Nasdaq Composite** gives me a glimpse into the technology sector, and to some degree the small-company sector of the market, especially the smaller banking stocks. But the Nasdaq Composite is heavily weighted toward technology, and that's the primary focus of any analysis of this index.

- The **Nasdaq 100** is a good way to core down the largest stocks in the Nasdaq Composite as it looks at the largest 100 non-financial sector stocks in the index.

- Many blue-chip stocks get their start in the **Russell 2000 Index.** Small companies with strong growth characteristics make their home here.

Defining the Overall Trend

By analyzing the overall market before I go into analyzing sectors, I get a better idea about what to look for in my sector analysis. Above all, I look for strength and momentum — in the markets and in individual sectors. That means that when the market is rising, I'm looking to invest in the strongest sectors of the market. And if I'm buying individual stocks, I'm looking to buy the strongest stocks in each individual sector.

Timing is about two things: buying or selling as the new trend is emerging and staying with the trend as long as possible. Your ability to get into positions as early as possible is crucial. And the way you do that is to analyze the markets on a daily basis and to have a good idea about where each area of the market needs to go in order to trigger your entry point.

An excellent grasp of the concepts of support, resistance, and trend reversals is important for your success. (Turn to Chapter 4 to refresh your memory about these topics.)

Just remember the following when you start timing the sectors:

✔ Analyze the markets daily.

✔ Record key support and resistance levels for each individual sector index that you follow.

✔ Decide ahead of time where your entry point will be.

✔ Have a list of ETFs or individual stocks that you will purchase or short, depending on the market's trend ready before your entry point is reached.

✔ Decide ahead of time where your exit point will be. You do this by adjusting sell stops as the market moves higher in long positions and by adjusting buy stops if you're selling the market short. See Chapter 1 for more on buy stops and sell stops.

Building — and Watching — Your Sector List

In order to get started in sector timing, develop a list of sector indexes that you monitor frequently. These indexes will be your guide as to which sectors to choose from for your trades.

There is no real magic to what sectors to place on the list, but at the very least, you want to include the energy, technology, financial, pharmaceuticals, biotech, and metals sectors — a broad cross-section of sectors for getting started. As you get comfortable with these, you can add other sectors and some subsectors, which are more specific areas of the groups in your original list.

I check my list on a daily basis, and I recommend the same for you, although you can develop your own routine. The least amount of monitoring that I would suggest is once per week.

Find at least one ETF that tracks the performance of each of the indexes on your list. You can find a list of indexes and ETFs on the American Stock Exchange Web site, www.amex.com. The site's left sidebar has all the links you need to reach the ETF lists. The Nasdaq Web site (www.nasdaq.com) and the Philadelphia Stock Exchange Web site (www.phlx.com) also have complete index listings. Some indexes list the individual component stocks; others don't.

Don't try to learn everything about every single sector at once. As with any type of trading or investing that you do, you'll find that you have a greater affinity for some sectors than others. That's perfectly normal and could be to your advantage, as the more you know and understand about any one particular area of the markets, the more likely you'll be successful at timing. Becoming proficient at trading one sector before moving on to try to master another is a good idea. You also want to home in on sectors that are doing well at any one time.

After you build your list of the sector indexes you plan to monitor, the next step is to analyze it systematically, looking for timing ideas. Get into the following habits when checking your sector index list:

- ✔ **Look at your index charts frequently and determine the primary trend of each sector.** When the trend is up, you want to be long (betting on the up side). When the trade is down, you want to be out of that sector or shorting it (betting that it will fall in price). You can short ETFs or individual stocks in the sector.

   Some ETFs specialize in short selling individual sectors of the market, and you can use them instead of short selling ETF shares for any one sector.

- ✔ **Determine whether the trend is in an early stage, somewhere in the middle, or late in the game.** This is not always easy to figure out. Figure 16-1 shows the Amex Oil Index (XOI) over a decade — an example of a long-standing trend, as the energy markets started rallying in 2001, after the September 11, 2001, terrorist attacks, and oil prices rallied from low single digits to nearly $120 per barrel in April 2008.

Figure 16-1:
The Amex Oil Index (XOI) in a long-term up trend with resistance near 1,600.

Chart courtesy of BigCharts.com.

When a trend has been in place for a long time, consider the following:

- **How long has the major trend been in place?** In the example in Figure 16-1, you see a five-year rising trend. At some point it will have to take a break or will reverse, even if only for a while.

- **What has the trend been doing of late?** The trend line that traverses the chart in Figure 16-1 clearly shows that the trend remains to the up side. But it also shows that the index has run into overhead resistance and that the sector has been increasingly volatile, given the wide trading range that started in 2007. The latter is a sign that a change in trend is possible and that there might be better areas in which to invest.

- **What are different sectors doing?** As you scan through all your sector charts you'll notice sectors that are acting differently from the Oil Index. Figure 16-2 is a perfect example: The Amex Computer Technology Index (XCI) was forming a multi-year base (moving sideways) during the period when big money was moving into energy stocks. This is a good find because even though money was moving into energy, the technology stocks were breaking above a down trend line, which meant that money was moving into tech stocks, giving you another sector to consider.

- **What can you determine from the undervalued sector?** Do further homework on that sector. A good way to do so is to look at a shorter-term chart. Figure 16-3 shows that XCI has crossed above a down trend line. If you had looked for news right about this time you would have seen that demand for semiconductor chips was starting to rise, and that some technology companies, such as IBM, were forecasting improvement for their business in the future.

 **What's your plan of attack?** Research your corresponding ETF, or stocks in the sector, and start making decisions. I tell you more about how to go about this in Chapters 17 through 20 and in the sections in this chapter titled "Analyzing Index Components" and "Getting Fundamental Not Sentimental As You Time Sectors."

Figure 16-2:
The Amex Computer Index (XCI) forms a long-term base in this decade-long view.

Chart courtesy of BigCharts.com.

Figure 16-3:
The Amex Computer Index (XCI), a 12-month view nearing an intermediate-trend change.

Chart courtesy of BigCharts.com.

Analyzing Index Components

Aside from using ETFs to time sectors, you can also time individual stocks within sectors, which is a useful technique when one or two stocks in any area of the market are doing better than others in the related industry. That's why it pays to look inside each index, in order to see whether one or two stocks may be stronger than the rest of the sector.

The Amex Computer Index (XCI) is a diversified technology index. It has 30 components from multiple subsectors of technology, ranging from Apple Inc. to IBM, Intel, and lesser-known names such as Network Appliances and Computer Associates. Thus, it offers a pretty broad picture of the entire spectrum of high-tech stocks. By scanning all 30 charts, one after another, you can get an idea about which members of the index are doing well and find the following juicy bits of information:

- ✔ Which stocks in the index are doing better individually
- ✔ Which subsectors might be doing better than other areas of technology
- ✔ How broad is the advance in the technology arena

For example, when I looked at the 30 stocks in the index as I wrote this chapter, I saw two stocks that were breaking out (moving powerfully higher after moving sideways for some time) — Adobe Systems (ADBE) and Symantec (SYMC) — and seven charts that looked fairly good, including the two breakouts.

I also noted that most of the stocks in the index were either moving sideways or had just started to move higher. Another important tidbit: Of the stocks that were moving higher, several were running into resistance levels, while others looked to be struggling just a bit.

The failure of so many stocks at resistance levels suggested that technology might be a sector where it would be best to consider owning only those stocks that were acting well, and not necessarily one where I would want to make a sector-wide bet. The lack of sector-wide strength also told me that this would be a good area to keep an eye on for some time, as it could offer significant opportunities in the future, especially as other stocks in the index might start moving higher.

Figure 16-4 shows the break out in Adobe Systems. Note that the break out came on rising volume, and that Adobe broke out above its 20-, 50-, and 200-day moving averages. The stock had previously broken above a down trend line.

Figure 16-4:
Adobe
Systems
(ADBE)
breaks out.

Chart courtesy of AskResearch.com.

Stocks that break above down trend lines and then move above key moving average resistance levels in rising volume are *under accumulation,* which means that buyers are steadily moving in. These are the strong stocks that you want to own as a timer, because they often rally a fairly good amount in a relatively short period of time, such as a few days to a few weeks.

Getting Fundamental Not Sentimental As You Time Sectors

Market timers are not known for their reliance on the fundamentals of a sector or a stock. But if you're going to be successful as a timer, you need to know the basics of each sector that you're putting your money into.

Here are the basic questions to ask before you start timing individual sectors:

✔ **What are the laws of supply and demand in the industry or sector?** Each sector has its own general supply and demand equation. The financial sector is dependent on interest rates and the business cycle. Technology usually depends on the number of new gadgets available. The drug sector depends on the status of each individual company's product pipeline. And energy depends on seasonal demand and the economic cycle. Become familiar with this dynamic in all sectors in which you'll be putting your money.

✔ **What are the cycles in the sector and in which stage of the current one is it?** Each sector has a behavior cycle, and even cycles within the cycles. Both are due to the supply and demand for the products that the industry provides, and also the overall economic climate. One example is the housing sector. Demand for housing always exists. But as the subprime mortgage crisis showed, the cycles can get exaggerated, and when the boom busts, the ensuing crisis can be devastating. Look for historical events and compare them to the current situation. Look at your index charts, and look at individual components. Look for similarities and differences between past and present.

✔ **Do all stocks in the sector respond in the same way to external and internal factors?** Some sectors do experience fairly equal movement of most of their stocks in tandem. This is more common in the energy, metals, and financial sectors, and some subsectors in technology act the same way. For example, if the earnings news is good or bad for one or two major oil companies, the entire sector tends to fall, at least in the short term. The reaction can be subtle too, as in the technology area where bad news in semiconductors doesn't always translate into poor performance for software, although it can cross over to some areas of the hardware sector.

✔ **What key metrics or indicators do investors watch?** Individual sectors tend to have key metrics associated with them. Look for key reports, usually provided by the private industry groups. The Semiconductor Industry Association, for example, publishes a monthly report called the book-to-bill ratio, a measure of orders.

My favorite is the book-to-bill ratio in the semiconductor industry. This is a fractional measure of how many orders are on the books for how many orders are being shipped. When the number is above 1.0, the number of orders is greater than the number of shipments. This is bullish (positive); it means that companies are ordering more product than they're receiving, which means that sales for the product at the consumer or corporate level are growing and that demand is likely to remain robust. Bull markets in technology are fueled by robust book-to-bill ratios.

✔ **How economically sensitive is this sector?** This important question is applicable to most areas of the stock market. To answer it, figure out how the economic cycle affects any particular sector. I give you more details on doing so in the chapters that cover each sector (Chapters 17 through 20). But here are some basic hints: Some sectors tend to do better during a weak economy than others. And some do fairly well no matter what, while others require a booming economy to do well.

For example, consumer stocks tend to do better than industrial stocks during periods of slower economic growth while gold stocks tend to do best toward the end of a bull market in stocks, which is when inflationary pressures tend to start moving through the economy.

✔ **How do interest rates affect this area of the market?** Interest rates are probably the most important influence on the stock market, and not all sectors respond in the same fashion. For example, financial stocks tend to do better when interest rates are in a downtrend, while generally speaking drug stocks tend to be less sensitive to interest rates.

These general tendencies usually hold up but can vary, which is why you use this kind of information as background and watch the charts to confirm your analysis.

Every cycle is different. What spurred stocks to new highs five years ago may not have any effect in the next bull market. Sector analysis, by nature, is a risky game, because when you play it, you're not diversifying your investments. Attention to detail and good planning are necessary for a successful foray into sector timing.

Chapter 17

Timing Financial Service Stocks

*T*he *financial services sector* — banks, brokers, insurance companies, and mortgage brokers — is also known as the *interest sensitive sector*. But that term is sort of a misnomer. After all, just about all stocks are interest-rate sensitive. If interest rates fall far enough, most stocks eventually rise. And if interest rates rise far enough, most stocks eventually fall.

Some particular sectors of the stock market respond more rapidly and profoundly to major moves in interest rates. Most of the time, these are companies in the financial sector, such as banks, brokerages, and mortgage companies. The shares of these companies are particularly sensitive to the actions of central banks, especially when it comes to the direction of interest rates.

The pure financial services industry provides the candidates for this chapter. But before you get too cozy thinking that this is only about banks and brokers, consider that a lot of large conglomerates have significant portions of their businesses in financial services. Among the largest are General Motors (GM) and General Electric (GE). The former owns GMAC Financial Services, which provides auto financing, real estate and commercial financing, and insurance. The latter owns GE Financial services. Many consumers have one or more loans through these two financial services companies.

The potential for damage to the stock of companies beyond the traditional financial services sector exists because large conglomerates like GM and GE operate businesses in many sectors of the economy. Thus, if one or more of those businesses gets hit, the whole stock gets hit. And that can have consequences beyond the stock, especially if these companies are part of major indexes, such as the S&P 500, the Nasdaq Composite, or the Dow Jones Industrial average.

In this chapter, I tell you about the pros and cons of timing the financial services sector and how you can position yourself to make money in good times and bad. The goal remains the same: using a combination of technical and fundamental analysis to time these sectors properly, with an eye toward maximizing profits and limiting risk.

The financial services area, including the banks, is a double-edged investment and timing sword. In good times, it can be lucrative. But in bad times, look out below. It pays to be a cynic. New financial concepts, such as collateralized debt obligations (CDOs), derivatives, and securities that require three or four steps in order for the holder to get paid are likely to lead to trouble at some point in the future.

When the good times are in full swing, the next crisis has been forming for some time and is likely to be around the next bend. As a market timer you need to wear two hats. The first one is that of a trend follower. The second one is the one of the skeptic. It's also a good idea to keep your eye on the possibility that a bottom could be around any bend. This is especially true when the media's hysteria hits fever pitch, such as it did with the subprime mortgage crisis in July 2008.

Indexing the Banking Sector

The best place to start looking at the interest rate sensitive sector is with the banking sector, which has two components: money-center banks and regional banks. The former are, of course, the big-name banks that do a lot of international business and provide nontraditional banking sectors, such as selling mutual funds and offering investment advice, as well as selling insurance.

The Philadelphia KBW Bank Index (BKX) is the traditional benchmark for this important group of stocks and includes some heavy-duty players in this index, with three Dow Jones Industrial Average components in the mix: Bank of America, Citigroup, and JP Morgan Chase.

The Philadelphia KBW Regional Bank Index (KRX) is the leading index for regional banks in the United States. As opposed to the BKX index, this index has 50 components and is made up of much smaller banks. These are the banks that many consider their neighborhood banks, and where a significant portion of the population does business.

Here are some basic facts about all banks:

- ✔ The basic role of the banking system in the United States — and the world — is to provide a hub for money to be moved from one destination to another. This, of course, is in the form of savings and investment capital being made available to businesses and consumers as loans and lines of credit.

- ✔ Banks are also investors in public and private ventures, but most importantly, in government, corporate, and municipal markets. Thus, banks make money by collecting fees, collecting dividends, and receiving interest from bonds as well as from loan repayment.

- ✔ Any time one or more of those revenue streams gets damaged, bank earnings fall. And any time investors sense a threat to the revenue streams, the stocks of banks and financial services companies suffer.

- ✔ Regional banks, by definition, are not as likely to be involved in international finance, and thus theoretically may be safer investments. Yet, that is not a guarantee, as the repeal of the Glass-Steagall Act (which had separated banks from brokerages, insurance companies, and other financial services companies) also blurred the lines in that sector.

Banks make money when they make responsible loans and sensible investments. Otherwise, they get in trouble and those who invest in their stocks take a bath.

Looking for trades during tough times

Figures 17-1 and 17-2 paint a grim picture of the U.S. banking sector during the subprime mortgage crisis. The charts chronicle the action in both the money-center banks and the regional banks. The huge declines, both of which started in the spring of 2007, accelerated in October of the same year as the news of the subprime mortgage crisis began to break and investors began to factor in the potential losses to the sector. As each new quarter passed, the banks continued to deliver bad news about their balance sheets, non-performing assets, and the need to increase capital from outside sources.

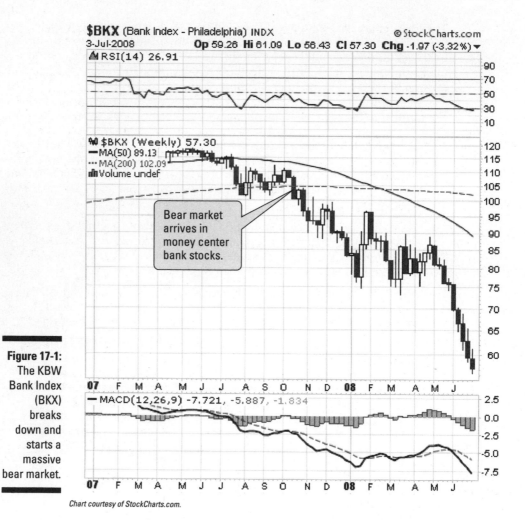

Figure 17-1:
The KBW
Bank Index
(BKX)
breaks
down and
starts a
massive
bear market.

Chart courtesy of StockCharts.com.

As the charts clearly show, the U.S. banking system lost more than 50 percent of its market capitalization in less than 12 months after the slide began to gather steam. Notice the following:

✔ Both banking indexes fell in lockstep, refuting the myth that regional banks are protected from the vagaries of money-center banks.

✔ Figures 17-1 and 17-2 show key technical turning points that served as clues that something significant was happening in the banking sector. Any time you see the banking stocks break key support, such as the breaks below the 50- and 200-day moving averages, it's a signal that the overall market may be in trouble and time to evaluate all of your open positions.

$KRX (KBW Regional Banking Index - Philadelphia) INDX © StockCharts.com
3-Jul-2008 **Op** 56.20 **Hi** 56.66 **Lo** 51.99 **Cl** 52.05 **Chg** -4.15 (-7.38%) ▼

RSI(14) 28.83

Selling accelerates as 50-day moving average crosses below 200-day line.

$KRX (Weekly) 52.05
—MA(50) 75.99
···MA(200) 91.62
Volume undef

New lows correspond to significant breaks in MACD histogram and oscillator

— MACD(12,26,9) -5.526, -4.251, -1.275

Figure 17-2:
The KBW Regional Bank Index (KRX) enters a bear market that's confirmed by trend and momentum indicators.

Chart courtesy of StockCharts.com.

You have two major opportunities when you see once-in-a-lifetime developments such as this one. One is to look inside each of the indexes, look for companies that were falling through key support levels, and sell them short. The other was to find an ETF that specializes in short-selling banking or financial stocks.

Figure 17-3 highlights the action of the UltraShort Financial ProShares ETF (SKF). This ETF came into existence in February 2007, just before the banking sector started to run into trouble. It is 200 percent leveraged, which means that it moves twice as much as the underlying stocks in the fund, both to the up side and to the down side. And that means volatility. But, if you have the guts to weather the occasional bout of selling, and the confidence to re-establish your positions when the dust clears, you can see that the overall trend of the ETF is essentially the opposite of the banking indexes.

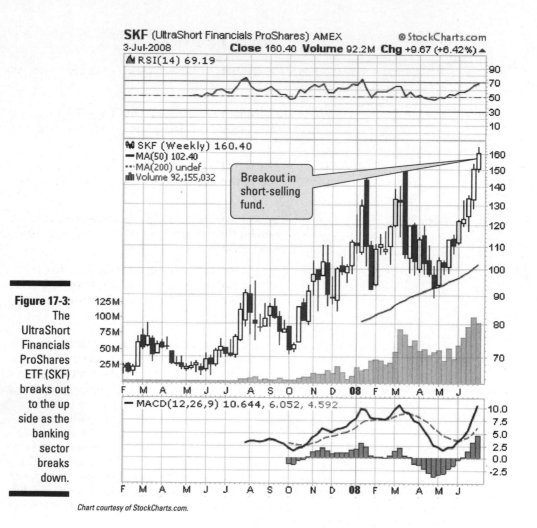

Figure 17-3:
The
UltraShort
Financials
ProShares
ETF (SKF)
breaks out
to the up
side as the
banking
sector
breaks
down.

Chart courtesy of StockCharts.com.

Because this ETF includes other financial sector stocks, it's not a pure short sale play on the banking system. Yet, as the chart clearly shows, it was a useful tool during a very difficult time for the banking system, one that offered a perfect opportunity to make money as the banking sector collapsed.

A less volatile, non-leveraged version of SKF, Short Financials ProShares (symbol SEF) became available in early 2008. Its general performance was also useful when looking to short sell the financial sector.

When the good times return

Here's what you need to know to prepare for the inevitable moment when the banking stocks rally:

- ✔ Some kind of new financial product will be unveiled that will capture the imagination of the public, the media, and the banking and investment community.

- ✔ The financial services sector will start to announce that its earnings have stabilized as the effects of the subprime mortgage crisis will have dissipated.

- ✔ The Federal Reserve will likely lower interest rates in order to stimulate the economy. Somewhere along the way the central bank will announce that the outlook for inflation has improved.

- ✔ The banking indexes will either form a base or start rallying. Look for the signs that usually accompany a major market bottom and buying opportunity. See Chapter 7 for more details about spotting important changes in the trend of the market and key sectors.

As with shorting the banking stocks, you can research and buy individual stocks from the indexes or those that turn up when you do research outside of the indexes, such as stocks featured in newsletters and Web sites that are good at what they do. See Chapter 22 for a list of good information resources.

Another sensible avenue is to look at ETFs. Several ETFs deal with the financial sector, but three of them are specific to banking stocks. They are KBW Bank ETF (KBE), KBW Regional Banking ETF (KRE), and the PowerShares Dynamic Sector Banking Portfolio ETF (PJB). All three ETFs essentially follow the general trend of the banking indexes, with PJB proving to be slightly less volatile than the other two. In a bull market, though, I would recommend following each of these ETFs closely and picking the one that tended to have the best performance on a regular basis.

Looking for Profit in the Brokerage Sector

Like the banking sector, the brokerage sector contains three distinct sub-sectors — investment banking, retail brokerage, and trading. Each sub-sector has its own role in the overall scheme of how Wall Street operates.

Investment banks are brokerage firms that specialize in making deals, whether arranging buyouts and mergers or bringing private companies public. Some of these institutions, such as Goldman Sachs, do nothing but investment banking and managing client money as their main business. Others, like Merrill Lynch, do retail investing, money management, mutual funds, and investment banking. All the major houses run hedge funds, manage money for wealthy clients, and trade for their own accounts.

Every bull market has its star firm — the one that can do no wrong, and the one that characterizes the key dynamic of the bull market. During the bull market that ran during the 2003–2008 period, it was Goldman's turn to lead the way; its forte is investment banking, and the bull market was driven by private equity funds and leveraged buyouts.

That was the factor that made Goldman the bellwether for the group. And the action in the stock was clearly a clue as to what the rest of the sector, and to some degree the market, was likely to do during this period. The company's and the stock's influence was a significant sign of investor confidence in the whole dynamic.

Goldman, as a company and a trading group, was a step ahead of the crowd during this bull market, as it cleverly diversified its assets and its business model away from just doing deals and managing money for wealthy clients. Goldman, already a large player, indeed became a business behemoth during this bull market, investing in a huge portfolio of sectors beyond the normal expected ratio of stocks and bonds. The company successfully branched out into real estate, as well as into key assets such as oil storage properties along the New York harbor, in addition to running a stable of very successful hedge funds, many of which were actually short the subprime mortgage market when the stuff hit the fan in 2007.

Figures 17-4 and 17-5 offer an excellent opportunity to analyze the dynamic between a market sector and the leader of the sector. Notice the following:

✔ The Broker Dealer Index (XBD) and Goldman topped out in the June-July 2007 time period, but Goldman actually topped out slightly ahead of the index. The fact that the number-one brokerage firm was starting to wobble was of concern, but Goldman recovered, while XBD did not. This sent a tricky message to timers On the one hand, it was good to see Goldman hold up. But on the other it made no sense to see Goldman hold up while XBD and the rest of the stock market looked top heavy.

✔ Eventually, as the charts show, the weight of the market brought Goldman shares down. Notice the technical divergence in the chart of Goldman Sachs. Even though the stock managed to make a new high, none of the oscillators (MACD or RSI) made new highs — a sign that the momentum driving prices is low. Eventually the weakness or the lack of conviction on the buy side became evident as the sellers took over and the stock broke.

✔ The RSI indicator gave a sell signal, but the index moved higher. That means that the index was getting so far ahead of itself that the buying was unreasonable. This kind of activity usually means that when the fall eventually comes it will be significant. This proved to be the case. Also notice the bearish moving average crossover as well as ability of the down trend line to keep prices from rising. These are all signs that the bears are well in control of the market.

Figure 17-4:
The Amex Broker Dealer Index (XBD) breaks down and remains below a falling trend line.

Chart courtesy of StockCharts.com.

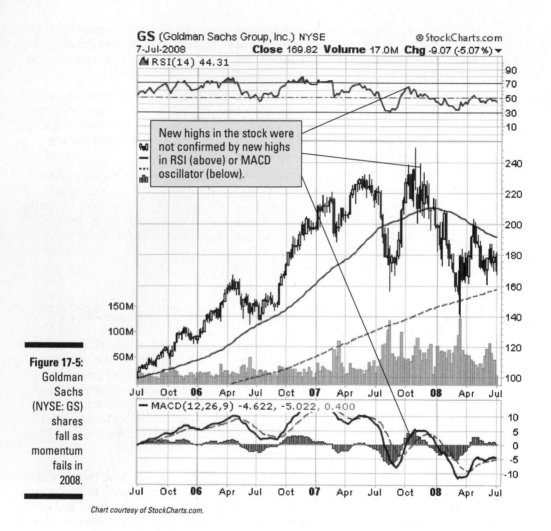

Figure 17-5:
Goldman
Sachs
(NYSE: GS)
shares
fall as
momentum
fails in
2008.

Chart courtesy of StockCharts.com.

Timing the brokerage sector is important from both an investment and an analytical point of view. As timing vehicles, brokerage stocks usually do well in a bull market. From an analytical standpoint, rallies without the brokerage stocks tend to be less robust; rising brokerage stocks signal that investors are confident in the prospects for all of Wall Street. And bull markets are pushed higher by confident investors. A lack of positive action in the broker stocks is a sign of low confidence.

When timing the brokerage stocks

✔ **Find the bellwether stock in the group.** Doing so enables you to invest in a strong stock and gives you a good clue about the overall brokerage sector and the overall market.

The bellwether is the one investment bank at the top of the heap for the current cycle — the one that has the best earnings and the highest profile, and is most mentioned. This changes every few years, but in the 2003–2008 bull market, the bellwether was Goldman Sachs.

✔ **Look for brokerage stocks to be market leaders in the early stages of a new bull market.** Traders know that when the Federal Reserve lowers interest rates far enough for a long enough period of time, brokerage houses start to make money. And as long as the brokers are making money, it's worth risking money on owning stocks.

✔ **Simplify your timing by trading the whole brokerage sector via the Dow Jones Broker Dealer ETF (IAI).** This ETF tracks the XBD index quite well and is an excellent vehicle for catching the trend, up or down, of the brokerage sector. As with any ETF, it's best to trade it when the market and the sector that it covers is trending, whether up or down. You can short this ETF and trade options on it as well.

Home Sweet Home: The Housing Sector

Far away from the bustle of Wall Street is Main Street. But the two are inextricably connected by one common factor — money. Of course, the housing sector is much more than homebuilders. Buy a house and after you sign on the dotted line and write a check, your bank or mortgage company puts your loan on the market. When someone buys it, the loan gets packaged into a bundle of mortgage-backed securities, essentially a bond, whose interest is paid for by your monthly mortgage payment along with the payments of thousands of others who actually make their monthly payment.

Your bank lends you a few hundred thousand dollars. You give them some of it as a down payment. Then you give them money every month for however long your mortgage is. But, just in case you default, your mortgage banker took out an insurance policy by passing your mortgage on to someone else as a bond.

The whole thing works pretty well until enough people miss their mortgage payments. Then the whole house of cards collapses. And that's what happened in the subprime mortgage crisis. Homebuilders built too many houses over too long a period of time. As a result, bankers had to help the homebuilders move inventory and so handed out loans to people who shouldn't have qualified. And there you go.

Under normal times, when builders and bankers act responsibly (it could happen), the whole thing can work. For argument's sake, in the following section, I fast forward time a few years and pretend that the subprime mortgage crisis has been resolved and that homebuilding is back to what it once was — a business with a nice bit of profit potential.

Finding a home in housing stocks

The Housing Index (HGX) houses (pun intended) the spectrum of the home-builders, including the top of the heap, the middle of the road, and even mobile home manufacturers.

I like to think in terms of bellwether stocks — companies that the market looks to for direction and leadership in any sector. And in the homebuilders, I have found that Centex (CTX) and Hovnanian (HOV) are quite good in the role of bellwethers.

Centex is a well-diversified builder that offers low- to moderately high-end homes, including custom home building. Centex also does commercial construction, giving the stock a bit of built-in diversification and some added meaning, as any potential problems in the commercial market would also affect the stock's price.

Hovnanian is a pure bet on the high end of building. I keep an eye on it to see whether expectations about big, expensive houses in hoity-toity locations are having problems.

Figure 17-6 shows the Housing Index; Figure 17-7 shows Centex. The charts reveal the following:

✔ The housing sector is what I call a *homogenous mover.* All the stocks in it tend to move in the same direction at any one time. That's because they are all affected by the same set of influences — interest rates, the general state of the economy, and the status of supply and demand in the sector.

At any one time, you can pick one or two stocks or buy the Homebuilders ETF in order to catch the general trend of the sector.

✔ As with any other change in the trend, a move below a key moving average is a key development. In Figure 17-6, you see that the Homebuilders Index broke below two key moving averages, the 50-day and the 200-day lines. When an index or a stock breaks above or below more than one moving average, the signal is more meaningful because two trends have been broken. In Figure 17-6, the long (200-day) and the intermediate (50-day) trends were broken.

✔ Centex (Figure 17-7) showed some weakness before the Homebuilders Index. In fact, careful examination of this particular chart shows that Centex was unable to rally above key resistance areas during two different time periods. The first is on the left of the chart during the June-July period of 2007. The second came during the September 2007 to April 2008 time period. MACD and RSI indicators reaching oversold levels and the underlying instrument (in this case, Centex) failing to rally show a sign of significant weakness in that stock or index.

Note that the 200-day moving average turned down in May of 2006 on CTX and the direction of the 200-day moving average is another indicator that shows whether a stock or index is in a bull or bear market. The XHB 200-day moving average turned down in July of 2007 and implied that the homebuilders sector was entering a bear market.

An excellent way to play the overall trend of the housing sector is the Homebuilders ETF (XHB). This ETF follows the trend of the homebuilder stocks very closely, both up and down, and allows short selling and options.

Figure 17-6:
The Home-builders Index (HGX) breaks below key support and starts a bear market.

Chart courtesy of StockCharts.com.

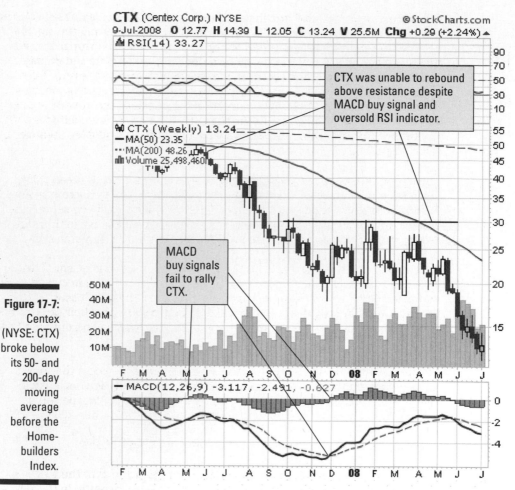

Figure 17-7:
Centex
(NYSE: CTX)
broke below
its 50- and
200-day
moving
average
before the
Home-
builders
Index.

Chart courtesy of StockCharts.com.

The mortgage sector

The week of July 7–11, 2008, may be the most notorious week in the history of the mortgage sector. Investors hit the panic button and sold shares of the government-sponsored but publicly traded companies Fannie Mae (Federal National Mortgage Association, FNM) and Freddie Mac (FRE) — two companies that form the backbone of the U.S. mortgage system.

Fannie Mae's and Freddie Mac's purpose is to buy mortgages from banks and mortgage companies and repackage them into securities (mortgage-backed bonds) that they sell to investors. Together, these companies own or finance 70 percent of the U.S. mortgage market, in one way or another. They're responsible for $5 trillion worth of mortgage-related investments.

During this week from hell for the sector (unless you were a short seller), *The New York Times* and other media outlets published reports suggesting that because these two companies had suffered some $11 billion worth of losses, their cash reserves were starting to be depleted and the government might bail them out. A huge sell-off in both stocks ensued, creating several days of general mayhem for the stock and bond markets. By the end of the week, after the market closed, the FDIC announced that it had taken over the operation of IndyMac Federal Bank. At the time, most investors were left to wonder whether the Fannie and Freddie news was related to the IndyMac takeover by federal regulators.

The major difference between mortgage companies and other areas of the financial services arena is that the mortgage sector is a very narrow investment sector. As a general rule, the more narrow the focus of any sector, the greater the potential for gains — and for losses. As a result, when the subprime mortgage crisis hit its peak in 2008, this sector was devastated.

Outside the realm of the major publicly traded mortgage banks, small mortgage companies were the first to take big hits, and many of them closed their doors, leaving employees out of work and a financial mess — losses on their books and collateral damage in the wake of their collapse as their obligations to other financial services companies were left unanswered and unfunded, in many cases.

At some point in the future, due to the subprime crisis, I expect that the damage to the publicly traded companies that have mortgages as a significant portion of their business will be so severe that the landscape will be quite different from what I could describe in this section in July 2008.

More important from a conceptual standpoint are these points:

- ✔ **Be ready for changes in companies, but remember that the mortgage business is not likely to change much conceptually.** In the years ahead, companies such as Washington Mutual and Wells Fargo, big regional banks that moved heavily into mortgage-related businesses, may not be around, at least not in the same way that they were in the early 2000s. Look for the new companies to make the same mistakes that their predecessors made. Just as Starbucks had a coffee shop on every street corner, Washington Mutual, and to some degree Wells Fargo, opened branches and offered loans and other sophisticated services at grocery stores.

- ✔ **Figure out the game as it evolves into the future.** Government regulation is going to increase and will make business harder to conduct for the mortgage sector. This will be negative in the long run and will eventually be reversed. But the damage will be done. And it could take as much as a decade or longer for the industry to recover. Meanwhile, some of the companies will survive, and those are the ones to put your money into when the charts signal buying opportunities.

Trusting the Real Estate Investment Trusts

Real estate investment trusts (REITs) are nice, easy-to-understand investment vehicles that usually are put together as *limited partnerships* (LPs) — where a bunch of rich guys put up enough money to start the partnership and then sell shares to the rest of us. The rich guys are the controlling partners. They take most of the risk and also make most of the money. They do, however, pass along some of the profits to us little guys based on the number of shares of the trust that we own.

The profits are paid out in *dividends* — periodic distributions to shareholders. Sometimes dividends are paid monthly, sometimes in a quarterly distribution, and rarely the profits get passed on every year. This is the key to REITs: By law the limited partners have to pass on all of the profits, after expenses, to the partners every year.

These investment vehicles are all about paying you dividends, which are measured in terms of yield. For example, an LP that has a net asset value (NAV or *price per share*) and pays a yearly dividend of 7 percent will pay you $7 for every share of the LP that you own.

Because the managing partners take more risk, they get to set the rules of how much money you receive after all the expenses are met, including their salaries and other operating expenses.

Here are some general facts about REITs:

- ✔ **REITs tend to do better when interest rates are falling or are relatively low.** This is because they usually pay a higher yield than treasury bonds and money market funds or bank accounts.

- ✔ **REITs can be risky investments, because the net asset value can fluctuate.** No matter how much of a dividend you collect, if you want to cash in your chips, you may get more or less than what you started with.

- ✔ **Investing in a diversified portfolio of REITs is your best bet.** This is where market timing comes in, as mutual funds and ETFs that invest in REITs are usually the best way to invest in this sector. As with any other vehicle, timers are only interested in them when they're moving, up or down. Remember, what timers want is a trend.

- ✔ **REITs are very economically sensitive investments.** In other words, an REIT is only good if its revenue stream is producing. If your REIT owns a bunch of empty apartment houses or strip malls, it isn't collecting rent, which means that unless it's getting interest from bonds or something else, you don't get paid. And as a rule, you don't invest in REITs to get bond interest passed through to you. You want rent money, because if your managing partners can't invest in good properties, the REIT isn't worth its salt.

You bet there's an REIT index. In fact there are several of them. One of the easiest to find and track is the Dow Jones Wilshire REIT Index (DWRTF). This index follows the general trend of the sector and is an excellent choice to add to your watch list. The REIT sector, like other areas of the financial services area, is a sector where most of the components tend to move in synch with one another, which means that when one security in the sector moves in one direction, the rest tend to move in the same general manner.

And yes, there are REIT ETFs — even an REIT short-selling ETF. In fact because the stocks in the sector move in tandem, it's better to own the whole sector, either via an ETF or a mutual fund, because your main goal as a timer is not so much to collect dividends but to track the general trend of the sector. Here are three vehicles that you can use to time the REIT sector — a great pair of ETFs and a great mutual fund:

- **The Ultra Real Estate ProShares (URE)** is a leveraged ETF that mirrors the trend but doubles the performance (200 percent leveraged) of the daily movements of the Dow Jones Wilshire REIT Index.

- **The UltraShort Real Estate ProShares (SRS)** gives you the opportunity to make money when the REIT index falls. This is also a 2000 percent leveraged fund, meaning that its price rises twice as much as the fall of the DWRTF Index on a daily basis.

- **Fidelity Real Estate Investment Trust Index (FRESX)** rises and falls directly with the general trend of the REIT sector. I've used this one with some success, but you can find a lot of REIT mutual funds.

Chapter 18

Timing the Technologies

• •

• •

*T*he technology sector made the bull markets of the 1980s and 1990s the place to be. But as time passed, the inevitable occurred: PCs became like refrigerators, and what used to be a growth industry became a commoditized industry, similar to the rest of the appliance sector — industries that are cyclical and depend on supply and demand as well the emergence of new must-have gadgets.

The Sony Walkman ruled the 1980s, but MP3 players have become the norm in the first decade of the 21st century; even sales of iPods, the ultimate MP3 player, have shown signs of slowing, as once again the "refrigeratorization" of the gadget continues.

Technology companies are in a constant and never-ending race to develop the next "killer" application, which means that investors in this far-ranging sector have to keep their eyes, ears, and noses fixed on what's happening.

Here are some important general facts about the technology sector:

✔ **It's not just one sector, it's quite fragmented, and you need to keep track of which subsector is doing what.** You hear commentators talk about the tech sector and you get a false sense of security about the whole thing. The big divisions of this area of the market are hardware, software, components, and media-related stocks; the latter includes Internet and telecommunications areas.

✔ **Each subsector of technology has its own set of supply-and-demand issues to contend with.** What drives the PC may not drive handheld devices or individual semiconductor chips. The PC is no longer the only driving force in this area of the market. Networking and telephony-related areas of the high-tech arena have made significant strides in the past decade.

✔ **Subsectors can move in tandem or individually.** For example, what moves the telecom sector may not have a whole lot of effect on the software sector but could move the Internet sector, because the Internet relies on phone lines to a great degree. Only when a major trend that affects most areas of the spectrum is in place are you likely to see an entire sector move in tandem. For example, the 1990s Internet bubble raised all boats at once.

✔ **Volatility is a reality in technology investing.** The software sector, where competition is fierce and profit margins are razor thin, is especially volatile.

✔ **As a timer in this area of the market, you have a wide variety of investment vehicles.** Choose from sector mutual funds, individual stocks, and exchange traded funds (ETFs). This chapter concentrates on stocks and ETFs, but you can apply similar principles to trading technology mutual funds.

Applying Timing to Technology

The technology sector was made for timing, as it tends to be volatile but can also trend for very long periods of time, both up and down, making decisions about the general direction of your trades fairly easy.

More than anything, you want to get a handle on supply and demand before you delve into technology timing. Most technology sectors and individual companies keep a key statistic, the *book-to-bill ratio*. This statistic measures the state of supply and demand in the technology sector and gives investors a good idea as to where in the business cycle the sector is at any time.

In general, a book-to-bill ratio above 1.0 is bullish and means that more orders are on the book than are being filled. In other words, demand exceeds supply. A ratio of 1.0 means that there is balance, and a ratio of less than 1.0 means that business is slow and that demand for product is falling. The book-to-bill ratio most widely watched by traders and industry watchers is that of the semiconductor industry, which is central to the entire technology sector.

You can get a lot of good information on the semiconductor book-to-bill ratio at the Web site of SEMI (www.semi.org), the trade association for the semiconductor (chip) industry. For example, the ratio is actually an average of the last three months of bookings for the chip industry. And the press release at Semi.org usually gives you a good amount of information on where the current number stands.

Stocks in the chip sector usually move in response to the semiconductor book-to-bill ratio. On May 20, 2008, the association released a book-to-bill ratio of 0.81, meaning that $81 worth of orders were being put on the books for every $100 being shipped. Yup, you got it: Business was slow. In fact, business was slowing down in a big way. As the press release put it, bookings were off 8 percent from the March reading, and 32 percent from the reading one year earlier.

What did the market do? Well, the Philadelphia Semiconductor Index (SOX) (Figure 18-1) sold off the day prior to the release, as traders feared that business was starting to slow down. And on May 20, the chip sector sold off a bit more.

Figure 18-1:
A market timing opportunity featuring the Philadelphia Semiconductor Index (SOX).

Chart courtesy of StockCharts.com.

In fact, a good look at Table 18-1 and Figure 18-1 shows that the book-to-bill ratio had been quite anemic in the time period ranging from November 2007 to April 2008. Yet the market had been rallying starting in February, in response to news from several chip makers during about their ability to raise prices on some components, such as memory chips.

Table 18-1	The Book-to-Bill Ratios Trend for Semiconductors		
	Billings (Three-month avg.)	*Bookings (Three-month avg.)*	*Book-to-Fill*
November 2007	1,383.2	1,130.7	0.82
December 2007	1,361.7	1,156.3	0.85
January 2008	1,279.3	1,141.0	0.89
February 2008	1,310.8	1,205.4	0.92
March 2008 (final)	1,344.9	1,165.6	0.87
April 2008 (prelim.)	1,318.9	1,073.8	0.81

Source: SEMI May 2008

Aggressive traders started to bid up the prices of the stocks in the SOX Index as a result. Yet, as Figure 18-1 clearly shows, the index ran into resistance at the 200-day moving average and failed. The news about the bad book-to-bill ratio hit one day later, and the rally was derailed.

This example raises several important points about timing the technology sector:

- ✔ **Markets that rise for no apparent reason are either very strong or very vulnerable.** If a market is rising and there's no news, money is moving in because it knows something or it expects something. In other words, the market is trading on momentum.

- ✔ **As a market timer, you should trade first and ask questions later.** The chip stocks were moving, and as a timer you needed to be in the sector that was moving.

  Figure 18-1 shows two buy points based on the index crossing above its 50-day moving average. The first one was in early April, and the second one was in mid-April. A positive MACD crossover preceded the first buy point. The chart also shows the failure of the index at the 200-day moving average — a good opportunity to sell.

✔ **Always remain suspicious, and be aware that such moves can come to a quick end.** In this case, if you'd have looked at the book-to-bill ratio on Semi.org, you'd have been scratching your head about the rally in the chip sector, and you would probably have been looking for something to happen near the release date of the next number. The charts were fairly clear about the potential for an intermediate-term trend.

Chips Without Chocolate: The Semiconductor Sector

The semiconductor sector has multiple subsectors, such as equipment manu-facturers and companies that specialize in very specific components. As with any complex sector of the market and the economy, the devil (or the trade) is often in the details.

A chip is a silicon wafer with a lot of circuits imbedded in it. These are the brains and nerve terminals of computers, cell phones, and just about anything that we use to enjoy life or to get something done these days. They are also used in defense systems, traffic lights, routers, modems, and the whole gamut of electronics.

The semiconductor industry includes the following important subsectors:

✔ **Equipment manufacturing:** These are the companies that make the machines that other companies use to make chips. The usual bell-wether of this subsector is Applied Materials. Other companies worth watching in this area are Teradyne and KLA-Tencor. All trade on the Nasdaq, and all are members of the SOX index. These are often the first companies to issue earnings warnings and potential business prob-lems when things start turning south in the industry as their orders for machinery start slowing.

✔ **Microprocessor manufacturers:** The most well-recognized names in this subsector are Intel and Advanced Micro Devices, at least when related to PCs, but Texas Instruments is a big part of this subsector because of its involvement in cell phones and other digital and analog areas such as digital movie projectors.

✔ **Logic chip manufacturers:** *Logic chips* are sort of chameleon chips that can be programmed to do one or more different tasks depending on who orders them and what their plans are. The companies that make these chips and are featured in the SOX index are Xilinx, Altera, Linear Tech. Corp., and National Semiconductor — hardly household names unless you're a tech-stock junky, manage a mutual fund, or need to know so that you can make money.

There are other subsectors in this arena and other companies that make specific chips for specific uses, as well as the gamut of other electronic components, such as transistors, diodes, and many other components of the things most of us take for granted in modern times. But, for the purposes of this section, these will suffice.

When one of these companies stumbles or shines, most of the others in the sector usually move in the same direction. This movement is called a *sympathy rally* or a *sympathy decline,* and each of the subsectors in the technology sector tends to rise and fall together; bad news for one software company likely affects most of the stocks in the sector, at least in the short term. The sympathy factor is why the technology area is well suited to be traded, as a sector or as individual subsectors, via ETFs.

Tracking down a trend

In order to succeed in timing, you really have to dig deeply into the business model of whatever area you're putting your money into. In the chip sector, figuring out what's important is pretty simple. Chips are components of devices. Some are popular. Others are not. You want to look for companies that take part in devices that sell well or that are blockbusters.

Using Apple's iPod as an example, here are some key questions to ask when you're working to identify a technology trend.

What is it?

In the 21st century, CDs are dying, and music downloading is hip. Apple's iPod rules the roost. Apple also morphed the iPod into a video player, developed podcasts, and spawned a whole new set of subindustries. Finally, we got the iPhone, and all things digital have never been the same.

A steady stream of new electronic devices will continue to grab the market and the consumers' attention. You can almost count on the company that makes the device of the moment and markets it successfully to have a winning stock for a significant period of time.

Who makes it?

Apple makes the iPhone, the iPod, and soon the iCoffee maker. (That's a joke, but it wouldn't surprise me.) Who makes a product is important, since you'll hear the buzz, and see the stock start moving. That's when you go and do research about the company, its finances, and so on. The key is that you want a good handle on the company's potential to have a long hit on its hand.

Who's buying it?

The broader the audience the better the chances of making money, especially because the company will be able to sell high-end stuff to those who can afford it. The big margins come when you sell not only the iPod but also the charger, the matching case, the speaker system, and so on. When the product is good, the loyal customer goes out and buys subsequent products as well (enter the iPhone), especially products with all the bells and whistles.

What's competing against it?

In the case of Apple and its iPhone, Research in Motion (RIMM) and its Blackberry are the leading competition. RIMM was formidable competition, as the Blackberry was more targeted to the business market, rather than the casual, hip market targeted by Apple. More important, you want good competition, especially if the competing companies have overlap but also their own individual audiences, which means that their opportunity for sales is plentiful.

What's inside?

As PC companies used to note in their commercials "Intel inside," so did Intel's fortunes as a brand become part of marketing history. What's inside is as important a question as any for those interested in investing in the chip industry. After all, who makes the chips that make the killer gadgets run is a vital part of the equation — worth finding out and considering investing in.

Here's a great example: Marvell Technologies (Nasdaq: MRVL) was a little-known company until its storage chips found their way into — you guessed it — iPods. As a result, Marvell went from unknown to Wall Street darling and major player in the chip sector.

Investing in semiconductor stocks

Investing in chip stocks is not much different from investing in any other sector. I like to start at the top and work my way down, and so my first stop is the Philadelphia Semiconductor Index (SOX; refer to Figure 18-1). As with any chart, I like to see the general trend, which in Figure 18-1 was pretty good until late May, when the book-to-bill ratio's release took the wind out of SOX's sails.

You also want to look at SOX within the context of the market, so compare it to the action in the S&P 500, which at the time was stunningly similar, as the S&P 500 also failed to rally above its 200-day moving average.

However, if you backtrack to March, you see that the index started showing signs of life. That's about the time when some of the chip companies in Asia started reporting that their bookings had improved and that they had been able to raise prices on memory chips. As Figure 18-1 shows, SOX followed classic technical behavior and moved above its 50-day moving average while remaining below its 200-day moving average.

The 200-day moving average is the defining line between bull and bear markets. So by definition, SOX was still in a bear market. Still, the action around the 50-day moving average was compelling enough for an intermediate-term trade. This was proven when the index pulled back after its initial foray above the 50-day line but found support there and moved higher after consolidating at the line.

The first move above the 50-day line was a warning that the trend had changed. At that point you should have been looking inside the SOX index for stocks that looked worthwhile and examining ETFs that specialize in semiconductor stocks to establish a small position in the sector.

The ETF solution

You have two simple ways to invest in the chip stocks. One is through ETFs; several exist, but the one that's most liquid, has the most activity, and tracks the SOX index most closely is the Semiconductors HOLDRS Trust (SMH), pictured in Figure 18-2.

I use this ETF as the basis for my technology-sector timing system. As Figure 18-2 shows, SMH follows SOX fairly closely. In other words, when SOX rises, SMH is likely to do the same, and vice versa when it falls, which gives you the opportunity to sell the ETF short.

Figure 18-2 shows plenty of clues to confirm an interest in buying shares of SMH. The MACD and the MACD histogram both turned up as SMH crossed above its 50-day moving average, a clear buy signal.

Volume was high on both up and down days as SMH backed and filled in March. But even though there was some aggressive selling, buyers stepped back in, as the ETF never broke to new lows. This is a great example of what traders call *accumulation,* or the aggressive and steady acquisition of shares by buyers. Eventually the buyers overwhelmed the sellers, and the ETF took off.

On the sell side, you also find a lot of clues. First, the rate of rise of the ETF was unsustainable. This was confirmed by the overbought reading on RSI, which preceded a bout of selling. Next MACD weakened, confirming the fact that more selling was coming.

Figure 18-2:
The Semi-
conductors
HOLDRS
Trust (SMH)
provides an
excellent
intermediate-
term timing
opportunity
based on
the 50-day
moving
average
and key
oscillator
relation-
ships.

Chart courtesy of StockCharts.com.

Stocking up on strength

A second way of owning chip stocks is to buy them individually. I keep a file
on tech stocks that includes some 60 or more stocks, including those in the
SOX index as well as those in the indexes that I describe later in this chapter. I also look at the "Stocks In The News" charts in *Investor's Business Daily*
every night, specifically looking for technology stocks. When I find new ones
that look promising, I add them to my list.

For illustrative purposes, in this section, I use the stocks in the SOX index.
A quick look through the SOX index pointed out that Linear Tech (Nasdaq:
LLTC) was the strongest stock in the sector at the time, as measured by

the index. (See Figure 18-3.) In fact, Linear was moving higher before SOX and even SMH took off to the races, showing a significant amount of relative strength. The chart shows that Linear hit a snag in April but recovered fairly quickly and regained its leadership position.

In bull markets, you want to own strength. And despite the fact that SOX was trading under its 200-day moving average, the rally was attractive enough on an intermediate-term basis to warrant using bull market criteria. In other words, if Linear was the strong stock, that was the one to own.

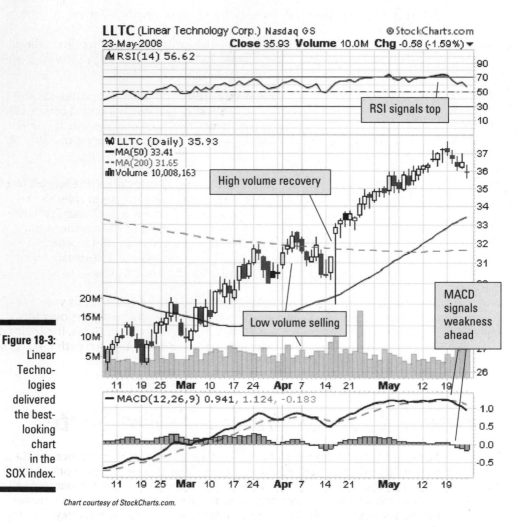

Figure 18-3:
Linear Technologies delivered the best-looking chart in the SOX index.

Chart courtesy of StockCharts.com.

When you own a stock and it acts better than the sector it's a part of, with a significant negative reversal along the way, it's best to let the market help you make the decision whether or sell the stock by using a sell stop. A good place to put a sell stop in technology stocks is somewhere near 5 to 8 percent below the purchase price. A *sell stop* is an order to sell that you instruct your broker to put in place. If the stock hits that price you'll be taken out of the position. It's an important part of timing, especially in volatile markets and sectors. You should continue to ratchet up the stop as the stock rises in order to protect your gains.

In Figure 18-3, the stock exhibited two important characteristics:

- **Volume on up days tended to be higher than volume on down days.** This was especially evident when the stock recovered in a few days after falling below its 200-day moving average.

- **The overall look of the chart was bullish.** It starts low on the left side and moves almost straight up the rest of the way. That kind of nice slope to the right, especially when accompanied by rising volume, is a sign that institutions are buying the stock. As a timer, you want to follow the big money.

Buy and sell any stock or ETF based on technical criteria. Let the market help you make decisions when it crosses above or below key support levels, or when stocks drop below your sell-stop point. In the case of Linear Tech., the stock moved so far, so fast that it was due for a pullback. When the entire sector, as measured by SOX, pulled back, so did the shares of Linear. Still, note that even though the RSI and MACD oscillators gave sell signals, the stock remained above its 50- and 200-day moving averages.

Even though you might have taken some profits or even sold out your position, Linear Tech would be a stock to keep a close eye on, as the overall action, on a longer-term basis is showing relative strength. Thus, it remains a strong stock, relatively speaking. And stocks with relative strength tend to be near the top of the leader board in the next rally.

Taking a Look at the Hardware Sector

Hardware is tech jargon for PCs, servers, drives, printers, monitors, and all the equipment that's required to connect them and help them work together. This is a mature sector of the technology index, and so the companies in the sector have to deliver extremely good results on a quarterly basis in order for their stocks to rise. Hardware is a difficult place to make money, barring the presence of a very strong market trend or a major catalyst driving the product cycle. The Computer Hardware Index (HWI) contains a traditional and fairly representative sampling of this sector.

Hardware is a highly commoditized sector of industry. Thus the companies that represent the sector in the stock market are essentially driven by the overall demand for computers and related equipment. Barring some new trend, such as the Internet in the late 1990s, this sector gets most of its orders from what is known as the *replacement cycle* — the demand for replacement computers and related equipment when the ones already in place wear out. In other words, hardware isn't a growth sector.

More importantly, key areas of the sector — the PC and server companies, such as Dell, Sun Microsystems, and Hewlett Packard — face intense competition from Asian companies that undercut prices just to gain market share. The two exceptions in those areas are Apple and IBM. But in fact, those two companies have a lot less to do with hardware than meets the eye. IBM makes most of its money from service contracts and business-related software, while Apple's money comes not from its MacIntosh line of computers, but from its line of MP3 players and phones.

Hardware stocks lagged the performance of the semiconductor stocks — SOX index (Figure 18-1) — which was in a smooth up trend. Note that the hardware index's advance was a lot more jagged that the smooth climb for the SOX, and that it took until very late in the rally for HWI to finally rally. This was a sign that investors were less enthusiastic about the prospects for this area of the market. Figure 18-4 shows the lackluster performance of the hardware stocks during this period of time.

A look at the components of the index shows that there were few market stalwarts in attendance. Other than Western Digital, IBM, and Apple, most of the other stocks in the index were clearly underperforming the market. That means that roughly 30 percent of the index's weight was doing all the work.

From an investment standpoint, other than considering owning shares of the above-mentioned trio, the comparison to SOX was rather tepid.

From a timing standpoint, HWI doesn't really have an ETF that matches its moves, so that leaves individual stocks as the only way to time this sector. As I describe in detail in the section "Chips Without Chocolate: The Semiconductor Sector," you should keep a list of hardware stocks, including the hardware index. By looking at the charts of the components when the action in the index looks favorable, you may be able to find some worthwhile timing opportunities. In this case, Western Digital, Apple, and IBM fit the bill.

Figure 18-4:
The
Computer
Hardware
Index (HWI)
lags the
perfor-
mance of
the Semi-
conductor
Index
(Figure 18-1)
until very
late in
the spring
2008 rally.

Chart courtesy of StockCharts.com.

Getting Soft on Software

Software is the Rodney Dangerfield of the technology sector: It gets no
respect, mostly because of the bad press garnered by Microsoft over the
years. But let's get real, without Microsoft, and without software, life would
be stuck in the '70s. I liked the '70s; that decade was a much simpler time. I
mean, there was no 24-hour news cycle, and Wall Street was something that
other people worried about. But we're not in the '70s, and Microsoft and
other companies that make software, such as Oracle and Adobe Systems,
have a lot to do with our lifestyle now.

The software sector is to some degree a commodity sector whose companies make money by selling software and by collecting subscription and maintenance fees from customers. The revenue stream for software varies generally with business conditions and the economy, and there is very stiff competition between companies, which makes it difficult for any one company to raise prices. Thus, the companies that make big money in software do so by owning large portions of their market share. All of this adds up to a sector that can be volatile and whose direction can move up or down from quarter to quarter depending on the interplay between all of these factors.

The Goldman Sachs CBOE Software index (GSO) in Figure 18-5 has 39 components and includes a wide spectrum of companies with products ranging from those in gaming to those in security, as well as the more common business uses — operating systems and database- and productivity-management software.

With 39 components in the index, it's hard to run through the charts by hand; fortunately, Yahoo! Finance (`finance.yahoo.com`) lets you look at the charts on one page. I like to scroll down the page and jot down those charts that look attractive. After I get a list, I go to my charting service and do more detailed study on the ones that make the cut before making decisions.

My scrolling expedition led me to five charts that were worth doing more work on: Adobe Systems, Ariba, Activision, BMC Software, and Oracle. The whole scrolling exercise took me less than five minutes — I just scanned the charts for up-trending stocks that looked strong. My second look removed Adobe and Oracle, because they had started to roll over, coring the list down to the last three, with Ariba being the strongest stock in a strong sector. Ariba is one of the few remnants of the old business-to-business (B2B) subsector, a major force during the Internet craze. B2B software enables companies to organize the supply chain and share data with their clients, simplifying the ordering and shipping of goods and services.

A simpler way to get into this sector is via the iShares Software ETF (IGV), which you see in Figure 18-6. The ETF closely mirrors the action in GSO, and its chart offers the same kind of analytic opportunities of the previous charts — moving average crossovers, confirmed by the oscillators, at both tops and bottoms.

I put some arrows on the chart of GSO, Figure 18-5, but did not put any signs on them. I did it on purpose so that you could write them in yourself and start getting some hands-on experience with the analysis you use to make your timing more realistic. I left Figure 18-6 blank so that you could analyze it without any hints, and see what you come up with. If you do need some hints, turn to Chapter 4.

Figure 18-5:
The Goldman Sachs CBOE Software Index (GSO) kept up with the Semi-conductor Index (SOX, Figure 18-1) during this rally.

Chart courtesy of StockCharts.com.

Figure 18-6:
Software
Ishares
ETF (IGV)
tracks the
Software
Index (GSO,
Figure 18-5)
well and
makes it
easy to buy
and sell
the whole
software
sector at
any one
time.

Chart courtesy of StockCharts.com.

Intersecting the Internet and Telecommunications Sectors

The Internet and telecommunications sectors of the market were among the biggest in the 1990s, during the heydays of the Internet bubble. I remember those days well, as my daily stock picks were all about bandwidth and revenue growth, but little about profits. Not too many companies are left from that era, and those that remain aren't always all that prominent.

The following three major indexes provide an excellent window into the tele-communications and related sectors:

- ✔ The North American Telecom Index (XTC)
- ✔ The Networking Index (NWX)
- ✔ The Interactive Week Internet Index (IIX)

The major focus in the telecom and Internet sectors — which have essentially melded into one sector — is wireless and broadband, and how to make content and communication reach as many people as possible for the least amount of money.

It's nearly impossible for companies in this space to make money, at least enough money to keep investors satisfied, because of the intense competition among companies and the different platforms, such as cable, traditional telephone, wireless, and voice over Internet (VOIP) that deliver voice and content.

The one thing that unifies this sector is the relative lack of profits for most of the participants, while the giants — companies like AT&T, Cisco Systems, and Time Warner — gather market share but fail to deliver the knockout punch to the smaller players.

MiStr Spicd

Chapter 19

Timing the Energy Sector

*A*nyone who's shivered, shook, and cussed while filling up his favorite gasoline-powered vehicle has at one point or another asked himself: How did we get here? How did gasoline go from $1.50 to $4 a gallon in the space of a few years? And the next question, of course, is how high will it go?

Until the late 1990s, the United States and Europe accounted for most of the world's oil consumption. But as globalization took hold, other countries began to increase their oil consumption. Among them were China and India, the two largest-growing emerging economies in the world. But they were not alone, as other Asian countries also increased their consumption. At the same time, OPEC, the cartel that accounts for 40 percent of the world's oil supply, began to experience a slowing rate of production, while non-OPEC producers like Mexico and the North Sea began to experience an outright drop in production.

The facts behind the decrease in production are controversial and in many cases are specific to the countries involved. For example:

✔ **Venezuela** claims that its production hasn't decreased and that its proven reserves have grown. But the truth is that because of the politics of the Hugo Chavez government, as many as 10,000 wells had to be shut down because of poor maintenance.

✔ **Nigeria's** production fluctuates on a frequent basis because militants routinely kidnap key personnel, and strikes at oil fields and related areas are common, as is pipeline sabotage.

✔ **Saudi Arabia's** oil fields are drying up, according to multiple reports from credible sources in the oil and energy community.

- **Mexico's** largest field, Cantorral, is in decline, losing significant amounts of production on a yearly basis.

- **Indonesia,** once an OPEC member, left the cartel in 2008 because it became an oil importer as its own production also began to decline.

- Meanwhile, in the **United States,** powerful special-interest groups with environmental agendas lobbied Congress successfully and created a highly difficult environment for oil exploration, drilling, and refinery building, leading the United States into a position where it became dependent on foreign oil.

As we move into the second decade of the 21st century, the following characteristics describe the supply and consumption of oil:

- The largest portions of the world's oil reserves are in places that are very unfriendly to the United States. Most of those countries want to charge as much as possible for oil, because it's their major source of income.

- World oil consumption is expected to average 87.7 million barrels per day in 2009, according to a July 2008 International Energy Agency (IEA) estimate.

- World oil production as of 2008 was somewhere around 86.1 million barrels per day, including both OPEC and non-OPEC sources, according to multiple estimates.

- World oil consumption is expected to continue to increase steadily over the next 20 years as emerging economies continue to grow and mature.

- The easy oil has been found. Any oil that can be extracted from now on will be very expensive and difficult to produce. Although prices may fluctuate, and although there will be periods where they fall significantly, the days of $20 per barrel oil are not likely to return anytime soon, if at all.

- From a trading standpoint, the opportunities to make money, on the long and the short side, are likely to be numerous over the next 20 to 50 years.

Factors Influencing the Price of Oil, Natural Gas, Heating Oil, and Gasoline

The energy complex and its components are influenced by similar factors: supply and demand, geopolitical issues, weather, and seasonal tendencies. I give you details about each of those factors, especially as the relate to timing, in the upcoming sectors.

Supply and demand

Just about any event from worker strikes to hurricanes and other natural disasters, accidents to spills to sabotage — even market manipulation by OPEC and other producers — affects supply, not demand.

Demand tends to be stable most of the time and rises during economic growth periods. In past cycles, demand in the United States and Western Europe used to be the major factor driving oil prices.

However, with other economies in the world growing to the point where they can make up for a significant amount of the demand losses from Europe and the United States when those economies slow, demand has another leg of support to contend with. In other words, it takes a lot more decrease in global demand to trigger a significant decrease in prices. The upcoming section "Finding Timing Vehicles for the Energy Sector" gives you more details.

Keep these important tidbits about the oil markets in mind as you trade:

✔ The world runs on oil, and any threat to the oil supply leads to rising prices.

✔ Demand fluctuates, but supply is finite — especially the supply of usable fuel that can be available at any time for real-time use because of the bottlenecks in refining, storage, and transportation. Ramping up supply or turning it back down takes weeks.

✔ As an oil timer, whether your focus is on oil itself or related stocks of companies in the sector, your primary goal is to consider the effects of events on supply and to correlate those effects with your charts.

The geopolitical equation

Aside from the Al-Qaeda factor and the "war on terrorism" (whatever the definition of that is at any one time), there is one significant change in the politics of the Middle East, one thing that generates the most action for oil: Iran.

The U.S. invasion of Iraq, along with neutralizing the global reach of Al-Qaeda, has given Iran an opportunity to expand its sphere of influence. That change keeps the Middle East boiling and is likely to do so for many years, regardless of what happens in Iraq.

From a strategic standpoint, aside from the nuclear question, Iran's geographic proximity to the Straits of Hormuz, where most of the oil from Saudi Arabia has to pass to reach larger waterways and move on to world markets, is the other lever that gives Iran leverage in global oil markets. Iran threatens to cut off or significantly obstruct oil tanker traffic through this important channel on a fairly regular basis. And it usually gets at least a small amount of attention from traders, depending on how tight is the rope around Iran at any one time as it jockeys for position against the European Union, the United States, and the United Nations.

When you throw in the fact that the largest non-OPEC producer of oil, Russia, is as unpredictable a global player as there is, and that Venezuela, a significant provider of crude oil and gasoline to the United States is also non-U.S.-friendly, you've got a recipe for constant volatility based on news releases and political posturing, aside from the real threats to global oil supply that could develop if any one of these players decides to make good on any threats to actually harm oil supplies.

Finally, just for added effect, throw in your run-of-the-mill strikes, attacks on pipelines in Nigeria, an occasional kidnapping, and threats of attacks against oil installations in Saudi Arabia or anywhere else in the world, and you've got myriad reasons, all geopolitically motivated, to affect the daily price of crude oil, natural gas, and related products.

The weather issues

The weather is a key influence on supply during certain times of the year. One is the Atlantic hurricane season, which runs from June until November. Any storm that threatens the Gulf of Mexico has the potential to affect the supply of crude oil as well as natural gas in the United States.

An important recent example of what can happen was Hurricane Katrina in August 2005. This storm devastated the New Orleans area, where a significant portion of the U.S. intake of oil from the Gulf of Mexico takes place. Yearly production of oil fell by almost 20 percent, natural gas by almost 15 percent.

Rita, a storm that hit Texas and parts of Louisiana, followed Katrina. And although Rita didn't do as much damage as Katrina, it did lead to a 48-hour Texas-size traffic jam, as much of Houston and the Gulf Coast were evacuated. Had Rita hit Houston as badly as Katrina hit New Orleans, it would have damaged as much as 23 percent of the U.S. refinery capacity. Oil and gasoline prices surged to record highs, $2 per gallon on gasoline and nearly $70 per barrel on crude oil. Man, how we miss those halcyon days. By July 2008, crude had reached $145 per barrel and gasoline at the pump was above $4 per gallon.

Here are some other weather- and temperature-related points to keep in mind:

 ✔ Crude oil prices tend to drift lower or sideways in the spring months when refineries convert production from heating oil to gasoline.

> ✔ Heating oil prices often drift lower in the first six months of the year as temperatures warm up. The only significant difference is when demand for diesel fuel overwhelms the normal supply-and-demand influences from weather.
>
> ✔ Gasoline prices often bottom in February and tend to move higher until March or April, but this can be a much more variable tendency than that of heating oil to fall in the first half of the year.
>
> ✔ Natural gas prices are much more volatile than heating oil and gasoline and are more susceptible to supply and demand at any given time, although weather and geopolitics can also affect prices.

All cycles are variable and other factors, such as geopolitics, weather, or other intangibles can override the usual tendencies of the market to move in a fairly predictable fashion. Still, you need to be aware of these cycles and watch for their presence.

Are we running out of oil?

Peak oil is the concept that the world is running out of oil. Over the years, I've come to see it in this way: Peak oil is real, but not because we're running out of oil. We *are* running out of the oil that's easy to get out of the ground; what's left to produce is far under the world's oceans, inside of rock formations or other inhospitable environments, or inaccessible because of political issues, such as with Russia, Venezuela, and Iran.

Thus, the real question is whether the tight supplies that we hear about are real because there isn't any more oil in the ground or under the ocean, or because it's profitable — financially and ideologically — for oil producers and oil companies to have us believe that we're running out of oil.

What we hear is that production is falling. But we don't hear details about why it's falling. Is it because there's plenty of oil left in the ground and our current technology isn't good enough to get it out? Or is it because at current prices producers are making so much money that they don't want to find more oil and get it out?

I'm not saying one way or another, because I don't know. The data is too conflicting. And finding someone neutral with regard to this question is nearly impossible. So, you and I are left with more questions than answers, as the markets act in an efficient manner, responding to the best information that they have available.

And that's where you and I need to be when we trade, and when we time the markets — in a zone where nothing matters except the ticks on the charts and the trends.

Charting an example

Energy is a natural for timing, because it's volatile and because it can be and often is influenced by seasonal factors, such as weather. You also find a smaller weekly cycle of energy activity based on the Wednesday morning releases of crude oil and natural gas supply statistics from the U.S. Energy Information Agency. When this data is released, the market tends to move, often in dramatic fashion. But that movement depends on expectations before the report and what the report actually shows. In some cases, the difference between expectations and the real number is significant enough to change the trend.

One such example came in July 2008. As Figure 19-1 shows, crude dropped 11.2 percent in price over four days. Although crude was already starting to show some weakness prior to the Wednesday report, the report confirmed what the market had already begun to suspect — that demand was starting to fall even as production remained stable.

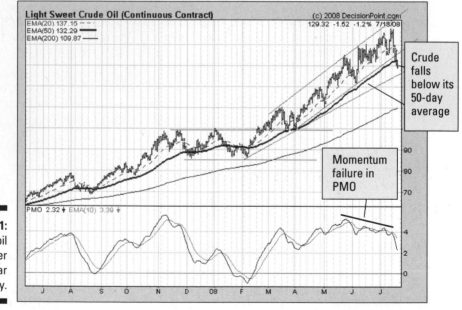

Figure 19-1:
Crude oil
breaks after
a multi-year
rally.

Crude
falls
below its
50-day
average

Momentum
failure in
PMO

Chart courtesy of DecisionPoint.com.

The rising trend was weakened and reversed by the report. On Wednesday, July 16, the EIA reported a 2.1 percent decrease in U.S. gasoline consumption over the prior four weeks, while also reporting a larger-than-expected increase in oil inventories, as oil imports rose during the period. The report was a double-barrel downer for the markets — decreased consumption and bloating inventories — a recipe for lower prices.

Here's how the charts and reality come together:

- Figure 19-1 shows an important market break, as crude fell below its 50-day moving average during this period. The 50-day moving average had been support for prices during the bull run that started in February. The average provided excellent support four times before giving in to selling pressure in July.

- The break also took out the support of a rising trend line that went back to February.

- The price-momentum oscillator (PMO), a proprietary momentum gauge from DecisionPoint.com, shows a loss of momentum that preceded the market's break. The second peak in PMO was lower than the first peak in the pair. At the same time, crude oil made a new high, which incidentally was hyped up to no end by the media, as prices flirted with $150 during this move up. This is a classic technical divergence that correctly predicted what was ahead.

- The big picture reveals that crude oil lost 11 percent of its value in four days but still had a lot of room to fall while remaining in a bull market: The 200-day moving average, the defining line of bulls and bear markets, was at 110, nearly another 20 percent below the July 18 close.

Relating Energy Stocks to the Underlying Commodities

Oil and oil service stocks are important bellwethers for the price of crude oil. Generally, changes in oil stocks tend to precede the moves in oil prices and should also confirm them. Sometimes oil stocks move along with or just after crude oil futures. The take-home message is that there should be a general agreement in the trend of oil and oil service stocks with the price of oil. Any divergence is a sign that one or the other will reverse its trend.

When oil and oil service stocks diverge from the general trend of oil, it can be positive or negative. For example, if the price of oil is moving sideways or is in a down trend, but oil and oil service stocks start to rally, there's a good chance that the price of crude will start to trend higher. And if oil doesn't rally after the stocks do, you'll probably see the price of the stocks fall at some point, and you were witness to a false start

If the underlying trend in crude or in the stocks is strong enough, you could trade that particular area — following the dominant trend — and choose to ignore the others.

Figures 19-2 and 19-3 are a huge source of trading information. The Oil Index (XOI), which houses stocks like Exxon Mobil and is a widely followed index, is in a volatile trading range while the Oil Service Index (OSX) is in a trading range of its own but isn't as volatile. Notice that the peaks and valleys in XOI, OSX, and the price of crude oil tend to correspond, despite differences in volatility, at least until the start of the year 2008, when crude oil (refer to Figure 19-1) consolidated in a very orderly trading range and the oil and oil service stocks became more disorderly.

Figure 19-2: The Oil Index (XOI) tops out after losing momentum.

Chart courtesy of DecisionPoint.com.

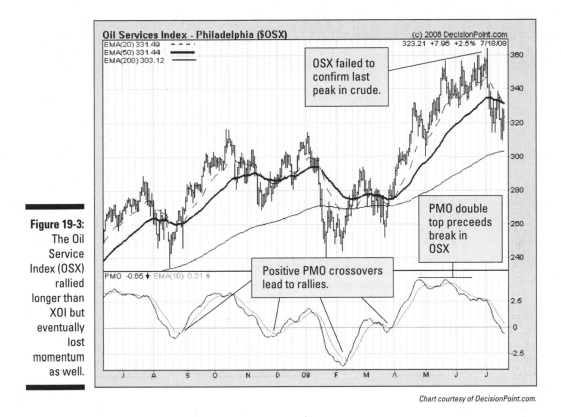

Figure 19-3:
The Oil Service Index (OSX) rallied longer than XOI but eventually lost momentum as well.

Chart courtesy of DecisionPoint.com.

By the month of March crude had started a legendary advance that led prices to levels near $150. But the confirmation from the major oil stocks in XOI was tepid at best. The confirmation from OSX was much better. That index confirmed all but the final high in crude. Still, a lack of confirmation is a lack of confirmation, and there were other signs as well that trouble was straight ahead.

The PMO indicator warned of future problems by giving a sell signal in XOI, in OSX, and eventually in the price of crude. The PMO indicator also comes in handy in giving buy signals, as I point out in Figure 19-3 of the Oil Service Index.

The bottom line is that you're looking for harmony, not dissonance between crude oil and the oil and oil service stocks. You want to see convergence, not divergence; they're both responding to the same fundamentals of supply and demand. When the prices of oil and oil service stocks deviate from the general trend of the price of crude oil, it's a sign that the stocks, crude oil, or all three are about to reverse trends.

Finding Timing Vehicles for the Energy Sector

You can time oil and oil stocks in real time via your online broker either by using exchange-traded funds or by buying individual stocks. You can also use sector mutual funds. But I prefer stocks and ETFs, because with sector mutual funds you have to wait until the end of the day to buy and sell, and in markets that can have big moves in short periods, you might miss big parts of both up and down action that can cost you money. In this section I show you how to time crude and energy stocks via ETFs.

Crude oil

The best way to time crude oil when it's rising, aside from directly buying futures contracts, is via the U.S. Oil Fund (USO). USO was the first ETF to allow the actual trade of crude oil futures without directly owning futures contracts, and it remains the most liquid ETF for timing crude, although it has some competitors.

But don't let the fact that USO is an ETF give you a false sense of security. USO is a commodity pool. It doesn't invest in oil companies but in crude oil futures; thus, it's a risky and volatile fund whose value is based on the value of the futures contracts owned by the management company that runs the fund. You can short shares of USO, as well as create option strategies based on this ETF. The key to success is to remember that USO follows the general price trend of crude oil, but that the price is not the same as the leading crude oil futures.

If you want to short sell crude oil, you can use an ETF that was introduced in July 2008, the MacroShares $100 Oil Down Shares (DOY). DOY isn't an ETF that sells crude oil short. It's a hybrid derivative fund that's paired with another fund, the MacroShares $100 Oil Up Shares (UOY). The funds operate as a pair. When oil prices fall, the issuer transfers assets, in the form of U.S. treasury securities, from the Up to the Down fund, with the goal being that it will transfer enough assets from one fund to the other to match as closely as possible the change in price of crude oil. When oil prices rise, the process is carried out in reverse.

If you're looking to diversify your exposure to energy futures, here's a good way to do it, the PowerShares DB Energy Fund (DBE). This ETF lets you trade West Texas Light Sweet Crude oil, Brent Crude, RBOB gasoline, heating oil, and natural gas futures under one banner.

And although diversification is a good concept, it doesn't always work. There's no guarantee that all five energy components will be in bullish or bearish trends at the same time. Diversification is okay if the five commodities' trends add up to a positive when in a single portfolio or even if they break even. But if losses in one or two components are significant, they can drag down the whole thing. As a result, this ETF may lag a single commodity fund such as USO (Figure 19-4).

Figure 19-4:
The U.S. Oil Fund (USO) invests exclusively in crude oil futures.

Chart courtesy of DecisionPoint.com.

Still, if the energy sector is firing on all cylinders, this ETF is a good one. Both crude grades get a 22.5 percent weighing here, as do gasoline and heating oil. The more volatile natural gas component gets a 10 percent weighing. As Figure 19-5 shows, during this period of time, DBE's general trend was similar to that of crude oil.

Weight, in the context of indexing, refers to how much gains or losses in any one component add or subtract to the price of the index or ETF. In the case of DBC, for example, natural gas contributes 10 percent to the price of the ETF.

Figure 19-5: The Power-Shares Multi-Sector Energy ETF (DBE) lets you buy the entire energy commodity complex in one basket.

Oil and oil service ETFs

Another way to time the oil and oil service sectors is via ETFs or via individual stocks. In this section, I show you how to do both.

The Oil Service HOLDRS Trust (OIH) and the Energy Sector (SPDR) XLE are two of a fairly large list of ETFs that you can use to time the general trend of the oil (XLE) and oil service (OIH) sectors. These are two well-established, highly liquid ETFs that have stood the test of time as far as following the general trend of the sectors that they are designed to follow.

As with any timing strategy, you want to pay special attention to both the technical and the fundamental aspects of the time in which you're trading.

To short the energy stocks, you can use the UltraShort Oil & Gas ProShares ETF (DUG). This is a diversified and leveraged ETF that specializes in matching twice the inverse performance of the Dow Jones U.S. Oil & Gas Index. In other words, when the index falls 1 percent, DUG rises 2 percent.

This ETF is an excellent way to make money when the trend in oil and gas stocks is to the down side and is an excellent complement to XLE. Figure 19-6 shows the close correlation between the inverse trends of XLE (right) and DUG (left).

Figure 19-6:
The UltraShort Oil & Gas ProShares ETF (DUG) and the Select Sector SPDR Energy ETF (XLE) let you short sell (DUG) and/or buy (XLE) oil and natural gas stocks.

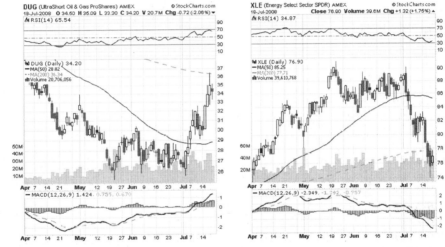

Chart courtesy of StockCharts.com.

 I look at XOI, OSX, and the price of crude oil on a daily basis. Depending on the overall trend of these important benchmarks, I then decide whether the best trend to time is up or down. After I make that decision I move on to the next stage, which is to decide which ETF is best to use at the time.

Stocking up on oil and oil service

To time individual stocks in oil and oil service, follow the general principles of technical and fundamental analysis outlined in this chapter.

Oil service stocks, the stocks of companies that provide support to companies such as Exxon and Chevron, are a separate subsector of energy and tend to move in tandem. For example, when Halliburton (HAL), one of the largest oil service stocks in the world, warns about its earnings, it usually leads to selling in Schlumberger (SLB), another big oil service contractor, and the rest of the sector. If you own one and something happens to the other, your position might be affected by the buying or selling, at least temporarily.

If you decide to time individual stocks, I suggest that you save your individual stock adventures for times when the price trend is clearly to the up side. If the chart for OSX or XOI looks to be in a good groove to the up side, look for individual stocks in these sectors. Otherwise, you're better off going long or shorting the ETFs.

The best place to find the biggest bang for your money on individual stocks in oil and oil service is in *Investor's Business Daily*'s NYSE or Nasdaq Stocks in the News sections. If the oil and oil service sectors are hot during the time, IBD will find the fastest growing stocks in the sectors and apply the CANSLIM (see Chapter 10) criteria to them. Using this resource is probably the best way to capitalize on oil and oil service during a bull market.

My best advice for timing oil and oil service stocks is to stick with ETFs, unless you find good ideas in IBD.

Natural gas

Natural gas is thought by many to be the fuel of the future. Just look at all the things that natural gas has going for it:

- ✔ It's cheaper than oil.
- ✔ It's plentiful in the United States.
- ✔ It burns more cleanly than oil.
- ✔ It can be used to power homes, electrical systems, power cells, and automobiles.

So what's not to like? For one thing, natural gas is extremely volatile to trade, with the trend changing on a fairly frequent basis and the intraday volatility making for a difficult environment for professionals as well as individual investors.

Still, it's worthwhile to consider both the commodity and the natural gas stocks. As with crude oil, you can trade the commodity via futures (least agreeable for most folks because of the volatility), ETFs (not bad but also volatile), or stocks (okay when the trend is correct).

Natural gas, no matter which vehicle you use to time it, is a tall order in the best of hands because of its volatility.

But in case you want to try timing natural gas despite its volatility, here are two options for doing so:

- **The United States Gas Fund (UNG) ETF** is the only pure play on the commodity that invests in natural gas futures contracts, other than buying futures directly. UNG actually works pretty well at moving along with the fortunes of natural gas futures; it rises and falls with the price of the underlying futures contract with a decent correlation to the price moves.

  The major problem with UNG is that natural gas is hugely volatile. Even in an indirect vehicle such as this ETF, you could experience big intraday volatility. If natural gas ever hits a bull market like crude oil has had since 2001, this would be a good way to play it.

- **The Natural Gas Index (XNG)** is the benchmark for the stock sector that encompasses natural gas stocks. Like OSX and XOI, the benchmark indexes for the oil and oil service sectors, XNG is a good bellwether for natural gas. As with other commodity complexes that include stocks and the commodity, you want to see the stocks and the commodity in the same general trend, and any divergence by one or the other is usually a sign that a change in the trend is coming. This is the most widely accepted benchmark for prices in natural gas stocks.

Heating oil

Heating oil used to be a winter commodity, but with demand rising for diesel fuel to power automobiles and trucks, and special formulations of this commodity used to power airplanes, the traditional seasonal patterns and other individual factors that used to be specific to the movements of this sector aren't as reliable as they once were. Still, it's likely that cold winters and high demand for diesel fuel from a strong economy will still be positive influences on prices in this sector.

Also important when timing heating oil is the oil supply data, which is released by the Energy Information Agency (EIA) of the U.S. Department of Energy every Wednesday. Heating oil supply numbers, included in the data released by the EIA, can move heating oil prices, especially in the fall and winter months, if the weather is a factor.

The best way to time heating oil, other than directly through futures contracts, is via an ETF that was introduced in July 2008 — the U.S. Heating Oil ETF (UHN). The ETF, even in its short history, has proven to be reliable in matching the general trend of heating oil futures.

Gasoline

Gasoline is another important energy-related commodity that you can trade via the futures markets or an ETF — the U.S. Gasoline Fund (UGA). UGA is an excellent vehicle for timing gasoline, as it offers options and can be sold short.

Another way to profit from gasoline is to time the refinery stocks. Refinery stocks tend to move higher when oil prices are cheap enough, demand is robust, and supply is fairly well balanced. The key to these companies is that they need to buy oil in the market, refine it, and be able to sell it to its customers at a price that isn't seen as being too expensive but that has a nice profit margin built into it.

There is no magic formula to how these companies meet this equation, but as their earnings start to improve, and as the companies guide analysts as to how well business is doing, so do their stock prices move higher. An excellent bellwether stock for the refinery sector is Valero Energy (VLO).

The flip side is that niche sectors, such as refining, tend to trend in one single direction for extended periods of time. After the trend is established, you can tailor your approach to that particular direction of the market.

There is no substitute for a sound and solid trading plan that involves constant review of all key sectors of the market, including oil and the related energy subsectors. By constantly and systematically looking at your charts and keeping up with developments in the market, you will be on the right side of most major intermediate- and long-term trends.

Perusing the Oil Supply Data Report: A Nice Routine for Wednesday Morning

I've mentioned the oil supply data report from the EIA throughout this chapter. In this final section, I'd like to give you some specific ideas that can help you make the most of it by adapting this weekly ritual to your timing routine.

Before every report, you hear the TV anchors and reporters and the print- and Web-based chatter focusing on analyst expectations about the report. You hear talk about a build or a drawdown in supplies and whether there is demand or demand destruction in the system.

Here's what all that stuff means:

- A *build* means that supply is expected to rise.
- A *drawdown* is the opposite of a build and means that supplies are expected to decrease.
- *Demand destruction* just means that demand is falling. (Leave it to Wall Street to come up with a dramatic buzzword that the media can gravitate to.)

Even if you can push through the chatter to the message, you don't gain a lot. Analysts almost never get their predictions for the oil supply data right. The market usually jumps up or down after the data are released, as traders adjust their own perceptions to the data by bidding prices up or down, or leaving them mostly unchanged. I do just about everything I can to rearrange my schedule so I can be in front of my trading screen when that report is released.

Checking other sources before Wednesday

In order to give yourself the best chance at making the right decision, I encourage you to prepare for Wednesday morning.

Here's what I do: On Monday and Tuesday, I scan my favorite news sources for analysts' opinions about what the numbers are expected to be when they are released on Wednesday. I do this so that I get a feel as to what the traders on the floor might be looking for when the report is released. By doing this, I have a good idea about what may happen if the market is priced wrong regarding current supply levels and what the reaction might be when the numbers are released.

 MarketWatch.com (www.marketwatch.com), Reuters (www.reuters.com), and Bloomberg (www.bloomberg.com) usually cover the pre-report period pretty well. If your broker gives you access to good news data, Dow Jones Newswires is about as good as any source to get the same data. Dow Jones Newswires is a subscriber service that is accessible online, usually through brokers and financial service institutions. See Chapter 22 for more great information resources.

Reacting to the report

Above all things, you don't want to be the first guy out of the gate when the report hits. More importantly, you probably won't trade after each report, since the market's response may be muted, or things will move so fast that trading is too risky. In other words, you should exercise a good amount of judgment before trading on this or any report.

After the number comes out, remember that making trades based on the supply reports isn't an exact exercise, because analysts usually are clueless about what's coming up. What you want to look for are instances when they all agree one way or another.

For example, if they're all leaning toward a build-up of crude, be ready for the market to go higher if the report even hints of a supply shortage. The same is true for when the market gets set up for a drawdown. If this is the case, be ready for the market to go lower.

When the report comes out, stay patient and give the market some time to digest the number before you jump in, if you jump in at all. The first few trades can be volatile. After a minute or two, your real-time chart should start to show you the way the market is headed. Then, if you see an important move, based on your knowledge of technical analysis, you can move in.

The report is an important market-moving event, and it can set the tone for the market. But trading on reports is probably a 50-50 bet, and you might as well go to Vegas for that. Technical analysis is about probabilities, and a report may be just a blip in an up trend or down trend.

My advice is to trade the technicals, but to be aware of the market's reaction to the report, as it will affect the technicals in many cases.

Wednesdays can be hairy days, especially if the markets are caught way off guard by the numbers. In those instances the moves can be huge, and prices can gap up or down as the figure is released. Instead of panicking, you should be ready for anything. Consider the following options before you set up any potential trades:

- ✔ If you're already out of the market, you may miss a chance to make some money. However, don't go chasing prices trying to get into the market. You'll end up sorry.

- ✔ If you have an established position on the right side of the market, stay with it and manage it. A good way to take advantage of the data being in your favor is by adjusting your sell stops periodically so you can take as much profit as possible if the market happens to turn against you. If the trend is down, and you're short, just drop your sell stop as the market moves. If the move is to the up side, just raise your stop periodically.

- ✔ If you were in the market but were stopped out because you guessed wrong or the market got a little volatile, be glad you're out. Rather than being in a hurry, take your time and reassess your position while you wait for a better opportunity.

Chapter 20

Timing the Health Care Sector

*T*iming the health care sector is one of the most challenging tasks in investing because the story is a paradox. If you look at global demographic trends, buying and holding health care stocks seems like a no-brainer. After all, the world's population is growing, and the number of aging people who are living longer is simultaneously growing. Intuitively, this seems like a recipe for success for investors and health care companies.

The problem is in the fine print: Although the world's population is growing and aging, the aging population is in the developed world; the growing population is in the developing — and often in the most underdeveloped — areas of the world. Further complicating matters, the aging populations in the developed world are living longer, and thus spending more money on health care.

In the developed world, governments are burdened by budget deficits brought on by too many social problems and the expensive and often wasteful programs put in place to attempt to solve them, large amounts of defense spending, and generally irresponsible policies about many issues. In the developing world, especially the areas where population growth tends to be greatest, little money is available for health care or anything else.

Although money goes into health care, the amounts aren't necessarily enough to grow company profits at previous rate. Much of the money is spent on program administration and bureaucracies; in the United States, entirely new corporations and agencies now exist just to administer prescription plans, keep records, and so on.

Health care companies, although they tend to be highly profitable, rarely meet or beat Wall Street earnings expectations because of the general state of health care in the United States, the former piggy bank of the sector. What it boils down to, for you as a timer, is that you have to be meticulous about when you invest in these companies, how you analyze the opportunities that present themselves, and how you execute your strategy.

In this chapter, I give you all the tools you need to get started and to build and develop your own strategies for timing the health care sector beginning with an overview of what you're up against, as well as an insider's view of the best way to approach timing in this area of the market.

The Real World of Health Care

The supply side of health care has two major components: those that provide products and services to the public (for our purposes these are the hospitals and other health care delivery companies, along with the drug and medical equipment companies), and those that pay for services, the state and federal governments and private insurers.

Patients make up the demand side of the equation, the side that dominates the whole dynamic. As populations age, studies show that chronic illnesses, such as high blood pressure, heart disease, diabetes, and chronic obstructive pulmonary disease (COPD) are the biggest spenders in the system. Drug and equipment companies have correctly diagnosed this trend and have capitalized on it for decades, producing drugs and equipment to treat them, while hospital medical wards are often full taking care of those who suffer from the acute complications of these illnesses and others.

Aging, chronically ill patients require and want health care, but the payers are less willing to pay for their care — at least not at rates that were considered reasonable in the past — as the rising numbers of patients who require products and services continue to grow.

So, although the rate of growth of health care spending continues to rise, the growth rate is selective. Lower-cost pharmaceuticals and bare-bones medical equipment often are the only services covered, as the largest payers for health care — the U.S. Federal Government, via Medicare, and state governments, via Medicaid — have made some important changes aimed at cutting costs. They now may require patients to pay for expensive new drugs, for example, or deny or reduce payments for products that are deemed to be too expensive or inappropriate. The federal government's actions are often the basis used by private health insurers to control the care patients receive.

You can get a good amount of information by visiting company Web sites as well as reading company summaries at Web sites such as www.market watch.com. From a market-timing standpoint, you need to understand the following about each subsector of health care:

- ✔ **The business model of each area:** How the companies in any one area of health care make money.

- ✔ **What influences the business:** What makes the companies deliver on the expectations of Wall Street, including the internal and external influences like market forces and factors specific to the industry.

- ✔ **Whether there's an index that monitors the performance of each subsector:** An index enables you to look at each subsector as a whole before wasting time on any further analysis.

- ✔ **Differentiation among companies:** Not all companies that make the same product are the same. At some point one or two of them will break away from the pack because their product is better than the others. For example, if two anti-cholesterol pills reduce cholesterol equally, the one with the fewest side effects is the one that will likely grab the major share of the market.

If an ETF serves the sector, you may want to trade the entire sector instead of spending time on individual companies.

Diagnosing the Health Insurers

Health insurers are just like any other insurance company. They make money when their investments do well and when they pay as few claims as possible. The health insurance sector is a hybrid sector: The insurance companies have to make money but are also expected to provide a service to their policyholders. The give and take between those two factors is what creates the fluctuation in prices in this sector. Here are some key factors to remember:

- ✔ Health insurance companies are subject to some of the same market-related pressures that other insurance companies are exposed to. As Figure 20-1 shows, this index was rocked as hard as other sectors of the financial industry as a result of the liquidity crisis brought on by the subprime mortgage crisis. As a timer, you need to understand that these are financial companies that provide health-related services. Events in both sectors — financial and health care — can move these stocks.

- ✔ These companies make significant choices about who gets care and how much care they get. As a result, litigation is a nearly constant part of their business. News of lawsuits and investigations that include these companies can make the shares of these companies volatile.

✔ Another key to the fortunes of these companies and their stocks is the tone of public policy from Washington. In an election season, HMOs are often fodder for politicians on the campaign trail, which can be another source of volatility for the sector.

✔ As unemployment rises, so often the number of those who can afford health insurance falls. This can be a negative for this sector.

✔ Once in a while an individual company runs into trouble — a contract goes bad, or a set of investments fails to pay off. The market often spreads the guilt to the entire sector, which can lead to significant volatility.

Figure 20-1:
The Morgan
Stanley
Health Care
Payor index
(HMO)
breaks
down in
2008.

Chart courtesy of AskResearch.com.

Introducing the big players

As of April 2008, 11 companies made up the HMO index. Table 20-1 gives you a rundown of these companies. United Health Group, Aetna, Wellpoint, Humana, and Cigna are the most recognizable names, and they account for a significant number of lives covered. That means that any news that affects one or more of these companies tends to spread throughout the sector.

Table 20-1	The Morgan Stanley Health Care Payors Index (HMO)	
Company Name	*Symbol*	*% Weighting*
WellCare Group Inc.	WCG	11.41%
Cigna Corp	CI	10.72%
Amerigroup Corp	AGP	10.59%

Company Name	Symbol	% Weighting
Coventry Health Care	CVH	9.80%
Aetna Inc	AET	9.75%
Molina Healthcare	MOH	8.78%
Unitedhealth Group	UNH	8.62%
Health Net	HNT	8.12%
Humana Inc	HUM	7.74%
Wellpoint Inc	WLP	7.39%
Centene Corp	CNC	7.08%

These stocks tend to trade as a block, with the others sometimes going along for the ride, but at other times they march to their own drum. Especially important situations include

✔ Earnings reports, earnings warnings, and future outlook for the company's businesses.

✔ Interest rates. As financial stocks, these companies are also moved by the general direction of interest rates

✔ The state of medical innovation. If new drugs or products are available and in high demand, this may also affect these companies as they eventually have to bow to public pressure in order to provide coverage, which costs them money.

Timing the HMOs

The health insurance sector can be a good timing vehicle because when it starts trending it tends to move in one direction for a good, long time. Your best bet is to buy these stocks when

✔ **Interest rates are favorable.** Health insurers are financial sector stocks. Traditionally the entire financial sector — banks, savings and loans, brokers, property and casualty, re-insurers, and health insurance companies — tends to rise when interest rates fall, as investors start betting on higher market prices improving the earnings potential for the sector.

✔ **Earnings are on a roll.** You want to keep track of the company's quarterly earnings. Large mutual funds like to buy companies that deliver rising earnings for long periods of time. When things are going well for this sector they can steam roll for a long time.

✔ **The technicals support the earnings trends.** The best combination here is when the big institutions are hot and heavy on the earnings momentum. That's usually when these stocks are in up trends for months or years at a time. Figure 20-1 shows one of those periods, starting in August 2007 and extending until February 2008. The figure shows how the whole sector recovered from a fall below the 20-, 50-, and 200-day moving averages and was able to trend higher for an extended period of time.

Use technical analysis to buy the strongest stocks in the group when the trend is on your side. See the next section, "Glimpsing Big Pharma and Biotech" for the nuts and bolts of applying technical analysis to buying index components. You can also buy HMO stocks via the SPDR Select Sector Health ETF. Its symbol is XLV. It's not a direct play on the HMOs, but it does include some HMO stocks (close to 8 percent of the portfolio) along with other sectors. That means that for HMO stocks, you might do better by looking at the individual stocks in the index (Table 20-1), and choosing the strongest of stocks.

HMO stocks are favorites of the big-money boys and girls. When you see them start to jump, you want to start following them very carefully because they can stay in up trends for very long periods of time. The same goes for the down side, as Figure 20-1 clearly shows. In other words, you're better off avoiding the HMO sector when the index chart looks as it does in the figure. When all else fails, look at the chart. If it doesn't look inviting, the underlying sector is best avoided.

Glimpsing Big Pharma and Biotech

The market used to view pharmaceutical and biotech companies separately, but after the human genome was deciphered the lines blurred. Most large traditional pharmaceutical companies now have some exposure to biotech, either because they started their own biotech divisions or because they bought one or more biotech companies.

From an investment standpoint, the distinction between biotech and the pharmaceuticals sector doesn't matter much, because times are fairly hard for growth investors in this area due to the constraints on spending for expensive drugs and treatments. Biotech is all about being expensive.

Developing one drug takes billions of dollars. How the company gets that money back is an important issue. Traditionally, but not always, old-line pharmaceutical companies make money by developing treatments for diseases of the masses, such as high blood pressure, infections, and diabetes. These companies make money by selling a lot of pills, ointments, powders, and other mixtures to as many people as possible.

Biotech companies, because they use biology to develop products, have had the opportunity to develop treatments for the masses and for small niche markets. Genzyme (Nasdaq: GENZ), a company that made its initial money by developing enzymes to treat rare diseases, is a perfect example. By charging large amounts of money to treat rare diseases, the company grew and diversified its focus to more mass markets such as kidney failure and drugs used to treat patients on dialysis.

The problems faced by the pharmaceutical industry as a whole have to do with — you guessed it — money. Who's going to pay the thousands of dollars required for one course of chemotherapy or the rare enzyme to keep someone alive? The government, at least in the United States, decided that it would be willing to pay a smaller price than the companies were asking for, and most of these stocks fell hard in result.

In fact, through Medicare, the government reduced the amounts it pays for drugs that formerly drove the major portion of earnings for major biotech companies such as Amgen and Genzyme, driving stock prices down in the process and making life difficult for those patients who could no longer get their drugs, and for investors whose longer-term price projections suffered significantly after the reimbursement reductions.

Getting to the technicals

Three major indexes enable you to track the drug and biotech sector: the Amex Biotechnology Index (BTK), the Amex Pharmaceuticals Index (DRG), and the Nasdaq Biotech Index (NBI). Here are some important things to understand about these indexes:

✔ Both BTK and DRG are heavily concentrated on large capitalization stocks, which means that they may give you a skewed view of their respective sectors.

You can find the components for DRG and BTK at the Amex Web site, www.amex.com. Use the "other products" link on the left navigation bar and the indexes link on the drop-down menu to get to the indexes and then their components.

✔ NBI, on the other hand, includes all the biotech stocks that trade on the Nasdaq, including large-, medium-, and small-cap stocks. Thus, it's a much broader measure of the biotech sector and often a better picture than BTK.

You can find the index, updated daily and with links to all of its components at http://dynamic.nasdaq.com/dynamic/nasdaqbiotech_activity.stm.

Top-to-bottom analysis

Figure 20-2 shows the three indexes stacked one on top of the other. BTK is on top. DRG is in the middle. And NBI is at the bottom. All three charts have three straight moving averages coursing through them, the 20-, 50-, and 200-day moving averages. The key to making money in timing biotech, or any other sector, is to define the trend of the sector and to figure out whether there is any strength to be found.

The three charts in Figure 20-2 reveal the following:

✔ DRG is the weakest index, which means that the large drug stocks are weaker than biotech and that your buying interest should be concentrated elsewhere.

You want to regularly compare this index to another non-related index, such as the HMO index in Figure 20-1. DRG looks better than HMO, which means that if you had to choose between the two subsectors, you should choose to buy something related to DRG over something related to HMO.

✔ NBI has more strength than BTK, as NBI is trading above its 50-day moving average. This is a sign of growing strength, as the index has crossed toward bull market territory (above the 200-day line), and the 20-day moving average has crossed above the 50-day moving average, a positive crossover. (See Chapter 4 for more on bullish crossovers.)

Your next move is to match the ETF to the index. With biotech stocks, your best bet is to buy the entire sector in order to protect your portfolio from any negative surprises that affect any one company, such as a denial for a new product from the Food and Drug Administration. Chapter 16 lists ETFs that correspond to biotech indexes.

If you were going to buy individual stocks, you'd have to look through NBI and look for strong stocks that were breaking out of their base formation. (See Chapter 4 for more on bases.) After you have your list of prospects then you can make your final decision and buy your ETF and/or your group of stocks.

Chart courtesy of AskResearch.com.

Figure 20-2: The Amex Biotech index (BTK, top), the Amex Pharmaceuticals Index (DRG, middle), and the Nasdaq Biotech Index (NBI, bottom).

Minding Medical Care Delivery and Hospitals

Hospital and other care delivery companies are another challenging area of the health care system. Aside from the reimbursement cuts from Medicare and private insurers, the medical delivery sector had the following issues to deal with:

- ✔ **Large numbers of uninsured patients choose emergency rooms as their primary care destinations.** By law, patients cannot be turned away, thus many get free care by default. Hospitals therefore run large amounts of uncollected and uncollectible debt on their balance sheets and often run their operations at a deficit.

- ✔ **Other subsectors are also under pressure.** For example, companies that perform kidney dialysis, run outpatient surgery centers, and operate nursing homes or senior care centers are also under pressure from the combination of rising costs, rising demand, and decreased reimbursement. And costs will probably continue to rise. Home health care beyond what is covered by Medicare commonly runs up to $4,000 per month. Similar costs can be expected for retirement homes and other senior-care centers.

- ✔ **The sector has been marred by fraud over the past 20 years.** Two major corporations, Columbia Health Care (now the closely held HCA) and Tenet Inc., have been prosecuted, fined, and had to return funds to the government for alleged billing schemes against Medicare. Full disclosure: I have worked at hospitals for both corporations in the past. HealthSouth, another large delivery organization also had internal fraud problems and had to fire its CEO, Richard Scrushy, before reorganizing its operations. These run-ins with law enforcement and the government, along with the other factors in this list, have led to increased auditing pressure and continued ratcheting down of reimbursements.

- ✔ **Costs are rising for the sector.** Profit margins are shrinking as operating budgets must grow to meet demand.

- ✔ **Competition from the nonprofit world is bearing down on the for-profit hospitals.** Charity and teaching hospitals are competing effectively in many markets against the for-profit hospitals, making the operation of profitable businesses.

The investment reality, not to mention the reality facing the health care system, is that hospitals and related medical delivery institutions are difficult places to operate — much less operate profitably. Here are some important steps to consider before investing:

✔ **Compare the performance of RXH to the S&P 500, a broad market benchmark.** Figure 20-3 shows that the S&P 500 and RXH both bottomed out in March 2008, and that both have moved higher, nearly in lock step. This is positive, as it shows that RXH is participating in the market's rally. RXH lagged the S&P 500 slightly, as it had not crossed above its 200-day moving average as of May 2, 2008, when the chart ended; still, when you consider the prospects for the business of running a hospital, it's positive that the sector has rallied along with the market.

✔ **Look at the index components to determine whether any are worth investing in.** Of the 16 stocks in the index, one — Kindred Health Care (KND, Figure 20-4) — had the key characteristics you look for when timing on the long side. It broke well above the 20-, 50-, and 200-day moving averages in rising volume.

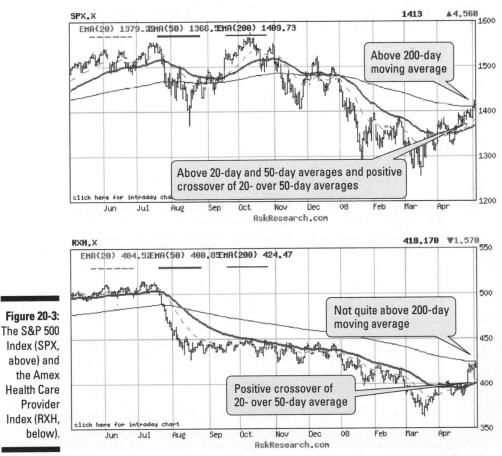

Figure 20-3:
The S&P 500
Index (SPX,
above) and
the Amex
Health Care
Provider
Index (RXH,
below).

Chart courtesy of AskResearch.com.

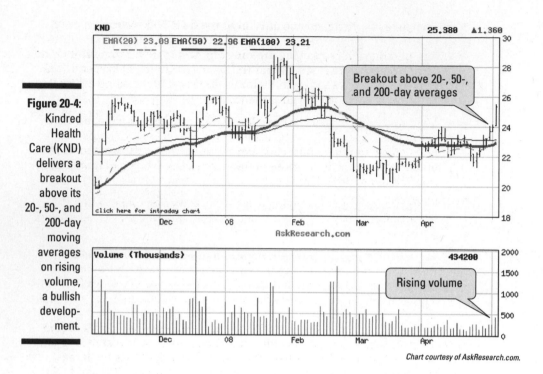

Figure 20-4: Kindred Health Care (KND) delivers a breakout above its 20-, 50-, and 200-day moving averages on rising volume, a bullish development.

Kindred operates long-term health care hospitals for very ill patients, including those on long-term ventilator care with needs of intensive care.

Your conclusion is fairly easy. The sector is holding up to your analysis. You found the strongest stock. And its business is not going away any time soon. The only unknown, as with the rest of the sector, is whether it will be able to grow its reimbursement along with its business. The answer lies with management, and with its ability to figure out the right plan. You won't know that, though, until the company communicates with the markets, via SEC disclosures, media interviews, or earnings reports.

Making Moves on Medical Equipment

The medical equipment sector is represented by the Medical Product index (RXP). The index is not a pure play on equipment, as it houses companies that have other products beyond medical equipment. Many of these companies are diversified, large pharmaceutical companies that have expanded their revenue streams beyond pharmaceuticals.

Here are the overwhelmingly positive influences for this sector:

- ✔ **The demographics of aging are on the side of these companies.** The population makeup ensures that joint-replacement surgeries will increase; pacemakers, defibrillators, and laboratory testing equipment and supplies will be in high demand.

- ✔ **Most of these companies have highly trained, aggressive, and efficient sales forces.** These teams form long-term relationships with physicians and hospitals. (Compare that with the pharmaceuticals industry, where staff turnover often makes the forging of long-term relationships difficult.)

- ✔ **Medical equipment lobbying arms are as good as there is in Washington.** Even if the pie shrinks, this sector will get a good slice of what's left.

- ✔ **The medical equipment subsector is the most likely candidate to deliver growth to investors in the health care sector.** Advances in engineering, electronics, and biotechnology all work their way into this sector much faster than into the pharmaceuticals industry.

Aside from the technical aspects of timing, as I've described previously in this chapter, the best way to decide which companies to invest in is to pick out the pure equipment plays from the index. Table 20-2 lists the largest pure plays in medical equipment. I have personally had contact with and had the opportunity to observe the professionals that work for many of these companies in the field and can attest to the fact that they are at the top of the heap in the business with regard to knowledge of their product and sales craft and service. That means that this is a sector that should be taken seriously in every bull market, because at some point, one or more of these companies can, and often does deliver surprising results, or a blockbuster new product.

Table 20-2	Pure Medical Equipment Stocks Found in the RXP Index	
Company Name	*Symbol*	*Business Segment*
C.R. Bard	BCR	Urological supplies, catheters, monitoring equipment
Becton Dickinson	BDX	Injection and infusion equipment
Boston Scientific	BSX	Cardiac, vascular, pain management
Medtronic	MDT	Cardiac, pain management, orthopedics (spine) equipment
St. Jude	STJ	Cardiac (valves, pacemakers, etc.)
Stryker	SYK	Orthopedics (joint replacements)

Note: Another notable company in the sector isn't included in the RXP Index. Zimmer (ZMH) produces orthopedics, or joint replacements.

As with other sectors, the best way to keep up and to raise your chances of making money is to follow the fortunes of the index. But that's not enough, because a lot of companies in the index are not pure plays in medical equipment. Thus, I suggest a more careful scrutiny of the companies that I list in Table 20-2. Consider doing the following:

✔ Become familiar with the fine points of each company's business and its ability to deliver on its business plans and expectations. You can do this by following how well they meet or beat their sales, revenues, and earnings expectations and how the market responds to the company's ability to deliver or not deliver. Companies that deliver the goods tend to do so for extended periods. You want to own the companies that don't disappoint every other quarter.

✔ Structure your analysis routine to pay special attention to this sector, as here is where a good deal of the growth in health care has migrated.

✔ Look beyond these companies to smaller firms that either do the same kind of business or compete with these giants. These large companies tend to grow by acquisition. And smaller companies that have something special are often takeover targets, which can make you money in a hurry.

The companies in Table 20-2 are the largest companies in the field but are not all of the companies in the sector. Some very good gems are out there to be discovered.

If you take a liking to this sector, I suggest that you either pick up a copy of *Investor's Business Daily* or subscribe to its online edition (www.investors. com), and look through their sector index sections. You're likely to find other, lesser-known, and smaller companies that have significant amounts of growth potential, and that you may want to add to those in Table 20-2.

Part V
The Part of Tens

"Sell."

In this part . . .

This is where I give you the pearls of wisdom that tie the rest of the book together. I show you the resources that I use to get my trading information and give you tips on trading philosophy.

Chapter 21

Ten Game Savers
to Know and Trust

*I*n my 18 years of trading, I've discovered that trading is 90 percent preparation and 10 percent good fortune. If you prepare, you will be successful. Does that mean that you will make money every time you trade? Of course not, but it does mean that you will have a much better chance of staying in the game than those who just shoot from the hip.

If you see Wall Street as a professional sports tour, timing as a tennis match, and yourself as a pro, you can develop a good set of habits — *game savers* — that help you survive any kind of trading environment and to stay sane during those periods when you don't take home the first-place trophy. In this chapter, I give you my favorite game savers and show you how to use them.

You can't win on every trade, but you can be sure that if you prepare for every trade, at the end of the year you too could have the best results of your career.

Embrace Chaos Theory

There is nothing random about the financial markets. Markets follow the rules of chaos, which actually is nonlinear order — not the order you experience when your desk is clean, or when you line up all your pencils in a row.

It is a peculiar type of order, a more loosely organized yet coherent set of circumstances that to the untrained eye looks disorderly. Chaos is the same set of rules that governs the behavior of a hurricane and makes the weather predictably unpredictable.

To see what I mean, just look at a real-time chart, with its seemingly never-ending set of ticks moving in what to the untrained eye are disorderly patterns. In fact, those ticks represent order — order as dictated by the active filtering of information that comes across the eyes and ears of the trading public, the institutions, and the market makers. It is order defined as the sum of all the opinions about the markets at any one time.

A closer look at real-time quotes shows that prices follow a nonlinear yet orderly pattern, and that they tend to stay within defined channels or trading ranges until something moves them toward another set of circumstances, where eventually they again stabilize and return to their nonlinear orderly pattern. When they rise above or fall below the range, they enter an area of temporary disorder before they re-enter a new price range.

You can make big bucks when you learn to spot the limits of chaos and the transitions from chaos to disorder and back to chaos. You can do this by learning to identify resistance and support levels and clearly marking them with trend lines and other tools such as Bollinger bands, which I describe in Chapter 4.

If you accept this scientific concept and make it a central tenet of your timing, you'll find that spotting meaningful trend changes in the market is a much easier and risk-averse approach to investing than buying and holding stocks forever, and hoping that their price eventually goes up.

By accepting chaos theory as the centerpiece of your trading philosophy you'll be able to cope with volatility and the angst that it can bring to your life a whole lot better.

Don't Trade if You Don't Have Enough Money

Sure, it's possible to make big money from small amounts, but the odds are not in your favor unless you're lucky. Those people who open online trading accounts with $5,000 or less and don't manage their money appropriately can lose 10, 20, or 50 percent of their stake in a short while, get discouraged, and quit. It happened to me once when I tried to trade futures without having enough equity to do the job right. I was washed out in about a month, even though I was experienced.

Is it impossible to start with a little and end up with a lot? Not if you use the following simple principles to get — and stay — in the timing game:

- ✔ **Watch your pennies.** Even if you have only $1,000, you can time the markets with mutual funds or even small share lots of ETFs. Just be very conscious of how much money you have and make the preservation of your capital the number-one goal by avoiding big losses.

- ✔ **Never invest in stuff that you don't understand.** I've never made money trading retail stocks, although I've tried many times. Why is that? Because I don't get the dynamics of the sector. I make money consistently in energy, technology, and health care. That's what's natural to me. Find what's a good fit for you and go with it.

- ✔ **Take your profits if that's what your gut says.** If you're having trouble sleeping because you bought something and it's up 50 percent, go ahead and sell a portion of it or close out the position. If your trading is affecting your health and well being, you've got to re-evaluate and make changes in your life and/or your trading.

Avoid Impatience to Live and Trade Another Day

Being impatient will cost you money. Don't rush into every single chart that looks attractive during your first week of technical analysis.

Start instead with some paper trades, track your progress, and evaluate your mistakes and your successes. If you note that you're doing well after a couple of weeks, then you can start making real money trades. Again, take small positions at first, and use the same methods for your real-money trades that made your paper trades successful.

Don't expect perfection. You learn with experience, and if you don't make mistakes, you never get that experience. The key is to start off small and give yourself time.

A significant issue with today's markets is that you can find too much information, and you can get into a bad habit — overtrading. If you find yourself trading for the thrill of it, or because you're bored, you're asking for trouble.

I've had periods where I haven't traded for days or weeks at a time, because I haven't found anything worth trading. And as I've become more experienced, these periods have come more often. As a result, I've cut my chances of making costly mistakes and have stayed in the game longer.

Never Trade Against the Trend

You and I are unlikely ever to outsmart the market, at least not for an extended period of time. But anyone who becomes proficient with technical analysis eventually can figure out the major direction in which the market is headed. And that trend is the one you want to go with until it changes.

The dominant market trend, your trading time frame, your entry and exit points, and the protection of your capital between trades (money management) are the most important aspects of your timing.

When trading with the trend, never lower your sell stops just because you think that the market will turn around and you were too tight in setting them. Likewise, when selling short, never raise your stops if the market starts going against you. For example, if you're in a long position and the stock drops and gets close to the sell stop, it's a sign that the stock is weakening — not a sign that you need to lower your stop to give yourself more time to be right. Making money, or in this case saving yourself from losing money, is better than being right.

Trade with Your Plan Instead of Your Emotions

Being emotional while you trade is a recipe for disaster, as joy and sorrow can both cloud your judgment. There is only one absolute truth in the markets: price. If price is in your favor, stay with the position. If it's going against you, get out by following your trading rules.

Although you want to consider your instincts in some situations, like walking down a dark alley, or canceling a date with a person who makes you uncomfortable, market timing works best when you follow your trading plan, not your emotions. The only exception to this rule is when you're holding a position that makes you uncomfortable. That's fear, and you should pay attention to it.

Markets trade on the willingness of all participants to take a chance on their perception of current conditions. Perceptions and opinions can reach extremes. And extremes in the markets lead to greed and fear — either of which can bring volatility, and volatility often is a signal that a change in trend is coming.

The best course of action is to have a sound trading plan and to rely on your charts, not your emotions. Emotional market timers are usually out of the game a lot sooner than they thought was possible.

Don't Be Afraid of the Big Bad . . . Cash

There's no such thing as too much cash, although Wall Street wants you to avoid the stuff as if it were the big bad wolf. The Wall Street "engulf and devour machine" will tell you that you should own stocks 100 percent of the time whether they're rising or falling in price. Their story, which is proven wrong with every bear market, is that the stock market will always come back and you'll be made whole. But these are the same guys that told you WorldCom and Enron were good companies and that sold you auction-rate securities backed by subprime mortgages that they said were safe.

As I see it, and as most market timers see it, sometimes, you'll own no stocks at all. And sometimes you'll own no bonds, currencies, or commodities. During those times your portfolio will be 100 percent in cash, sitting in a money market account waiting for better times.

It's okay to have no investments during some periods because some markets are so bad that the risk is beyond the potential reward, and earning a little interest is better than losing a whole lot of money.

If conditions are negative in one or more markets, and you're losing money and sleep, you can and should hold up to 100 percent of your portfolio in cash. Contrary to popular Wall Street lore, nobody ever went broke collecting interest in a money market fund, unless of course your money market fund had subprime mortgage assets. But that's another story.

Know When to Say When

Hope may spring eternal according to the poets, but on Wall Street, hope is for suckers, and it seems to run out as you lose everything on a position you should have sold months ago. Kind of like in politics — after the election.

Knowing how big a loss you're willing to take is a key part of any timer's trading plan. You should know this before you enter any position, and apply this limit to your setting of sell stops A fairly common loss limit in the stock market is 5 to10 percent, depending on your risk tolerance and how often you want to trade. Placing sell stops 1 to 2 percent below moving averages or above the moving averages for short sales is another useful practice.

Cutting losses at 5 percent may save you trouble some of the time, but being willing to take a 10 percent loss can sometimes keep you in a position long enough for the position to rebound and start a new up trend. Figure out which approach is best for you.

You can figure out where your loss limit is by watching the price of your stock frequently or by setting sell stops below your positions. If you do the former, you have to be watching all the time. It's easier to instruct your broker about where to put your sell stop when you first buy the stop. If you use a phone broker, you just tell them over the phone. Online brokers have drop-down menus that let you put in and adjust your stops.

Fear the Reaper, Not Adaptation

I love Blue Oyster Cult, but I should tell you that I don't agree with their "Don't Fear the Reaper" song title. If I see that guy heading my way, I'm gonna run. And part of successful timing is the ability to adapt your methods and your expectations to the general conditions of the market and your own situation at any time. If a reaper of a bear market is coming, don't be afraid to get out of its way.

Get a dose of reality into your trading. If you have only a little money, there's no point in taking big risks. And even if you have a lot of money, there's no point in being foolish. That means that trading along the lines of what the market gives you, in the sense of choices, and keeping a good line on your own financial status is a good strategy.

For example, in a bull market, I often have 20 or 30 positions open, with each lot being no more than 500 shares. That's how I protect myself against news that can affect any individual stock position. In a bear market, I hold large amounts of cash, look to the commodities markets for alternatives and look for short positions while generally holding positions for shorter periods of time.

A good rule of thumb in a bull market, where the pickings are plentiful, is to buy larger lots of cheaper stocks and smaller lots of more expensive stocks. For example, if I like a stock that's trading at $15, I may buy 500 shares, for $7,500. If I also like a stock that's trading for $37.50, I may buy 200 shares, also $7,500. In that way, no position exerts any greater effect on the overall portfolio than any other.

This is an especially good strategy in the early part of a bull market. As things develop, I may start to add more shares to any position that is acting better than others, adding a bit more pop to the portfolio and playing more aggressively toward the stronger components of my holdings.

Set Low Expectations but Avoid Low Self-Esteem

Casey Kasem always said to "keep your feet on the ground, but aim for the stars." And that's pretty good advice for those who want to time the markets, as long as you have a good trading plan and a pretty thick skin.

Although you should try to make as much money as you can, you should also know that the odds are always against you and that you should never expect to trade flawlessly.

Good traders are masters of the low-expectations game, as they never get too excited about spectacular gains if they have them. This is what being disciplined is all about. By having low expectations you can keep a lid on the emotions of trading that can come from the highs, the lows, and the dull periods that you are likely to encounter, and continue to function at an efficient level of trading proficiency.

If It Ain't Fun, Forget It

Aside from making money, I enjoy trading and market timing because it lets me put my wits up against incredible odds and the collective investment opinion of the entire trading world.

Yup, it's a rush. But it's a controlled rush and is one that I take seriously. If I ever stop enjoying the preparation, analysis, and management of a trade, I'll quit.

If you don't enjoy it, find something else to do.

Chapter 22

Ten-Plus Awesome Resources

In This Chapter

▶ Exploring timing Web sites

▶ Getting market info from TV

▶ Checking out newsletters and magazines

*L*iterally hundreds of Web sites, books, magazines, and newsletters claim to be able to double and triple your money in days, weeks, and months. I contend that although doubling or tripling your money is plausible — even possible — it's difficult. And if it's difficult, very few can actually deliver. That means that the rest of them are lying.

This chapter describes some of the more reliable information sources available, based on my personal experience.

Timing Web Sites

Several great Web sites focus on delivering the tools you need for timing, along with discussion of trends, advice for investing, piles of data, and commentary.

FibTimer.com

This one's run by Frank Kollar, a good friend of mine who works hard at his craft and who's as honest as they come — not to mention a damn good market timer for over 30 years. You won't get any hype here, just good, steady advice and recommendations on what's working, both up and down in the markets. You can get long and short recommendations from Frank, for timing stocks, ETFs, and even mutual funds.

PMFM.com

PMFM is a pure timing mutual fund family. This site is a no-nonsense place where you get the real deal on what's happening. Subscribe for free updates, which provide some nice views on the market and hints on trends.

DecisionPoint.com

DecisionPoint is a subscription service that features reams of data about technical indicators, including the mainstream ones I talk about in Chapter 4, and many more that become more interesting as you get more experienced. The site also features weekly comments from market timers around the world, including yours truly.

StockCharts.com

StockCharts.com is an excellent, free charting site that also offers commentary for subscribers from John Murphy, one of the elder statesmen of technical analysis. John, whom I've met and spoken with on multiple occasions, offers excellent market insights in easy-to-follow language.

Joe-Duarte.com

My Web site features my widely read daily column Market IQ, which deals with both the broader issues of the current market cycle — including intelligence, commodities, and economic problems — and important trends emerging and existing. The Web site also features timing for technology, energy, undervalued and growth stocks, as well as a wide array of ETF timing systems. I offer free and paid subscriber content at the site. Hope to see you there.

General Investment Information Web Sites

The following sites are great places to look through reports, do research on economic indicators, and look at long-term trends of important things such as the Fed Funds rate.

FederalReserve.gov

The Federal Reserve Web site is the home of the Fed's Beige Book, a great summary of where the Fed thinks the economy has been and is headed. The Beige Book is the Fed's roadmap for interest rates, and it sets the stage for much of the action in the bond and stock markets. The site includes plenty of data on Fed policy and for-beginners information about how a central bank works.

StLouisFed.org

If you're a data hound, the St. Louis Federal Reserve Bank's Web site is the place for you. The site is full of charts and statistics that I like to use when I'm doing my history homework, such as when I want to see a chart of interest rates for the past several years. This site is also different from the Fed's main Web site, as it has a more news-oriented and less academic feel to it.

WSJ.com

The online edition of *The Wall Street Journal* connects you to the premier financial publication in the world — still the best, even if Dow Jones no longer owns it. It might get racier in the future, but it's hard to get past the top-notch editorial content and thoughtful editorial content. For timing, the Economy section of the Journal's Web site is one of my favorites. It's an excellent resource for catching up on the big picture before you trade. I also like the economic calendar and the data library, where you can find charts of the major economic indicators. The Journal online also gives you links to the full economic reports released so you can actually dive into them and look for nuance and detail.

Investors.com

In my opinion, if you're a market timer, Investors.com — the Web site of *Investor's Business Daily* (IBD) — is the must-have subscription. You won't get any better or a larger number of trading ideas for the stock market anywhere. A column on the site, "The Big Picture," has an excellent record of timing calls on the buy side. I particularly like the "NYSE" and "Nasdaq Stocks in the News" sections, a huge number of preselected charts with attractive timing characteristics.

Marketwatch.com

Marketwatch.com is probably the best free market content in the world. My favorite column here is the commodity summary, where I get a good feel for what the oil, natural gas, gasoline, and heating oil markets are doing, and what traders are fretting about. Other good areas of the site include summaries of individual company stocks. Finally, if you register, you can get news updates e-mailed to your mailbox about important news items on your stocks or sectors.

Trading Books

Over the years, I've read a good selection of trading books that have helped me develop into a successful market timer. Here is a sampling of some of the better books that I've run across:

- *Trading for a Living* (Wiley) by Dr. Alexander Elder

  This one is one of my all-time favorites and one of the first trading books that delved into details of how to examine oscillators and other indicators, as well as how to set up your trading plan and how to understand the psychology of trading.

- *The Complete Guide to Market Breadth Indicators* (McGraw-Hill) by Gregory L. Morris

  This book is an excellent reference for anyone interested in improving their knowledge and understanding of the market's trend, which is the key for succeeding in market timing; highly recommended.

- *How to Make Money in Stocks: A Winning System in Good Times or Bad* (McGraw-Hill) by William J. O'Neil

  This is the bible of CANSLIM investing, the widely used momentum-based trading system espoused by *Investor's Business Daily* that I introduce in Chapter 10.

Newsletter Resources

You can get some good information free of charge in your e-mail box just by signing up for a subscriber service's free periodic newsletter. Sure, it's a marketing tool, but most services give you the real deal in these free letters, because they want you to like what you see and subscribe to the paid service. Newsletters offer a way to get in on good sales, as most services drop prices at least once or twice a year to replenish their coffers and improve cash flow.

I offer a free look at my Market IQ column on Mondays at www.joe-duarte.com. You can sign up with just your e-mail address, and you get the same stuff that the paid subs get on Monday, plus or minus an ad or two. Other services do the same thing as well, including

✔ **FibTimer.com** (www.fibtimer.com) gives you a weekly article about the psychology of trading that's worthwhile reading.

✔ **StockCharts.com** (www.stockcharts.com) has excellent charting — most of it free.

✔ **BigTrends.com** (www.bigtrends.com) provides good detail about the goings on in the major indexes every week.

Index